HTML5

for Masterminds

How to take advantage of HTML5
to create amazing websites
and revolutionary applications

D1414082

HTML5

for Masterminds

J.D. Gauchat
www.jdgauchat.com

Edited by: Laura Edlund
www.lauraedlund.ca

The source code for this book is available at **www.minkbooks.com**

Registration Number: 1086517

ISBN-13: 978-1463604059
ISBN-10: 146360405X

1st Edition 2011

For those who are not here
with me anymore

Table of Contents

Chapter 12—File API

Chapter 13—Communication API

Chapter 14—Web Workers API

Chapter 15—History API

Chapter 16—Offline API

Conclusion

Introduction

HTML5 is not a new version of an old markup language—not even an improvement on this already "ancient" technology—but instead a new concept for the construction of websites and applications in the era of mobile devices, cloud computing and networking.

It all started a long time ago with a simple version of HTML proposed to create the basic structure of web pages, organize their content and share information. The language and the web itself were born primarily with the intention of communicating information through text.

The narrow scope of HTML motivated companies to develop new languages and software to add characteristics to the web that had never been seen before. These initial developments grew into powerful and popular plugins. Simple games and animated jokes soon turned into sophisticated applications, providing new experiences that changed the concept of the web forever.

Of the options proposed, Java and Flash were the most successful; they were massively adopted and widely considered to be the future of the Internet. However, as soon as the number of users increased and the Internet changed from a way to interconnect computer lovers to a primary field for business and social interaction, limitations present in both technologies proved to be a death sentence.

The main inconvenience of Java and Flash may be described as a lack of integration. Both were conceived from the beginning as plugins, something that is inserted into a structure but basically shares with that structure only some space on the screen. There was no communication and integration between applications and documents.

The lack of integration turned out to be critical and paved the way for the evolution of a language that shares space in the document with HTML and that is not affected by plugin limitations. Javascript, an interpreted language embedded in browsers, clearly was the way to improve the user's experience and provide functionality for the web. However, after a few years of failed attempts to promote it and misuses, the market never fully adopted the language and its popularity declined. The detractors had good reasons to oppose its adoption. At that moment, Javascript couldn't replace the functionality of Flash and Java. And even when it was evident that Java and Flash were limiting the scope of web applications and isolating the web's content, popular features such as video streaming were becoming a big part of the web and were only effectively offered through those technologies.

Despite this success, Java was declining. The language's complex nature, slow evolution and the lack of integration diminished its importance to the point that today Java is hardly used any more in mainstream web applications. Without Java, the market turned its attention to Flash. However, the fact that Flash shares the same basic characteristics with its competitor on the web makes it also susceptible to the same fate.

Meanwhile, the software to access the web continued to evolve. Along with new features and faster techniques for Internet access, browsers also were improving their Javascript engines. More power brought more opportunities, and this scripting language was ready to embrace them.

At some point during this process, it became evident to some developers that neither Java nor Flash would be enough to provide the tools they needed to create the applications demanded by an increasing number of users. These developers started to apply Javascript in their applications in a way that was never seen before. The innovation and the amazing results attracted the attention of more programmers. Soon what was called the "Web 2.0" was born, and the perception of Javascript in the developers' community radically changed.

Javascript was clearly the language that allowed the developers to innovate and do things that nobody had done before on the web. Over the last years, programmers and web designers all over the world came up with the most incredible tricks to overcome the limitations of this technology and its initial deficiencies in portability. Javascript along with HTML and CSS was obviously the most perfect combination for the necessary evolution of the web.

HTML5 is, actually, the improvement of that combination, the glue that puts everything together. HTML5 proposes standards for every aspect of the web and also a clear purpose for each technology involved. From now on, HTML provides the structural elements, CSS is concentrated on how to turn that structure into something visibly attractive and usable and Javascript has all the power necessary to provide functionality and build full web applications.

Boundaries between websites and applications have finally disappeared. The required technologies are ready. The future of the web is promising, and the evolution and combination of these three technologies (HTML, CSS and Javascript) into one powerful specification is turning the Internet into the leading platform for development. HTML5 is clearly leading the way.

IMPORTANT: At the moment, not every browser supports HTML5 features, and most of these features are currently in the design stage. We recommend you read the chapters and execute the codes with the latest version of Google Chrome, Safari, Firefox or Internet Explorer. Google Chrome and Safari are both based on WebKit, the open source browser engine that supports almost all the features already implemented in HTML5, and they are good testing platforms. Firefox is one of the best browsers for developers and its engine, Gecko, provides full support for HTML5 as well. Finally, the new version of Internet Explorer, IE9, is HTML5 ready and supports most of the new features as well.

Whatever browser you use, always keep in mind that a good developer installs and tests his or her codes in each program available on the market. Test the codes provided in this book with each and every browser.

To download the latest versions, visit the following links:

- www.google.com/chrome
- www.apple.com/safari/download
- www.mozilla.com
- windows.microsoft.com
- www.opera.com

In the book's Conclusion, we explore different alternatives to making your websites and applications accessible from old browsers and those that are not yet HTML5-ready.

Chapter 1
HTML5 Documents

Basic Components

HTML5 provides basically three features: structure, style and functionality. It was never officially declared but, even when some APIs and the entire CSS3 specification are not part of it, HTML5 is considered the product of the combination of HTML, CSS and Javascript. These technologies are highly dependable and act as one unit organized under the HTML5 specification. HTML is in charge of the structure, CSS presents that structure and its content on the screen and Javascript does the rest, which (as we will see later in this book) is quite significant.

Despite the integration of these technologies, the structure is still the essential part of a document. It provides the elements necessary to allocate static or dynamic content, and it is also a basic platform for applications. With the variety of devices to access the Internet and the diversity of interfaces used to interact with the web, a basic aspect, the structure, turns into a vital part of the document. Now the structure must provide shape, organization, and flexibility, and it must be as strong as the foundations of a house.

To work and create websites and applications with HTML5, we need to know first how that structure is constructed. Creating strong foundations will help us later apply the rest of the components to take full advantage of these new possibilities.

So let's start with the basics, step by step. In this first chapter you will learn how to build a template for future projects using the new HTML elements introduced in HTML5.

> **Do It Yourself:** Create a new empty document with your favorite text editor to test in the browser every code reviewed in this chapter. This will help you remember the new tags and get used to this new markup.

> **Review the Basics:** An HTML document is a text file. If you don't have any developer software, you can simply use Notepad in Windows or any other text editor. The file must be saved with the `.html` extension and the name you wish (e.g., `mycode.html`).

> **IMPORTANT:** In order to have access to the additional information and listing examples, visit our website at www.minkbooks.com

Global Structure

HTML documents are strictly organized. Every part of the document is differentiated, declared and enclosed in specific tags. In this part of the chapter, we are going to see how to build the global structure of an HTML document and the new semantic elements incorporated in HTML5.

Doctype

First, we need to indicate the type of document we are creating. In HTML5 this is extremely simple:

```
<!DOCTYPE html>
```

Listing 1-1: using the <doctype> element

> **IMPORTANT:** This line must be the first line of your file, without any space or line before. This is a way to activate the standard mode and force browsers to interpret HTML5 when it's possible or ignore it otherwise.

> **Do It Yourself:** You can start writing the code right now into your HTML file and add every new element studied later.

<html>

After declaring the type of document, we have to build the HTML tree structure. As always, the root element for this tree is the **<html>** element. This element will enclose all our HTML code.

```
<!DOCTYPE html>
<html lang="en">

</html>
```

Listing 1-2: using the <html> element

The attribute `lang` in the opening tag `<html>` is the only attribute we need to specify in HTML5. This attribute defines the human language of the content of the document we are creating—in this case, `en` for English.

> **Review the Basics:** HTML uses markup language to build web pages. These HTML tags are keywords and attributes surrounded by angle brackets —for example, `<html lang="en">`. In this case `html` is the keyword, and `lang` is the attribute with the value `en`. Most HTML tags come in pairs, one tag is the opening tag and the other one is the closing tag, and the content goes in between. In this case `<html lang="es">` indicates the start of the HTML code, and `</html>` indicates the end. Compare the opening and closing tags and you will see that the closing tag is distinguished by a slash before the keyword (e.g., `</html>`). All the rest of our code will be inserted between these two tags: `<html>` ... `</html>`.

> **IMPORTANT:** HTML5 is extremely flexible regarding the structure and the elements used to build it. The `<html>` element may be included without any attributes or even ignored at all. For compatibility, and for a few more reasons not worth mentioning here, we recommend you follow some basic rules. We are going to teach you how to build HTML documents according to what we consider best practices.

To find other languages for the `lang` attribute, you can follow this link: www.w3schools.com/tags/ref_language_codes.asp

<head>

Let's continue building our template. The HTML code inserted between the `<html>` tags has to be divided into two main sections. As it happened in previous HTML versions, the first section is the head and the second the body. So the next step is to create these two sections in the code using the already known elements `<head>` and `<body>`.

The `<head>` goes first, of course, and like the rest of the structural elements, it has an opening and a closing tag.

```
<!DOCTYPE html>
<html lang="en">
<head>

</head>

</html>
```

Listing 1-3: using the `<head>` element

The tag itself didn't change from previous versions, and its purpose will be exactly the same. Within the **<head>** tags we will define the title of our web page, declared the character encoding, provide general information about the document, and incorporate external files with styles, scripts or even images needed to render the page.

Except for the title and some icons, the rest of the information incorporated to the document between the **<head>** tags is usually not visible.

<body>

The next big section that is part of the main organization of an HTML document is the body. The body is the visible part of the document and is specified with the **<body>** tag. This tag didn't change from previous versions of HTML:

```
<!DOCTYPE html>
<html lang="en">
<head>

</head>
<body>

</body>
</html>
```

Listing 1-4: *using the* <body> *element*

> **Review the Basics:** So far we have a simple code but an already complex structure. This is because the HTML code is not a sequential set of instructions. HTML is a markup language, a set of tags or elements that usually come in pairs and can be nested (fully contained within something else). In the first line of the code in Listing 1-4, we have a single tag with the definition of the document and immediately next the opening tag **<html lang="en">**. This tag and the closing tag **</html>** at the bottom are indicating the start and end of the HTML code. Between the **<html>** tags we inserted other tags specifying two important parts of this basic structure: the **<head>** and the **<body>**. These two tags also come in pairs. Later in this chapter you will see that more tags are inserted between the **<head>** and the **<body>**. This structure is tree-like, with the **<html>** tag as its root.

<meta>

Now it is time to build the document's head. There are a few changes and innovations inside the head, and one of them is the tag that defines the character encoding of the document. This is a **meta** tag and it specifies how the text has to be presented on the screen.

```
<!DOCTYPE html>
<html lang="en">
<head>
  <meta charset="utf-8">

</head>
<body>

</body>
</html>
```

Listing 1-5: using the `<meta>` *element*

The innovation for this element in HTML5, like in most cases, was just simplification. The new **meta** tag for the character encoding is shorter and simpler. Of course you can change **utf-8** for the encoding you prefer to use, and other **meta** tags like **description** or **keywords** may be added, as shown in the next example:

```
<!DOCTYPE html>
<html lang="en">
<head>
  <meta charset="utf-8">
  <meta name="description" content="This is an HTML5 example">
  <meta name="keywords" content="HTML5, CSS3, Javascript">

</head>
<body>

</body>
</html>
```

Listing 1-6: adding more `<meta>` *elements*

> **Review the Basics:** There are several **meta** tags that may be used in a document to declare general information, but this information is not shown in the browser's window; it is only important for search engines and devices that need to preview or get a summary of the relevant data of our document. As we commented before, aside from the title or some icons, most of the information inserted between the **<head>** tags is not visible to users. In the code in Listing 1-6, the attribute **name** inside the **<meta>** tag specifies its type and **content** declares its value, but none of these values are shown on the screen. To learn more about **<meta>** tags, go to our website and follow the links for this chapter.

In HTML5, it is not necessary to self-close tags with a slash at the end, but we recommend self-enclosing for compatibility reasons. You might write the last code this way:

```
<!DOCTYPE html>
<html lang="en">
<head>
    <meta charset="utf-8" />
    <meta name="description" content="This is an example" />
    <meta name="keywords" content="HTML5, CSS3, JavaScript" />

</head>
<body>

</body>
</html>
```

***Listing 1-7:** self-closing tags*

\<title\>

The `<title>` tag, as usual, simply specifies the title of the document, and there is nothing new to comment about it.

```
<!DOCTYPE html>
<html lang="en">
<head>
    <meta charset="utf-8">
    <meta name="description" content="This is an HTML5 example">
    <meta name="keywords" content="HTML5, CSS3, JavaScript">
    <title>This text is the title of the document</title>

</head>
<body>

</body>
</html>
```

***Listing 1-8:** using the `<title>` element*

> **Review the Basics:** The text between `<title>` tags is the title of the entire document we are creating. Usually this text is shown by browsers at the top of the window.

\<link\>

Another important element that goes in the head of the document is `<link>`. This element is used to incorporate styles, scripts, images or icons from external files within a document. One of the most common uses of `<link>` is to incorporate styles inserting an external CSS file:

```
<!DOCTYPE html>
<html lang="en">
<head>
  <meta charset="utf-8">
  <meta name="description" content="This is an HTML5 example">
  <meta name="keywords" content="HTML5, CSS3, JavaScript">
  <title>This text is the title of the document</title>
  <link rel="stylesheet" href="mystyles.css">
</head>
<body>

</body>
</html>
```

Listing 1-9: using the `<link>` element

In HTML5, it is no longer necessary to specify what kind of style sheet we are inserting, therefore the **type** attribute was eliminated. We only need two attributes to incorporate our styles' file: **rel** and **href**. The attribute **rel** means relation and this is about the relation between the document and the file we are incorporating. In this case the attribute **rel** has the value **stylesheet** that tells the browser that the file **mystyles.css** is a CSS file with styles required to render the page (In the next chapter, we will study and incorporate CSS styles.).

> **Review the Basics:** A style sheet is a group of formatting rules that will help us change the appearance of our document—for example, the size and color of the text. Without these rules, the text and any other element will be shown on the screen using standard styles provided by browsers (default sizes, colors, etc.). Styles are simple rules, usually requiring only a few lines of code that may be declared in the same document. As we will see later, it is not strictly necessary to get this information from external files, but we recommend it as a best practice. Loading the CSS rules from an external document (another file) will let us organize the main document, increase the load speed of our website, and take advantage of the new HTML5 features.

With the last insertion, we can consider the work on the head of our template finished. Now we are able to work on the body, where the magic happens.

The Body Structure

The body structure (the code between **`<body>`** tags) will generate the visible part of our document. That's the code that will produce our web page.

HTML always offered different kinds of ways to build and organize the information in a document's body. One of the first elements provided for this purpose was **`<table>`**. Tables allowed authors to arrange data, text, images and tools into rows and columns of cells, even when they weren't conceived for that purpose.

In the early days of the web, tables were a revolution, a big step forward in visualizing the document and improving the users' experience. Later on, gradually, other elements replaced the function of tables, providing a different way to do the same thing with less code and faster thus facilitating creation, portability and maintenance.

The **`<div>`** element started to dominate the field. With the emergence of more interactive web applications and the integration of HTML, CSS and Javascript, the use of the **`<div>`** tag became a common practice. But the **`<div>`** element, as well as **`<table>`**, doesn't provide much information about the parts of the body that the element is representing. Anything from images to menus, text, links, scripts, forms, etc., could go between the opening and closing **`<div>`** tags. In other words, the keyword **`div`** only specifies a division in the body, like the cell in a table, but it doesn't give a clue about what kind of division that is, what is the purpose of that division, or what is inside.

For users, those clues and indications are not important, but for browsers the right interpretation of what is inside the document being processed may be crucial. After the revolution of portable devices and the emergence of different ways for people to access the web, the identification of every part of the document has become more relevant than ever.

With that in mind, HTML5 incorporates new elements that help identify each part of the document and organize the body. In HTML5, the most important sections of a document are differentiated, and the main structure no longer depends on **`<div>`** or **`<table>`** tags.

How we use these new elements is up to us, but the keywords selected for each one will give us a hint about their function. Usually a web page or web application is divided into several visual areas in order to improve the users' experience and interactivity. The keywords representing every new HTML5 element are closely related to these visual areas, as we will see soon.

Organization

Figure 1-1 represents a regular layout found in most websites at the moment. Despite the fact that every designer creates his or her own designs, in general we will be able to identify every website studied in terms of the following sections:

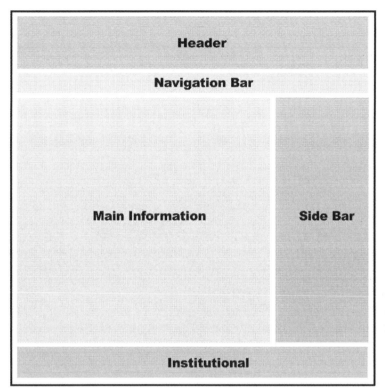

Figure 1-1: visual representation of a typical web page layout

At the top, described as the **Header**, is the place where you usually have your logo, name, subtitles and short descriptions of your website or web page.

Below, you can see the **Navigation Bar** in which almost every developer offers a menu or list of links for navigation purposes. Users are led from this bar to different pages or documents, usually in the same website.

The most relevant content of the page is usually placed in the middle of the layout. This section presents important information and links. Most of the time, it is divided into several rows and columns. In the example of Figure 1-1 you can see only two columns, **Main Information** and **Side Bar**, but this section is extremely flexible and designers normally adapt it according to their needs by inserting more rows, splitting the columns into smaller blocks or generating different combinations and distributions. The content presented in this part of the layout is usually top priority. In the example layout, **Main Information** could have a list of articles, product descriptions, blog entries or any other important information, and **Side Bar** could show a list of links pointing to each of those items. In a blog, for example, this last column will offer a list of links pointing to every blog entry, information about the author, etc.

At the bottom of the typical layout we have one more bar named the **Institutional** bar. We name it as such because this is the area of the layout often with general information about the website, the author or the company, plus links regarding rules, terms and conditions, maps, and all additional data the developer considers worth sharing. The **Institutional** bar is the complement to the **Header**, and it is part of what is considered these days as the essential structure of a web page.

Figure 1-2: visual representation of a typical blog layout

Figure 1-2 is an example of a regular blog. In this example, you can easily identify every part of the design we were considering before.

1. **Header**
2. **Navigation Bar**
3. **Main Information** section
4. **Side Bar**
5. the footer or **Institutional** bar

This simple representation of a blog can help us understand that every section defined in a website has a purpose. Sometimes that purpose doesn't look clear but the essence is always there, and you will still be able to recognize any of the sections described above everywhere.

HTML5 considers this basic structure and layout, and it provides new elements to differentiate and declare each one of them. Now we can say to browsers what every section is for:

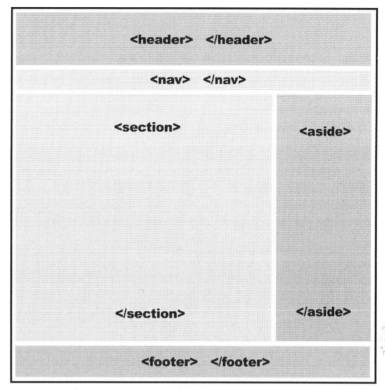

Figure 1-3: visual representation of section arrangement using HTML5 tags

Figure 1-3 shows the typical layout we used before, but this time with the corresponding HTML5 elements for every section (both opening and closing tags).

<header>

One of the new elements incorporated in HTML5 is **<header>**. The **<header>** must not to be confused with the **<head>** tag used before to build the head of the document. In the same way that the **<head>** does, the **<header>** is intended to provide introductory information (such as titles, subtitles or logos), but the two tags differ in scope. While the **<head>** tag has the purpose of providing information about the entire document, the **<header>** is intended to be used only for the body or for sections within the body.

```
<!DOCTYPE html>
<html lang="en">
<head>
  <meta charset="utf-8">
  <meta name="description" content="This is an HTML5 example">
  <meta name="keywords" content="HTML5, CSS3, JavaScript">
  <title>This text is the title of the document</title>
  <link rel="stylesheet" href="mystyles.css">
</head>
```

```
<body>
  <header>
    <h1>This is the main title of the website</h1>
  </header>

</body>
</html>
```

Listing 1-10: using the `<header>` *element*

In Listing 1-10, we are defining the title of the web page using the **<header>** tag. Remember that this header is not the same as the general title of the document defined previously in the head. The insertion of the **<header>** element represents the beginning of the body and the visible part of the document. From now on we will be able to see the results of the code on browser's window.

> **IMPORTANT:** If you followed the instructions from the beginning of this chapter you should already have a text file with the codes studied so far and ready to be tested. If not, all you have to do is copy the code found in Listing 1-10 into an empty text file using any text editor (such as Windows' Notepad) and save the file with the name of your choice and the **.html** extension. To see the script working, open the file from an HTML5 compatible browser. You can do that from inside the browser by using the File menu or simply double-click the file from the file explorer.

> **Review the Basics:** Between the **<header>** tags on Listing 1-10 there is an element that you probably don't know. The element **<h1>** is an old HTML element used to define a heading. The number indicates the importance of the heading and its content. The element **<h1>** is the highest in importance and **<h6>** is the lowest in importance, therefore **<h1>** will be used to show the main title and the rest are used for a main subtitle or internal subtitles. We will see how these elements work in HTML5 later.

<nav>

The next section of our example is the **Navigational Bar**. This bar is generated in HTML5 with the **<nav>** tag.

```
<!DOCTYPE html>
<html lang="en">
<head>
  <meta charset="utf-8">
  <meta name="description" content="This is an HTML5 example">
  <meta name="keywords" content="HTML5, CSS3, JavaScript">
  <title>This text is the title of the document</title>
  <link rel="stylesheet" href="mystyles.css">
</head>
```

```
<body>
  <header>
    <h1>This is the main title of the website</h1>
  </header>
  <nav>
    <ul>
      <li>home</li>
      <li>photos</li>
      <li>videos</li>
      <li>contact</li>
    </ul>
  </nav>

</body>
</html>
```

Listing 1-11: *using the* <nav> *element*

As you can see in Listing 1-11, the **<nav>** element is between the **<body>** tags but falls after the closing tag of the header (**</header>**), not in between **<header>** tags. This is because **<nav>** is not part of the header, but instead a new section.

We said before that the structure and the order we choose to use with HTML5 is up to us. That means HTML5 is very versatile, and is only giving us the parameters and basic elements to work with, but how to use them will be our decision. One example of this versatility is that the **<nav>** tag could be inserted within the **<header>** element or in any other section of the body. However, you must always consider that these new tags were created to provide more information to browsers and help every new program and device in the market to identify the most relevant parts of the document. To keep our code portable and readable, we recommend the best practice of following the standards and keeping it as clear as possible. The **<nav>** element is intended to contain navigation aids like the main menu or major navigation blocks, and you should use it that way.

> **Review the Basics:** In the example of Listing 1-11, we are listing the menu options for our web page. Between the **<nav>** tags, there are two elements that are used to create a list. The purpose of the **<ul>** element is to define a list. Nested between the **<ul>** tags you can see several **<li>** tags with different text to represent the menu options. The **<li>** tags, as you probably already realized, are used to define each item in the list. The purpose of this book is not to teach you basic concepts of HTML. If you need more information about regular elements of the language, please visit our website and follow the links for this chapter.

<section>

Next in our standard design are what we called the **Main Information** bar and the **Side Bar** on Figure 1-1. As we explained before, the **Main Information** bar contains the most relevant information of the document and can be found in different forms—for example, divided into several blocks or more columns. Because the purpose of these columns and blocks is more general, the HTML5 element that specifies these sections is simply called **<section>**.

```
<!DOCTYPE html>
<html lang="en">
<head>
  <meta charset="utf-8">
  <meta name="description" content="This is an HTML5 example">
  <meta name="keywords" content="HTML5, CSS3, JavaScript">
  <title>This text is the title of the document</title>
  <link rel="stylesheet" href="mystyles.css">
</head>
<body>
  <header>
    <h1>This is the main title of the website</h1>
  </header>
  <nav>
    <ul>
      <li>home</li>
      <li>photos</li>
      <li>videos</li>
      <li>contact</li>
    </ul>
  </nav>
  <section>

  </section>

</body>
</html>
```

Listing 1-12: *using the* <section> *element*

Like the **Navigation Bar**, the **Main Information** bar is a separate section. Therefore the section for the **Main Information** bar goes below the **</nav>** closing tag.

> **Do It Yourself:** Compare the last code in Listing 1-12 and the layout in Figure 1-3 to understand how the tags are located in the code and what section those tags are generating in the visual representation of the web page.

> **IMPORTANT:** The tags that represent every section of the document are located in the code in a list, one over another, but in the website some of these sections will be side by side (The **Main Information** and **Side Bar** columns are examples.). In HTML5, the presentation of these elements on the screen has been delegated to CSS. The design will be achieved by assigning CSS styles to every element. We will study CSS in the next chapter.

\<aside\>

In the typical website layout (Figure 1-1), a bar called **Side Bar** sits beside the **Main Information** bar. This is a column or section that usually contains data related to the main information but not as relevant or not as important.

In the example of a standard blog layout (Figure 1-2), the **Side Bar** contains a list of links (number 4). In that example, the links were pointing to every blog entry and providing additional information about the author of the blog. The information inside this bar is related to the main information but is not relevant by itself. Following the blog example, we can say that the entries of the blog are relevant, but the links and short previews of those entries are only a navigational aid, and not what the reader or user will be most interested in.

In HTML5, we are able to differentiate this secondary kind of information with the **\<aside\>** element.

```
<!DOCTYPE html>
<html lang="en">
<head>
  <meta charset="utf-8">
  <meta name="description" content="This is an HTML5 example">
  <meta name="keywords" content="HTML5, CSS3, JavaScript">
  <title>This text is the title of the document</title>
  <link rel="stylesheet" href="mystyles.css">
</head>
<body>
  <header>
    <h1>This is the main title of the website</h1>
  </header>
  <nav>
    <ul>
      <li>home</li>
      <li>photos</li>
      <li>videos</li>
      <li>contact</li>
    </ul>
  </nav>
  <section>

  </section>
  <aside>
    <blockquote>Article number one</blockquote>
    <blockquote>Article number two</blockquote>
  </aside>

</body>
</html>
```

Listing 1-13: *using the* `<aside>` *element*

The **<aside>** element could be located at the right or left side in our sample page; the tag doesn't really have a predefined position. The **<aside>** element is only describing the information that is enclosed, not a place in the structure. The **<aside>** element may be located in any part of the layout, and it may be used as long as its content is not considered the main content of the document. For instance, we can use the **<aside>** element inside a **<section>** element, or even within relevant information—for example, for a quotation in a text.

<footer>

To finish the construction of the template or elemental structure of our HTML5 document, we only need one more element. We already have the header of the body, sections with navigation aids and important information, and additional information in a side bar. The only thing left is to close the design and give an end to the document's body. HTML5 provides a specific element for this purpose called **<footer>**:

```
<!DOCTYPE html>
<html lang="en">
<head>
  <meta charset="utf-8">
  <meta name="description" content="This is an HTML5 example">
  <meta name="keywords" content="HTML5, CSS3, JavaScript">
  <title>This text is the title of the document</title>
  <link rel="stylesheet" href="mystyles.css">
</head>
<body>
  <header>
    <h1>This is the main title of the website</h1>
  </header>
  <nav>
    <ul>
      <li>home</li>
      <li>photos</li>
      <li>videos</li>
      <li>contact</li>
    </ul>
  </nav>
  <section>

  </section>
  <aside>
    <blockquote>Article number one</blockquote>
    <blockquote>Article number two</blockquote>
  </aside>
  <footer>
    Copyright &copy; 2010-2011
  </footer>
```

```
</body>
</html>
```

Listing 1-14: *using the* `<footer>` *element*

On the typical web page layout (Figure 1-1), the section named the **Institutional** bar would be defined with **`<footer>`** tags. This is because the bar represents the end (or foot) of our document, and this part of the web page is commonly used to share general information about the author or the company behind the project, like copyright, terms and conditions, etc.

Usually, the **`<footer>`** element will represent the end of the body of our document and have the main purpose described above. However, the **`<footer>`** tag may be used several times within the body to represent also the end of different sections (The **`<header>`** tag may be used several times within the body as well.). We will study this characteristic later.

Deep Inside the Body

The body of our document is ready. The basic structure of our website is finished, but we still have to work on the content. The HTML5 elements studied so far help us identify every section of the layout and assign an intrinsic purpose for each one of them, but what is really important for our website is what is inside those sections.

Most of the elements already examined were created to provide a structure to the HTML document that can be identified and recognized by browsers and new devices. We learned about the **<body>** tags to declare the body or the visible part of the document, the **<header>** tags to enclose important information for the body, the **<nav>** tags to supply navigational aids, the **<section>** tags containing the most relevant content, and the **<aside>** and **<footer>** tags to provide additional information. But none of these elements are declaring anything about the content itself. All of them have a very specific structural purpose.

The further inside the document we go, the closer we get to defining the content. This information will be composed of different visual elements such as titles, texts, images, videos, and interactive applications among others. We need to be able to differentiate these elements and establish relationships between them.

<article>

The layout considered before (Figure 1-1) is the most common and essential structure for websites on the Internet these days, but it is also representative of how key content is shown on the screen. In the same way that blogs are divided into entries, websites usually present relevant information divided into parts that share similar characteristics. The **<article>** element let us identify each of these parts.

```
<!DOCTYPE html>
<html lang="en">
<head>
  <meta charset="utf-8">
  <meta name="description" content="This is an HTML5 example">
  <meta name="keywords" content="HTML5, CSS3, JavaScript">
  <title>This text is the title of the document</title>
  <link rel="stylesheet" href="mystyles.css">
</head>
```

```
<body>
  <header>
    <h1>This is the main title of the website</h1>
  </header>
  <nav>
    <ul>
      <li>home</li>
      <li>photos</li>
      <li>videos</li>
      <li>contact</li>
    </ul>
  </nav>
  <section>
    <article>
      This is the text of my first post
    </article>
    <article>
      This is the text of my second post
    </article>
  </section>
  <aside>
    <blockquote>Article number one</blockquote>
    <blockquote>Article number two</blockquote>
  </aside>
  <footer>
    Copyright &copy; 2010-2011
  </footer>
</body>
</html>
```

Listing 1-15: *using the* `<article>` *element*

As you can see in the code in Listing 1-15, the **<article>** tags are between the **<section>** tags. The **<article>** tags belong to that section. They are its children, in the same way that every element between the **<body>** tags is a child of the body. But, as with every child of the body, the **<article>** tags are placed one after another, because each one is an independent part of the **<section>**, as shown on Figure 1-4.

> **Review the Basics:** As we said before, the HTML structure can be described as a tree, with the **<html>** element as its root. Another way to describe the relationships between elements is to name them as parents, children or siblings according to their position in the tree structure. For example, in a typical HTML document the **<body>** element is child of the **<html>** element and sibling of the **<head>** element. Both, **<body>** and **<head>**, has the **<html>** element as their parent.

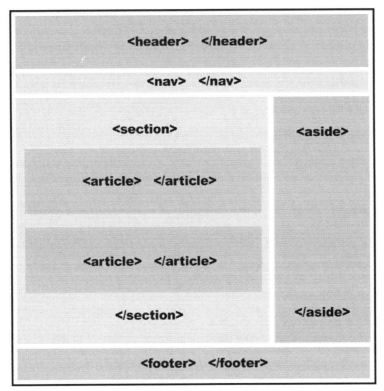

Figure 1-4: *visual representation of the* `<article>` *tags inside the section created to hold the relevant information of the web page*

The **<article>** element is not limited by its name—so not limited to news articles, for example. The **<article>** element is intended to contain an independent item of content so can include a forum post, a magazine article, a blog's entry, user's comment, etc. This element will group portions of information that are related to each other regardless of the nature of that information.

As an independent part of the document, the content of every **<article>** element will have its own independent structure. To define this structure we can take advantage of the versatility of the **<header>** and **<footer>** tags studied before. These tags are portable and can be used not only in the body, but also in every section of our document.

```
<!DOCTYPE html>
<html lang="en">
<head>
  <meta charset="utf-8">
  <meta name="description" content="This is an HTML5 example">
  <meta name="keywords" content="HTML5, CSS3, JavaScript">
  <title>This text is the title of the document</title>
  <link rel="stylesheet" href="mystyles.css">
</head>
```

```html
<body>
  <header>
    <h1>This is the main title of the website</h1>
  </header>
  <nav>
    <ul>
      <li>home</li>
      <li>photos</li>
      <li>videos</li>
      <li>contact</li>
    </ul>
  </nav>
  <section>
    <article>
      <header>
        <h1>Title of post One</h1>
      </header>
      This is the text of my first post
      <footer>
        <p>comments (0)</p>
      </footer>
    </article>
    <article>
      <header>
        <h1>Title of post Two</h1>
      </header>
      This is the text of my second post
      <footer>
        <p>comments (0)</p>
      </footer>
    </article>
  </section>
  <aside>
    <blockquote>Article number one</blockquote>
    <blockquote>Article number two</blockquote>
  </aside>
  <footer>
    Copyright &copy; 2010-2011
  </footer>
</body>
</html>
```

***Listing 1-16:** building the structure of the* `<article>`

Both posts inserted in the code in Listing 1-16 were built with the **<article>** element and have a specific structure. First we have the **<header>** tags containing the title defined with the **<h1>** element. Below is the content itself, the text of the post. And finally, after the text comes the **<footer>** tag specifying the number of comments.

<hgroup>

Inside each **<header>** element, at the top of the body or at the beginning of every **<article>**, we already incorporated **<h1>** tags to specify a title. Basically **<h1>** tags are what is needed to create the head line of every part of the document. But sometimes we will also need to add subtitles or more information to declare what the web page or the section is about. In fact, the **<header>** element is intended to contain other elements as well—for example, a table of contents, search forms, or short texts and logos.

To build the header, we can take advantage of the rest of the H tags: **<h1>**, **<h2>**, **<h3>**, **<h4>**, **<h5>** and **<h6>**. But for internal processing purposes, and to avoid generating multiple sections or subsections during the interpretation of the document, these tags must be grouped together. To do this HTML5, provides the **<hgroup>** element.

```
<!DOCTYPE html>
<html lang="en">
<head>
  <meta charset="utf-8">
  <meta name="description" content="This is an HTML5 example">
  <meta name="keywords" content="HTML5, CSS3, JavaScript">
  <title>This text is the title of the document</title>
  <link rel="stylesheet" href="mystyles.css">
</head>
<body>
  <header>
    <h1>This is the main title of the website</h1>
  </header>
  <nav>
    <ul>
      <li>home</li>
      <li>photos</li>
      <li>videos</li>
      <li>contact</li>
    </ul>
  </nav>
  <section>
    <article>
      <header>
        <hgroup>
          <h1>Title of post One</h1>
          <h2>subtitle of the post One</h2>
        </hgroup>
        <p>posted 12-10-2011</p>
      </header>
      This is the text of my first post
      <footer>
        <p>comments (0)</p>
      </footer>
    </article>
```

```
    <article>
      <header>
        <hgroup>
          <h1>Title of post Two</h1>
          <h2>subtitle of the post Two</h2>
        </hgroup>
        <p>posted 12-15-2011</p>
      </header>
      This is the text of my second post
      <footer>
        <p>comments (0)</p>
      </footer>
    </article>
  </section>
  <aside>
    <blockquote>Article number one</blockquote>
    <blockquote>Article number two</blockquote>
  </aside>
  <footer>
    Copyright &copy; 2010-2011
  </footer>
</body>
</html>
```

Listing 1-17: using the `<hgroup>` *element*

H tags must keep their hierarchy, which means that you must first declare the title with the **<h1>** tag, then use **<h2>** for the subtitle, and so on. However, unlike the older versions of HTML, HTML5 lets you reuse the H tags and build this hierarchy again and again in every section of the document. In the example of Listing 1-17, we added a subtitle and metadata to each post and grouped the title and subtitle together with **<hgroup>**, reusing the **<h1>** and **<h2>** hierarchy in every **<article>** element.

> **IMPORTANT:** The element **<hgroup>** is necessary when we have a title and subtitle or more H tags together in the same **<header>**. This element can only contain H tags and that's why we kept the metadata outside in the example. If you only have the **<h1>** tag or the **<h1>** tag along with metadata, you don't have to group these elements together. For example, in the **<header>** of the body we didn't use this element because we only have one H element inside. Always remember that **<hgroup>** is only intended to group H tags together just as its name clearly specifies.

Browsers and programs that execute and render websites read the HTML code and create its own internal structure to interpret and process every element. This internal structure is divided into sections that have nothing to do with the divisions in the design or the **<section>** element. These are conceptual sections generated during the interpretation of the code. The **<header>** element doesn't create one of these conceptual sections by itself; this means that the elements inside the **<header>** will represent different levels and could generate internally different sections. The

<hgroup> element was created with the purpose of grouping H tags together and avoiding misinterpretations by the browser.

> **Review the Basics:** Metadata is a set of data that describes and provides information about another set of data. In the example, the metadata is the date when the articles were inserted.

<figure> and <figcaption>

The **<figure>** tag was created to help us be even more specific in declaring the document's content. Before this element was introduced, we couldn't identify content that was part of the information but self-contained—for example, illustrations, pictures, videos, etc. Usually those elements are part of the relevant content but can be moved away without affecting or interrupting document's flow. When this type of information is present, **<figure>** tags may be used to identify it.

```
<!DOCTYPE html>
<html lang="en">
<head>
  <meta charset="utf-8">
  <meta name="description" content="This is an HTML5 example">
  <meta name="keywords" content="HTML5, CSS3, JavaScript">
  <title>This text is the title of the document</title>
  <link rel="stylesheet" href="mystyles.css">
</head>
<body>
  <header>
    <h1>This is the main title of the website</h1>
  </header>
  <nav>
    <ul>
      <li>home</li>
      <li>photos</li>
      <li>videos</li>
      <li>contact</li>
    </ul>
  </nav>
  <section>
    <article>
      <header>
        <hgroup>
          <h1>Title of post One</h1>
          <h2>subtitle of the post One</h2>
        </hgroup>
        <p>posted 12-10-2011</p>
      </header>
      This is the text of my first post
```

```
    <figure>
      <img src="http://minkbooks.com/content/myimage.jpg">
      <figcaption>
        This is the image of the first post
      </figcaption>
    </figure>
    <footer>
      <p>comments (0)</p>
    </footer>
  </article>
  <article>
    <header>
      <hgroup>
        <h1>Title of post Two</h1>
        <h2>subtitle of the post Two</h2>
      </hgroup>
      <p>posted 12-15-2011</p>
    </header>
    This is the text of my second post
    <footer>
      <p>comments (0)</p>
    </footer>
  </article>
</section>
<aside>
  <blockquote>Article number one</blockquote>
  <blockquote>Article number two</blockquote>
</aside>
<footer>
  Copyright &copy; 2010-2011
</footer>
</body>
</html>
```

Listing 1-18: *using the* `<figure>` *and* `<figcaption>` *elements*

In Listing 1-18, in the first post, we inserted an image (**`<img src="http://minkbooks.com/content/myimage.jpg">`**) after the text of the post. This is a common practice; often text is enriched with images or videos. The **`<figure>`** tags let us enclose these visual complements and differentiate them from the most relevant information.

Also on Listing 1-18, you can see an extra element inside **`<figure>`**. Usually units of information like images or videos are described with a short text below. HTML5 provides an element to place and identify this descriptive caption. The **`<figcaption>`** tags enclose the caption related to the **`<figure>`** and establish a relationship between both elements and their content.

New and Old Elements

HTML5 was developed in order to simplify, specify and organize the code. To achieve these purposes, tags and attributes were added, and HTML was integrated with CSS and Javascript. These incorporations and improvements from previous versions relate not only to new elements, but also to the way we use the old ones.

<mark>

The **<mark>** tag was added to highlight part of a text that originally wasn't considered important but is now relevant according to the user's current activity. The best example is a search result. The **<mark>** element will highlight the part of the text that is matching the search string.

```
<span>My <mark>car</mark> is red</span>
```

Listing 1-19: *use of the* <mark> *element to highlight the word "car"*

An example is if someone performed a search for the word "car"; the results might be shown with the code in Listing 1-19. The short text represents the results of the search, and the **<mark>** tags in between enclose what was the text searched— the word "car." In some browsers, this word will be highlighted with a yellow background by default, but you can always overwrite those styles with your own using CSS, as we will see in later chapters.

In the past, we usually achieved the same result as above using a **<b>** element. However, the addition of **<mark>** helped change the meaning and set up a new purpose for these and other related elements.

- **<em>** should be used to indicate emphasis (replacing the **<i>** tag we have been used before)
- **<strong>** is for importance
- **<mark>** to highlight text that is relevant according to the circumstances
- **<b>** should be used only when there is no other element most appropriate for the situation

<small>

The new specificity of HTML is also evident in elements such as **<small>**. Previously this element was intended to present any text with small font. The keyword was referencing the size of the text, independently of its meaning. In HTML5 the new purpose of the **<small>** element is to represent small print, like legal print, disclaimers, etc.

```
<small>Copyright &copy; 2011 MinkBooks</small>
```

Listing 1-20: legal print with `<small>`

<cite>

Another element that has changed its nature to become more specific is **<cite>**. Now the **<cite>** tags enclose the title of a work such as a book, movie, song, etc.

```
<span>I love the movie <cite>Temptations</cite></span>
```

Listing 1-21: citing a movie with `<cite>`

<address>

The **<address>** element is an old element turned into a structural element. We didn't have to use it before to build our template. However, it could fit perfectly in some situations to represent the contact information for the content of an **<article>** element or the entire **<body>**.

This element should be included inside a **<footer>**, as in the next example:

```
<article>
  <header>
    <h1>Title of post Two</h1>
  </header>
  This is the text of the article
  <footer>
    <address>
      <a href="http://www.jdgauchat.com">JD Gauchat</a>
    </address>

  </footer>
</article>
```

Listing 1-22: adding contact information to an `<article>`

<time>

In every **<article>** in our last template of Listing 1-18, we included the date to indicate when the article was posted. We used a simple **<p>** element inside the

\<header\> of the articles to show the date, but there is a special element in HTML5 for this specific purpose. The **\<time\>** element lets you declare a machine-readable timestamp and a human-readable text representing the date and time.

```
<article>
  <header>
    <h1>Title of post Two</h1>
    <time datetime="2011-10-12" pubdate>posted 12-10-2011</time>
  </header>
  This is the text of the article
</article>
```

Listing 1-23: date and time using the <time> *element*

In Listing 1-23, the **\<p\>** element used in previous examples was replaced by the new **\<time\>** element to show the date when the article was posted. The attribute **datetime** has the value that represents the machine-readable timestamp. The format of this timestamp might follow a pattern as in this example: **2011-10-12T12:10:45**. We also included the attribute **pubdate**, which is just added to indicate that the value of the attribute **datetime** represents the publication date.

Quick Reference
HTML5 Documents

In the HTML5 specification, HTML is in charge of the structure of the document and provides a whole set of new elements for this purpose. There are also a few elements that remain just for styling. Here is the list of what we consider the most relevant:

IMPORTANT: For a complete reference of the HTML elements incorporated in the new specification, visit our website and follow the links for this chapter.

<header>—This element represents a set of introductory aids and can be applied to different sections of the document. It is intended to contain the section's headings, but also could be used to wrap indexes, search forms, logos, etc.

<nav>—This element indicates a section of links that have navigational purposes, such as menus or indexes. Not all the links in a web page have to be inside a **<nav>** element; only those parts of major navigation blocks must be.

<section>—This element represents a generic section in the document. It is usually used to build several blocks of content (for example, columns) in order to group content that shares a specific theme, such as chapters or pages of a book, groups of news articles, a set of articles, etc.

<aside>—This element represents content that is related to the main content but not part of it. Examples might be quotations, information on side bar, advertising, etc.

<footer>—This element represents additional information related to its parent element. For example, a footer inserted at the end of the body will provide additional information about the document, like a regular footer of a page. The element can be used not only for the **<body>** but also inside different sections in the body, providing additional information about those specific sections.

<article>—This element represents a self-contained portion of relevant information—for example, every article of a newspaper or every entry of a blog. The **<article>** element can be nested and used to show a list within a list of related items —for example, users' comments in a blog entry.

<hgroup>—This element is used to group a set of H elements when the heading has multiple levels—for example, a heading with a title and a subtitle.

<figure>—This element represents an independent portion of content (for example, images, diagrams or videos) that is referred to in the main content. This is information that could be removed from the main content without affecting its normal flow.

<figcaption>—This element is to show a caption or legend to be used along with the **<figure>** element. An example is the description of an image.

<mark>—This element highlights a text that has relevance in a particular situation or that is shown in response to user's input.

<small>—This element represents side comments, such a small print (for example, disclaimers, legal restrictions, copyrights).

<cite>—This element is used to show the title of a work (book, movie, poem, etc).

<address>—This element encloses contact information for an `<article>` or the entire document. It should be inserted within a `<footer>`.

<time>—This element is intended to show date and time in formats readable by humans and machines. The human-readable timestamp is placed between the tags, while the machine-readable timestamp is set as the value of the attribute `datetime`. A second optative attribute called `pubdate` is used to indicate that the value of `datetime` is the publication date.

Chapter 2
CSS Styling and Box Models

CSS and HTML

As we made clear before, the new specification of HTML is not only about tags and HTML itself. The web demands design and functionality, not just structural organization and sections definition. In this new paradigm, HTML comes together with CSS and Javascript as one integrated instrument. The function of every technology has been explained and the new HTML elements responsible for a documents' structure have been already studied, so now is time to see the relevance of CSS in this strategic union and the influence it has over the presentation of HTML documents.

Officially CSS has nothing to do with HTML5. CSS is not part of the specification and never was. It was in fact a complement developed to overcome the limitations and reduce the complexity of HTML. At the beginning, attributes within HTML tags provided some essential styles to every element, but as the language evolved the code became more complicated to write and maintain and HTML alone no longer could meet the demands of web designers. As a result, CSS soon was adopted as the way to separate structure from presentation. Since then, CSS has thrived but developed in parallel, always focused on designers and their needs rather than necessarily be part of HTML evolution.

The version 3 of CSS followed the same path, but this time with much more compromise. The HTML5 specification was developed implicitly considering CSS in charge of the design. Due to this consideration, the integration between HTML and CSS3 is now vital for web developing and that's why every time we mention HML5 we are also making reference to CSS3, even when officially these are two independent technologies.

At this moment, CSS3 features are being implemented and incorporated into HTML5 compatible browsers along with the rest of the specification. In this chapter we will study basic concepts of CSS and the new CSS3 techniques already available for presentation and structuring. We will also learn about new selectors and pseudo-classes that make easier the selection and identification of HTML elements.

> **Review the Basics:** CSS is a language that works along with HTML to provide visual styles to the elements of the document, such as size, color, backgrounds, borders, etc.

IMPORTANT: At this moment CSS3 features are being incorporated in the last versions of the most popular browsers, but some of them are still in an experimental stage. For this reason, these new styles must be preceded by prefixes like `-moz-` or `-webkit-` to be effectively used, depending on browser's engine. We will talk again about this issue later in this chapter.

Styles and Structure

Although each browser grants styles by default to every HTML element, those styles do not necessarily agree with each designer's expectations. Usually the styles are very distant from what we want for our websites. Designers and developers often have to apply their own styles to get the look and organization on the screen they really want.

> **IMPORTANT:** In this part of the chapter, we are going to review CSS styling and explain basic techniques to define a document's structure. If you are familiar with these concepts, you might feel comfortable skipping over the parts you already know.

Block Elements

Regarding the structure, basically every browser orders the elements by default according to their type: block or inline. This classification is associated with the way the elements are displayed on the screen.

- **Block elements** are positioned one under another down the page
- **Inline elements** are positioned side-by-side one after another in the same line, without any line break unless there is not enough horizontal space

Almost every structural element in our document will be treated like a block element by default. That means that every HTML tag that represents a part of the visual organization (for example, `<section>`, `<nav>`, `<header>`, `<footer>`, `<div>`) will be positioned one under another.

In Chapter 1, we created an HTML document with the intention of replicating the layout of a typical website. The design included horizontal bars and two columns in the middle. Due to the way browsers render these elements by default, the result on the screen is far from what we expected. Once you open the HTML file with the code on Listing 1-18 of Chapter 1 in your browser, you can immediately identify the wrong position on the screen of the two columns defined by `<section>` and `<aside>`. One column is under the other instead of side by side. Every block is rendered by default as wide as possible, as tall as the information it contains, and one over another as shown in Figure 2-1.

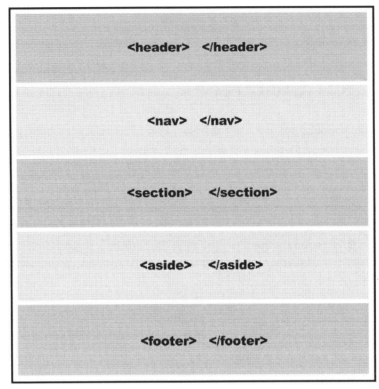

Figure 2-1: *visual representation of the page layout rendered with default styles*

Box Models

To learn how we can create our own layout, we need to understand first how browsers process HTML code. Browsers consider every HTML element as a box. A webpage is actually a group of boxes put together following certain rules. These rules are made by styles provided by browsers or by designers using CSS.

CSS has a predetermined set of properties to overwrite browsers' styles and get the design wanted. These properties are not specific; they have to be combined to form rules that later are used to group boxes together and get the right layout. The combination of those rules is usually called a model or layout system. All the rules put together constitute a box model.

There is only one box model that is considered standard these days, and several others are experimental. The valid and widely adopted model is the one called Traditional Box Model, which has been used since the first version of CSS. Although this model has proven to be effective, some experimental models are trying to address its shortcomings. The most important, and the one that is considered part of HTML5, is the new Flexible Box Model, introduced with CSS3.

Basics About Styling

Before we start typing CSS rules in our style sheet and experimenting with box models, we have to review the basic concepts about CSS styling that are going to be used in the rest of the book.

Applying styles to HTML elements changes the way they are presented on the screen. As we said before, browsers provide by default a set of styles that in most cases are not enough to satisfy the needs of designers. To change that, we can overwrite them with our own styles using different techniques.

> **Review the Basics:** In this book, you will find just a brief introduction to CSS styles. We only mention the techniques and properties you need to know to be able to understand the subjects and codes studied throughout the book. If you don't have any experience with CSS, go to our website and follow the links for this chapter.

> **Do It Yourself:** Into an empty text file, copy every HTML code from the following listings and open the file in your browser to check how they work. Note that the file must have the `.html` extension to be open properly.

Inline Styles

One of the simplest techniques is to assign styles inside the element as an attribute. Listing 2-1 provides a simple HTML document showing the element **<p>** modified by the attribute `style` with the value `font-size: 20px`. The attribute `style` changes the default size of the text inside the element **<p>** to the new size of 20 pixels.

```
<!DOCTYPE html>
<html lang="en">
<head>
  <title>This text is the title of the document</title>
</head>
<body>
  <p style="font-size: 20px">My text</p>
</body>
</html>
```

Listing 2-1: *CSS styles within HTML tags*

To use the technique outlined previously is a fine way to test styles and have a quick look to its effects, but is not recommended for an entire document. The reason is simple: when using this technique, we have to write and repeat every style in every element, increasing the document to an unacceptable size and making it impossible to update and maintain. Just imagine if you decide that instead of 20 pixels the size of the text in every **<p>** element should be 24 pixels. You would have to change every style in every **<p>** tag in the whole document.

Embedded Styles

A better alternative is to insert styles in the head of the document and then use references to affect the proper HTML elements:

```
<!DOCTYPE html>
<html lang="en">
<head>
  <title>This text is the title of the document</title>
  <style>
    p { font-size: 20px }
  </style>
</head>
<body>
  <p>My text</p>
</body>
</html>
```

Listing 2-2: styles listed in the head of the document

The **<style>** element (shown in Listing 2-2) allows authors to insert CSS styles within documents. In previous HTML versions, it was necessary to specify what kind of styles would be inserted. In HTML5, the default style is CSS, therefore we don't need to add any attribute to the opening **<style>** tag.

The highlighted code in Listing 2-2 has the same function as the line of code in Listing 2-1, but in Listing 2-2 we didn't have to write the style inside every **<p>** tag in the document because all **<p>** elements are already affected. With this method we are reducing our code and assigning the style we want to a specific element using references. We will look at references later in this chapter.

External Files

Declaring the styles in the head of the document saves space and makes the code more consistence and maintainable, but it requires us to make a copy of the styles in every document of our website. The solution is to move all the styles to an external file and then use the **<link>** element to insert this file to any document that requires styling. This method also allows us to change a whole set of styles by simply including a different file. It also allows us to modify or adapt our documents to every circumstance or device, as we will see at the end of the book.

In Chapter 1, we studied the `<link>` tag and saw how to insert CSS files in our documents. Using the line `<link rel="stylesheet" href="mystyles.css">` we told the browser to load the file `mystyles.css` because it contains all the styles needed to render the page. This practice is widely adopted among designers that are already working with HTML5. The `<link>` tag referencing the CSS file will be inserted in any document where the styles are required:

```
<!DOCTYPE html>
<html lang="en">
<head>
  <title>This text is the title of the document</title>
  <link rel="stylesheet" href="mystyles.css">
</head>
<body>
  <p>My text</p>
</body>
</html>
```

Listing 2-3: applying CSS styles from an external file

Do It Yourself: From now on, we will be adding the CSS styles to a file called `mystyles.css`. You have to create that file in the same folder as the HTML file, and copy the CSS styles inside this file to see them working.

Review the Basics: CSS files are also regular text files. As well as the HTML files, you can create them using any text editor such as Windows' Notepad.

References

Putting all our styles together in one external file and inserting that file into every document is quite convenient. However, we need mechanisms to establish a specific relationship between these styles and the elements inside the document that will be affected by them.

When we were talking about how to embed styles in the document, we showed one of the techniques often used in CSS for referencing HTML elements. In Listing 2-2, the style to change the font size was referencing every `<p>` element using the `p` keyword. In this way, the style inserted between the `<style>` tags was referencing each `<p>` tag of the document and assigning that particular CSS style to all of them.

There are different methods to select which HTML element will be affected by a CSS rule.

- by the keyword of the element
- by the `id` attribute
- by the `class` attribute

However, we will see later that CSS3 is pretty flexible in this matter and incorporates new and more specific ways to do it.

Referencing by Keyword

Declaring the CSS rule with the keyword of the element will affect every similar element in the document. For example, the following rule will change the styles of the **<p>** elements:

```
p { font-size: 20px }
```

Listing 2-4: *referencing by keyword*

This is the technique already presented in Listing 2-2. With the keyword **p** in front of the rule we are telling the browser that this rule must be applied to every **<p>** element found in the HTML document. Now, all the texts surrounded by **<p>** tags will have the size of 20 pixels.

Of course, the same will work for any other HTML element in the document. If we specified the keyword **span** instead of **p**, for instance, every text between **<span>** tags would have the size of 20 pixels:

```
span { font-size: 20px }
```

Listing 2-5: *referencing by another keyword*

But what happens if we only need to reference one specific tag? Do we need to use the **style** attribute inside that tag? The answer is no. As we learned before, the **Inline Styles** method (using the attribute **style** within HTML tags) is a deprecated technique and its use should be avoided. To select a specific HTML element from the rules in our CSS file, we can use two different attributes: **id** and **class**.

Referencing by the Id Attribute

The **id** attribute is more like a name, an identification of the element. This means that the value of this attribute can't be duplicated. This name must be unique in the entire document.

To reference a particular element using the **id** attribute from our CSS file, the rule has to be declared with the sign **#** in front of the identification value.

```
#text1 { font-size: 20px }
```

Listing 2-6: *referencing by the value of the* id *attribute*

The rule in Listing 2-6 will be applied to the HTML element identified by the attribute `id="text1"`. Now our HTML code will look like this:

```
<!DOCTYPE html>
<html lang="en">
<head>
  <title>This text is the title of the document</title>
  <link rel="stylesheet" href="mystyles.css">
</head>
<body>
  <p id="text1">My text</p>
</body>
</html>
```

Listing 2-7: *identifying the element* <p> *by its* id *attribute*

The impact of this procedure is that every time we make a reference using the identification **text1** in our CSS file, the element with that id value will be modified, but the rest of the **<p>** elements, or any other element in the document, won't be affected.

This is an extremely specific way to reference an element and is commonly used for more general elements, such as structural tags. The **id** attribute and its specificity is in fact more suitable for Javascript reference, as we will see in further chapters.

Referencing by the Class Attribute

Rather than using the **id** attribute, it is better practice to use the **class** attribute for styling purposes most of the time. This attribute is more flexible and can be assigned to every HTML element in the document that shares a similar design:

```
.text1 { font-size: 20px }
```

Listing 2-8: *referencing by the value of the* class *attribute*

To work with the attribute **class**, we have to declare the rule with a period before its name. The advantage of this method is that inserting the **class** attribute with the value **text1** will be enough to assign this style to any element we want.

```
<!DOCTYPE html>
<html lang="en">
```

```
<head>
    <title>This text is the title of the document</title>
    <link rel="stylesheet" href="mystyles.css">
</head>
<body>
    <p class="text1">My text</p>
    <p class="text1">My text</p>
    <p>My text</p>
</body>
</html>
```

Listing 2-9: assigning styles through the `class` *attribute*

The **<p>** elements in the first two lines inside the body in Listing 2-9 have the attribute **class** with the value **text1**. As we said before, the same class can be applied to different elements in the same document. Therefore, these first two elements share the same class and both will be affected by the style in Listing 2-8. The last **<p>** element keeps the styles by default.

The reason for the period before the name of the class is because we can use the same name of the class in different elements and assign different styles to every one of them:

```
p.text1 { font-size: 20px }
```

Listing 2-10: referencing only <p> elements by the value of the `class` *attribute*

In Listing 2-10, we created a rule that references the class named **text1** but only for the elements **<p>**. If any other element has the same name for its **class** attribute, it won't be modified by this particular rule.

Referencing by Any Attribute

Although these reference methods cover a variety of situations, sometimes they are not enough to find the exact element we want to style. The last versions of CSS have incorporated new ways to reference HTML elements. One of them is the **Attribute Selector**. Now, we can reference an element not only by **id** and **class**, but also any other attribute:

```
p[name] { font-size: 20px }
```

Listing 2-11: referencing only <p> elements that has a `name` *attribute*

The rule in Listing 2-11 changes only elements **<p>** that have an attribute called **name**. To emulate what we were doing with the attributes **id** and **class**, we can also provide the value of the attribute:

```
p[name="mytext"] { font-size: 20px }
```

Listing 2-12: *referencing <p> elements that has a* name *attribute with the value* mytext

CSS3 lets us combined the symbol "=" with others to make a more detailed selection:

```
p[name^="my"] { font-size: 20px }
p[name$="my"] { font-size: 20px }
p[name*="my"] { font-size: 20px }
```

Listing 2-13: *new selectors in CSS3*

If you already know **Regular Expressions** from other languages such as Javascript or PHP, you will recognize the selectors used in Listing 2-13. In CSS3, these selectors produce similar results:

- the rule with the selector **^=** will be assigned to any **<p>** element with a **name** attribute value beginning with "**my**" (e.g. "**mytext**", "**mycar**")
- the rule with the selector **$=** will be assigned to any **<p>** element with a **name** attribute value ending with "**my**" (e.g. "**textmy**", "**carmy**")
- the rule with the selector ***=** will match any **<p>** element with a **name** attribute value containing the substring "**my**" (In this case, the substring could also be in the middle—for example, in "**textmycar**".).

In these examples, we used the element **<p>**, the attribute **name**, and some random text such as "**my**", but the same technique may be used with any attribute and value you need. You just have to write the square brackets and type inside the name of the attribute and value you are looking for to reference any HTML element.

Referencing by Pseudo-Classes

CSS3 also incorporates new pseudo-classes that make things even more specific.

```
<!DOCTYPE html>
<html lang="en">
```

```
<head>
  <title>This text is the title of the document</title>
  <link rel="stylesheet" href="mystyles.css">
</head>
<body>
  <div id="wrapper">
    <p class="mytext1">My text1</p>
    <p class="mytext2">My text2</p>
    <p class="mytext3">My text3</p>
    <p class="mytext4">My text4</p>
  </div>
</body>
</html>
```

Listing 2-14: *template to test pseudo-classes*

Let's take a look at the new HTML code in Listing 2-14. It has four **<p>** elements that, considering the HTML structure, are siblings, and all of them are children of the same element **<div>**.

Using pseudo-classes we can take advantage of this organization and reference a specific element no matter how much we know about its attributes or their values:

```
p:nth-child(2){
  background: #999999;
}
```

Listing 2-15: *pseudo-class* `:nth-child()`

The pseudo-class is added using a colon after the reference and before its name. In the rule of Listing 2-15, we are referencing **<p>** elements. This rule could also be written as **.myclass:nth-child(2)** to reference every element that is a child of another element and has the value of the **class** attribute equal to **myclass**. The pseudo-classes can be appended to any kind of reference that has been studied before.

The **nth-child()** pseudo-class let us find a specific child. As we already explained, the HTML document of Listing 2-14 has four **<p>** elements that are siblings. This means that all of them have the same parent that is the element **<div>**. What this pseudo-class is really indicating is something like: "the child in the position…" so the number between the parentheses will be the number of the position of the child, or index. The rule of Listing 2-15 is referencing every second **<p>** element found in the document.

> **Do It Yourself:** Replace the previous code in your HTML file with the one in Listing 2-14 and open this file in your browser. Incorporate the rules studied in Listing 2-15 into the file **mystyles.css** in order to test this example.

Using this reference method, we can, of course, select any child we want by changing the index number. For example, the following rule will have an impact only over the last **<p>** element of our template:

```
p:nth-child(4){
  background: #999999;
}
```

Listing 2-16: pseudo-class `nth-child()`

As you probably realized, it is possible to assign styles to every element by creating a rule for every one of them:

```
*{
  margin: 0px;
}
p:nth-child(1){
  background: #999999;
}
p:nth-child(2){
  background: #CCCCCC;
}
p:nth-child(3){
  background: #999999;
}
p:nth-child(4){
  background: #CCCCCC;
}
```

Listing 2-17: creating a list with the pseudo-class `nth-child()`

The first rule in Listing 2-17 uses the universal selector * to assign the same style to every element in the document. This new selector represents every single element in the document's body and is useful when we need to establish some basic rules. In this case, we set the margin of every element to 0 pixels to avoid any spaces or empty lines like the ones created by the **<p>** elements by default.

In the rest of the code in Listing 2-17, we used the **nth-child()** pseudo-class to generate a menu or a list of options that are clearly differentiated by the color of its line.

> **Do It Yourself:** Copy the last code into the CSS file and open the HTML document to check the effect in your browser.

Adding more options to the menu could be done by incorporating new **<p>** elements in the HTML code and new rules with the **nth-child()** pseudo-class and the proper index number. However, using this approach would generate lots of code and be impossible to apply in websites with dynamic content generation. An alternative to get the same result more effectively is to take advantage of the keywords **odd** and **even** available for this pseudo-class:

```
* {
  margin: 0px;
}
p:nth-child(odd){
  background: #999999;
}
p:nth-child(even){
  background: #CCCCCC;
}
```

Listing 2-18: *taking advantage of the keywords* odd *and* even

Now there are only two rules for the entire list. Even if more options or rows are incorporated to the list, the styles will be assigned automatically to every one of them according to their position. The **odd** keyword for the `nth-child()` pseudo-class affects the elements **<p>** that are children of another element and have an odd index, and the **even** keyword affects those that have an even index.

There are other important pseudo-classes related to this one, some of them recently incorporated, such as **first-child**, **last-child** and **only-child**. The **first-child** pseudo-class references only the first child, the **last-child** references only the last child, and the **only-child** affects an element if it's the only child of its parent. These pseudo-classes in particular don't require keywords or extra parameters and are implemented as in the following example:

```
* {
  margin: 0px;
}
p:last-child{
  background: #999999;
}
```

Listing 2-19: *using* last-child *to modify only the last* <p> *element of the list*

Another important pseudo-class is the negation pseudo-class, written **not()**.

```
:not(p){
  margin: 0px;
}
```

Listing 2-20: *applying styles to every element except* <p>

The rule in Listing 2-20 will assign a margin of 0 pixels to every element in the document except the elements **<p>**. Unlike the universal selector we used before, the **not()** pseudo-class let us provide an exception. The styles in the rules created with this pseudo-class will be assigned to every element but not the ones included between parentheses.

Instead of the keyword of the element, you may use any reference you want. In Listing 2-21, for example, every element will be affected except those with the value **mytext2** in their **class** attribute:

```
:not(.mytext2){
   margin: 0px;
}
```

Listing 2-21: exception using the `class` *attribute*

When you apply the last rule to the HTML code of Listing 2-14 the browser assigns the styles by default to the **<p>** element identified by the class value **mytext2** and provides a margin of 0 pixels to the rest.

New Selectors

There are a few more selectors that were added or considered part of CSS3 and could be useful for your designs. These selectors use the symbols >, + and ~ to specify a relation between elements.

```
div > p.mytext2{
   color: #990000;
}
```

Listing 2-22: selector >

The selector **>** is indicating that the element affected is the second element when it has the first element as its parent. The rule in Listing 2-22 modifies the **<p>** elements that are children of a **<div>** element. In this case, we were specific and referenced only the **<p>** element with the class **mytext2**.

The next selector is constructed with the symbol **+**. This selector references the second element when it is immediately preceded by the first element. Both elements must share the same parent:

```
p.mytext2 + p{
   color: #990000;
}
```

Listing 2-23: selector +

The rule in Listing 2-23 affects the <p> element that is after another <p> element identified with the class **mytext2**. If you open in your browser the HTML file with the code of Listing 2-14, the text in the third <p> element will appear on the screen in the color red because this particular <p> element is positioned immediately after the <p> element identified with the class **mytext2**.

The last selector is constructed with the symbol ~. This selector is similar to the previous one but the element affected is not necessarily immediately preceding the first element. Also, there may be more than one element.

```
p.mytext2 ~ p{
   color: #990000;
}
```

Listing 2-24: selector ~

The rule in Listing 2-24 is affecting the third and fourth <p> elements in our example. The style will be applied to all the <p> elements that are siblings and are after the <p> element identified with the class **mytext2**. It doesn't matter if other different elements are in between; the third and fourth <p> element will still be affected. You can experiment with the HTML code in Listing 2-14 by inserting a <span></span> element after the <p> element with the class **mytext2** to verify that only <p> elements are modified by this rule.

Applying CSS to Our Template

As we learned earlier in this chapter, every structural element is considered a box, and the structure is presented like a group of boxes. The boxes put together constitute what is called a box model.

We are going to study two different box models: the Traditional Box Model and the new Flexible Box Model. The Traditional Box Model has been implemented since the first version of CSS. This model is currently supported by every browser in the market and is actually a standard for web design. In contrast, the Flexible Box Model, incorporated in CSS3, is still under development, but its advantages over the Traditional Box Model could make it a standard, hence its importance as a subject of study.

Every model can be applied to the same HTML structure, but the structure has to be prepared to be affected by these styles in the right way. Our HTML documents have to be adapted to the box model selected.

> **IMPORTANT:** The Traditional Box Model presented next is not an HTML5 introduction. This model has been always available and probably you already know how to implement it. If this is the case, feel free to jump to the next part of the chapter.

Traditional Box Model

It all began with tables. Tables were the elements that unintentionally became the tools for developers to create and organize boxes of content on the screen. This can be considered the first box model of the web. The boxes were created by expanding cells and combining rows of cells, columns of cells, and entire tables, one next to another or even nested. When websites got bigger and more complex, this practice presented serious problems related to the size and how to maintain the code necessary to create them.

These initial problems started what we now see as a natural practice: the division between structure and presentation. Using `<div>` tags and CSS styles made it possible to replace the function of tables and effectively separate the HTML structure from the presentation. With `<div>` elements and CSS we could create boxes on the screen, position those boxes at one side or another, and give a specific size, border, color, etc. CSS provided specific properties to let us organize the boxes as we wished. These properties were powerful enough to create a model of boxes that turned to be what today is known as the Traditional Box Model.

Some deficiencies in this model kept tables alive for a while, but the mainstream, influenced by Ajax's success and a lot of new interactive applications, gradually turned `<div>` tags and CSS styling into a standard. Finally, the Traditional Box Model was adopted on a large scale.

Template

In Chapter 1, we already built our HTML5 template. This template has the necessary elements to provide structure for our document, but some things have to be added to make it ready for CSS styling and the Traditional Box Model.

The Traditional Box Model needs to wrap boxes together to provide horizontal order. Because the entire content of the body is created from a group of boxes that have to be centered and sized to a specific value, a `<div>` element has to be added as a wrapper.

The new template will look like this:

```
<!DOCTYPE html>
<html lang="en">
<head>
  <meta charset="utf-8">
  <meta name="description" content="This is an HTML5 example">
  <meta name="keywords" content="HTML5, CSS3, JavaScript">
  <title>This text is the title of the document</title>
  <link rel="stylesheet" href="mystyles.css">
</head>
```

```
<body>
<div id="wrapper">
  <header id="main_header">
    <h1>This is the main title of the website</h1>
  </header>
  <nav id="main_menu">
    <ul>
      <li>home</li>
      <li>photos</li>
      <li>videos</li>
      <li>contact</li>
    </ul>
  </nav>
  <section id="main_section">
    <article>
      <header>
        <hgroup>
          <h1>Title of post One</h1>
          <h2>subtitle of the post One</h2>
        </hgroup>
        <time datetime="2011-12-10" pubdate>posted 12-10-
2011</time>
      </header>
      This is the text of my first post
      <figure>
        <img src="http://minkbooks.com/content/myimage.jpg">
        <figcaption>
          this is the image of the first post
        </figcaption>
      </figure>
      <footer>
        <p>comments (0)</p>
      </footer>
    </article>
    <article>
      <header>
        <hgroup>
          <h1>Title of post Two</h1>
          <h2>subtitle of the post Two</h2>
        </hgroup>
        <time datetime="2011-12-15" pubdate>posted 12-15-
2011</time>
      </header>
      This is the text of my second post
      <footer>
        <p>comments (0)</p>
      </footer>
    </article>
  </section>
  <aside id="main_aside">
    <blockquote>Article number one</blockquote>
    <blockquote>Article number two</blockquote>
  </aside>
```

```
<footer id="main_footer">
   Copyright &copy 2010-2011
</footer>
</div>
</body>
</html>
```

Listing 2-25: new HTML5 template ready for CSS styling

Listing 2-25 provides a new template ready to be styled. Two important changes from Listing 1-18 of Chapter 1 can be spotted on this code. There are several tags identified with the attributes `id` and `class`. This means that now we can reference a very specific element with the value of its `id` attribute, or we can modify several elements at the same time using the value of their `class` attribute from the CSS rules.

The second important modification from the previous template is the addition of the `<div>` element mentioned before. This `<div>` was identified with the attribute `id="wrapper"`, and it is closed at the end of the body with the closing tag `</div>`. This wrapper will let us apply the box model to the content of the body and designate its horizontal position.

> **Do It Yourself:** Compare the code on Listing 1-18 Chapter 1 with the code on Listing 2-25 in this chapter, and find the opening and closing tags of the `<div>` element added as wrapper. Also check which elements are now identified with the `id` attribute and which with the `class` attribute. Confirm that the values of the `id` attributes are unique for every tag.
> You will also need to replace the code in the HTML file created before by the one on Listing 2-25.

With the HTML document ready, it is time to create our style sheet.

Universal Selector *

Let's start with basic rules that will provide some consistency to the design:

```
*  {
  margin: 0px;
  padding: 0px;
}
```

Listing 2-26: general CSS rule

Usually, for most elements, we need to customize margins, or just simply keep the margins to the minimum. Some elements by default have margins that are different from zero and sometimes too big. As we progress in the creation of our design, we will find that most of the elements' margins have to be set to zero. To avoid needing to duplicate styles, we can use the universal selector * studied before.

The first rule in our CSS file listed in Listing 2-26 assures that every element will have a margin of 0 pixels. From now on, we will only need to modify the margins of the elements that we want to be bigger than zero.

> **Review the Basics:** Remember that every element is considered a box. So the margin is the space around the element, outside the border of that box (The padding, on the other hand, is space around the content of the element and inside its border—for example, the space between the title and the border of the virtual box created by the <h1> element that contains that title. We address padding later in this chapter.). The margin size can be defined for selected sides of the element or every side. The rule **margin: 0px** in our style sheet is setting a zero or null margin for every side of the box. If the size was specified as 5 pixels, for example, the box would have a space of 5 pixels wide around it. That means that the box would be separated by 5 pixels from neighboring boxes.

> **Do It Yourself:** We have to write all the necessary CSS rules in the style sheet file. The file was already included in the head of the HTML code with the <link> tag, so all you have to do is create a new empty file with your text editor called **mystyles.css** and then copy the rules in Listing 2-26 and the following listings into it.

New Heading Hierarchy

In our template, we used the elements <h1> and <h2> to declare the titles and subtitles of different sections of the document. The default styles for these elements are always far from what we want, and in HTML5 (as we learned in the previous chapter), we can rebuild the H hierarchy over and over again in every section. The <h1> element, for example, will be used several times in the same document, not only for the main title of the entire document as happened before, but for some internal sections as well, so we have to style them properly:

```
h1 {
   font: bold 20px verdana, sans-serif;
}
h2 {
   font: bold 14px verdana, sans-serif;
}
```

Listing 2-27: adding styles for <h1> and <h2> elements

The property **font**, assigned to the elements <h1> and <h2> in Listing 2-27, lets us declare all the text styles in just one declaration. The properties that can be declared using `font` are: `font-style`, `font-variant`, `font-weight`, `font-size/line-height`, and `font-family` in that order. With these rules, we are changing the type, size and font family of every text inside `<h1>` and `<h2>` elements to the values we want.

Declaring New HTML5 Elements

Another basic rule that has to be declared from the beginning is the default definition of the HTML5 structural elements. Some browsers are not recognizing these elements or treating them like an inline elements. We need to declare these elements as block elements to assure that they will be treated like `<div>` tags, and that we are able to build our box model:

```
header, section, footer, aside, nav, article, figure, figcaption,
hgroup{
   display: block;
}
```

Listing 2-28: default rule for HTML5 elements

Now the elements affected by the rule in Listing 2-28 will be positioned one over another unless we specify something different later.

Centering the Body

The first element that is part of the box model is always the `<body>`. Usually the content of this element has to be positioned horizontally for one reason or another. We will also have to specify its size or a maximum size to get a consistent design through different configurations.

```
body {
   text-align: center;
}
```

Listing 2-29: centering the body

By default, the `<body>` tag has a width value of 100%. This means that the body will occupy the complete width of the visible screen in the browser. To center the page on the screen, we need to center the content inside the body. With the rule added in Listing 2-29, everything that is inside the `<body>` will be centered on the screen, thus centering the entire web page.

Creating the Main Box

Next, we have to specify the maximum size or a fixed size that the content of the body will have. If you remember, in Listing 2-25 of this chapter, a `<div>` element was added to our template to wrap the whole body's content. This `<div>` will be considered the main box that contains everything else inside. Therefore, the size of this box will be the maximum size of the rest of the elements.

```
#wrapper {
  width: 960px;
  margin: 15px auto;
  text-align: left;
}
```

Listing 2-30: defining the properties for the main box

The rule in Listing 2-30 is referencing for the first time an element by the value of its `id`. The character `#` is telling the browser that the element affected by these styles has the attribute `id` with the value `wrapper`.

This rule provides three styles for the main box. The first one is setting its fixed width to 960 pixels, therefore this box will always be 960 pixels wide (The common values for a website these days are between 960 and 980 pixels wide. However, this things change constantly through time, of course.).

The second style is part of what we call the Traditional Box Model. In the previous rule (Listing 2-29), we were specifying that the content of the body will be horizontally centered with the style `text-align: center`. But that only affects inline content such as text or images. For block elements such as `<div>`, we need to set a specific value for its margin that adapts them automatically to the size of the parent. The property `margin` used for this purpose can have 4 values: up, right, bottom and left, in that order. This means that the first value specified is the margin at the top of the element, the second is the right margin, and so on. However, if you only write the first two parameters, the rest will take the same values. In our example we are using this technique.

In Listing 2-30, the style `margin: 15px auto` assigns 15 pixels to the margin at the top and the bottom of the element `<div>` that it is referencing, and sets as automatic the size for the left and right margins. In this way, we will have a space of 15 pixels at the top and bottom of the body and the space at the left and right will be automatically calculated according to the size of the body and the size of the `<div>`, effectively centering the content on the screen.

The web page is now centered, and has a fixed size of 960 pixels.

The next thing to do is to prevent a problem that occurs in some browsers. The property `text-align` is hereditary. That means that all the elements inside the body will be centered, not only the main box. The style will be transferred to every child of the `<body>`. We have to change this style for the rest of the document back to its default value. The third and last style in the rule of Listing 2-30 accomplishes this purpose. The result is that the content of the body is centered, but the content of the main box (the `<div>` wrapper) is aligned back to the left, therefore all the rest of the code will inherit this style and have it by default.

> **Do It Yourself:** If you haven't already done so, copy every rule we listed to this point into an empty file named **mystyles.css**. This file must be placed in the same folder or directory as the HTML file with the code of Listing 2-25. At this point you should have two files, one with the HTML code and **mystyles.css** with all the CSS styles we studied since Listing 2-26. Open the HTML file in your browser and on the screen you will be able to notice the box created (In most systems you just need a double-click over the file name to open it.).

The Header

Let's continue with the rest of the structural elements. Following the opening tag of the `<div>` wrapper is the first HTML5 structural element: `<header>`. This element contains the main title of our web page and will be located at the top of the screen. The `<header>` was identified in the code with the attribute **id="main_header"**.

By default, every block element, as well as the body, has a width of 100%. That means that the element will occupy all the horizontal space available. In the case of the body, as we already said, that space is the width of the visible screen, but for the rest of the elements, the maximum space will be determined by the size of their parent. In our example, the maximum space of the elements inside the main box will be 960 pixels, because their parent is the main box, which has a width previously set as 960 pixels.

```
#main_header {
  background: #FFFBB9;
  border: 1px solid #999999;
  padding: 20px;
}
```

Listing 2-31: adding styles for `<header>`

Because the `<header>` will occupy all the available horizontal space in the main box, and will be already treated like a block element and positioned at the top of the page, the only thing left to do is assign styles that will let us recognize it when it is represented on the screen. In the rule shown on Listing 2-31, we gave the `<header>` a yellow background, a solid border of 1 pixel, and an inside margin of 20 pixels using the property **padding**.

Navigational Bar

Following the **<header>**, the next structural element is **<nav>**, which has the purpose of aiding navigation. The links grouped together inside this element will represent the menu of our website. This menu will be just a single bar below the header. Because of this, as well as the **<header>** element, most of the styles we need to position the **<nav>** element are already assigned: **<nav>** is a block element, therefore will be located under the previous element; the default width is 100% so it will be as wide as its parent (the wrapper **<div>**); and (also by default) it will be as tall as its content and specified margins. Therefore, the only thing we need to do is make it more appealing to the eyes. We do this by adding a gray background and a small internal margin to separate the options of the menu from the border:

```
#main_menu {
  background: #CCCCCC;
  padding: 5px 15px;
}
#main_menu li {
  display: inline-block;
  list-style: none;
  padding: 5px;
  font: bold 14px verdana, sans-serif;
}
```

Listing 2-32: *adding styles for* <nav>

In Listing 2-32, the first rule is referencing the **<nav>** element by its **id**, changing its background and adding internal margins of **5px** and **15px** with the property **padding**.

> **Review the Basics:** The property **padding** works exactly like **margin**. Four values can be specified: top, right, bottom and left, in that order. If you only specify one value, that same value will be assigned all around the content of the element. If you specify two values, then the first one will be assigned to the top and bottom, and the second one to the left and right side.

Inside the navigation bar, there is a list created with the tags **<ul>** and **<li>**. By default, the items of a list are positioned one over another. To change this and put every option of the menu side by side in the same line, we reference the **<li>** elements inside this particular **<nav>** tag with the selector **#main_menu li**, and then assign the style **display: inline-block** to turn them into inline boxes. Unlike the block elements, the elements affected by the **inline-block** parameter standardized in CSS3 don't generate any line breaks but let us treat the elements as blocks and declare a width value for them. This parameter also sets the size of the element according to the size of its content when no width is specified.

We also eliminated the small graphics generated in front of every item of the list (usually called "bullets") with the **list-style** property.

Section and Aside

The next structural elements in our code are two boxes ordered horizontally. The Traditional Box Model is built over CSS styles that let us specify the position of every box. Using the property `float` we can position these boxes on the right or the left side of the screen according to our needs. The elements we use in our HTML template to create them are `<section>` and `<aside>`, each one identified with the attribute `id` and the values `main_section` and `main_aside` respectively.

```
#main_section {
   float: left;
   width: 660px;
   margin: 20px;
}
#main_aside {
   float: left;
   width: 220px;
   margin: 20px 0px;
   padding: 20px;
   background: #CCCCCC;
}
```

Listing 2-33: *creating two columns with the property* `float`

The CSS property `float` is one of the properties that is widely used to apply the Traditional Box Model. It makes the element float to one side or the other in the available space. The elements affected by `float` act as block elements—with the difference that are laid out according to the value of this property and not the normal flow of the document. The elements are moved to the left or to the right of the available area, as far as possible, responding to the value of `float`.

With the rules on Listing 2-33, we are declaring the position of both boxes and their sizes thus generating the visible columns on the screen. The property `float` moves the box to the available space at the side specified by its value, **width** assigns a horizontal size, and **margin**, of course, assigns the margin of the element.

Affected by these styles, the content of the `<section>` element will be situated at the left of the screen, with a size of 660 pixels, plus 40 pixels of margins, occupying a total space of 700 pixels wide.

The `float` property of the `<aside>` element has also the value **left**. This means that the box generated will move to the space available at its left. Because the previous box created by the element `<section>` was also moved to the left of the screen, now the space available will be the space remaining. The new box will be in the same line of the first box but to its right, occupying the rest of the space in the line, creating a second column for the design.

We also declared a size of 220 pixels for this second box, added a gray background, and set an internal margin of 20 pixels. As a result, this box's horizontal size will be 220 pixels, plus 40 pixels added by the **padding** property (The margin of the sides has been set as **0px.**).

> **Review the Basics:** The size of an element and its margins are added to get the real value. If we have an element of 200 pixels wide and a margin of 10 pixels at each side, the real area occupied by the element will be 220 pixels. The total 20 pixels of the margins are added to the 200 pixels of the element, and the final value is represented on the screen. The same happens with the property **padding** and **border**. Every time we add a border to an element, or create a space between the content and the border with the property **padding**, those values will be added to the width of the element to get the real value when the element is shown on the screen. The real value is calculated with the formula: **size + margin + padding + borders**.

> **Do It Yourself:** Review Listing 2-25. Check every CSS rule we have created so far and find the HTML element in the template corresponding to each of those rules. Follow the references: elements' keywords (like **h1**) and **id** attributes (like **main_header**) to understand how the references work and how the styles are assigned to every element.

Footer

To finish the application of the Traditional Box Model, another CSS property has to be applied to the **<footer>** element. This property changes back the normal flow of the document and lets us position the **<footer>** under the last element rather than at the side:

```
#main_footer {
  clear: both;
  text-align: center;
  padding: 20px;
  border-top: 2px solid #999999;
}
```

Listing 2-34: styling the <footer> and recovering the normal flow

Listing 2-34 declares a border of 2 pixels at the top of the **<footer>**, the internal margin (or padding) of 20 pixels, and centers the text inside the element. As well, it restores the normal flow of the document with the property **clear**. This property simply clears the area occupied by the element not letting it position adjacent to a float box. The usual value is **both**, which means that both sides will be cleared, and the element will follow the regular flow (the element is not floating anymore). This, for a block element, means that it will be positioned below the last element, in a new line.

The property **clear** also pushes the elements vertically, making the float boxes occupy a real area on the screen. Without this property, the browser renders the document as if the float elements wouldn't exist, and the boxes are overlapped.

When we have boxes positioned side by side in the Traditional Box Model, we always need to create an element with the style **clear: both** to being able to continue placing other boxes below in a natural way. Figure 2-2 shows a visual representation of this model with basic CSS styles necessary to create the layout.

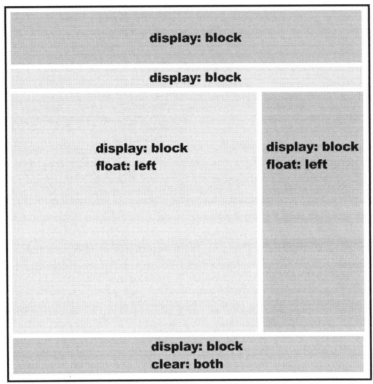

Figure 2-2: *visual representation of the Traditional Box Model*

The values **left** and **right** in the property **float** do not necessarily mean that the box must be positioned at the left or the right side of the window. What the values do is turn float that specific side of the element, breaking the normal flow of the document. If the value is **left**, for example, the browser will try to position the element at the left side of the available space. If there is space available next to a previous element, this new element will be situated at its right, because the left side of the element has been set to **float**. That will make it float to the left until it finds something that blocks it such as another element or the edge of its parent. This is important when we want to create a layout with several columns. In that case, every column will have the value **left** in the property **float** to assure that one column will be positioned next to the other in the correct order. Every column will be floating to the left until is blocked by another column or the edge of the parent. This practice will position the boxes side by side in the same line, creating a set of columns in the visual representation on the screen.

Last Touches

The only thing left is to work on the content's design. There are a few more HTML5 elements that can be styled for this purpose:

```
article {
  background: #FFFBCC;
  border: 1px solid #999999;
  padding: 20px;
  margin-bottom: 15px;
}
article footer {
  text-align: right;
}
time {
  color: #999999;
}
figcaption {
  font: italic 14px verdana, sans-serif;
}
```

Listing 2-35: *adding the last touches for the basic design*

The first rule in Listing 2-35 references all the **<article>** elements and provides them with some styles (background color, a solid 1 pixel border, padding, and a bottom margin). The bottom margin of 15 pixels has the purpose of separate one article from the next vertically.

Every article has also a **<footer>** element that shows the number of comments received. To reference a **<footer>** inside an **<article>** element, we used the selector **article footer** that means "every **<footer>** inside an **<article>** will be affected by the following styles." This reference technique was applied here to align the text inside the **<footer>** of every article to the right.

At the end of the code in Listing 2-35, we changed the color inside every **<time>** element and differentiated the caption of the image, inserted with the **<figcaption>** element, from the rest of the text in the article using a different font.

> **Do It Yourself:** If you haven't done so yet, copy every CSS rule listed in this chapter since Listing 2-26 one after another inside the file **mystyles.css**, and then open the HTML file with the template created in Listing 2-25. That will show you how the Traditional Box Model works and organizes the structural elements on the screen.

> **IMPORTANT:** You can also access these codes and execute them with just one click from our website. Go to www.minkbooks.com.

Box-Sizing

There is an additional property incorporated to CSS3 regarding the structure and the Traditional Box Model. The **box-sizing** property allows us to change how the size of an element is calculated and force browsers to include in the original value the padding and border.

As we explained before, every time the total area occupied by an element is calculated, the browser gets the final number through the following formula: **size + margin + padding + borders**. Therefore, if we set the **width** property equal to 100 pixels, **margin** to 20 pixels, **padding** to 10 pixels and **border** to 1 pixel, the total horizontal area occupied by the element will then be: **100+40+20+2= 162** pixels (Notice that we had to double the values of the **margin**, **padding** and **border** in the formula because we considered that the same values were assigned to each left and right side of the box.). This means that every time you declare the size of an element with the property **width**, you will have to remember that the real area necessary to place the element will usually be bigger than that.

Depending on your habits, it might be good to force the browser to include the **padding** and **border** in the value of **width**, so the new formula will be just: **size + margin**.

```
div {
    width: 100px;
    margin: 20px;
    padding: 10px;
    border: 1px solid #000000;

    -moz-box-sizing: border-box;
    -webkit-box-sizing: border-box;
    box-sizing: border-box;
}
```

Listing 2-36: including padding and border in the size of the element

The **box-sizing** property may take two values. By default, it is set to **content-box**, which means the browsers will add the **padding** and **border** to the size specified by **width**. Using the value **border-box** instead, this behavior is changed so that the padding and border are drawn inside the element.

Listing 2-36 shows the application of this property on a **<div>** element. This is just an example and we are not going to use it in our template, but it could be useful for some designers depending on how familiar they are with the traditional methods of calculation proposed from previous versions of CSS.

> **IMPORTANT:** At this moment, **box-sizing** is experimental in some browsers. To effectively apply it to your documents, you have to declare it with the proper prefix. We will return to this subject later.

Flexible Box Model

The main purpose of the box model is to provide a mechanism for dividing the window's space into several boxes and creating the rows and columns that are part of a regular web design. However, the Traditional Box Model implemented since the first version of CSS, and widely used these days, fails in this matter. Defining how boxes are distributed and specifying their horizontal and vertical sizes, for example, can't be done effectively with this model without using tricks or a set of intricate rules programmed by a clever guy somewhere in the world.

The difficulty in creating common design effects (for example, expanding several columns according to the space available, vertical centering the content, or extending a column from top to bottom independently of its content) made developers think about new possible models to apply to their documents. Several examples were developed, but no one got more attention than the Flexible Box Model.

The Flexible Box Model solves the previous model problems in a really elegant manner. With this new implementation, the boxes are finally representing those virtual rows and columns that are in fact what designers and users really see and care about. Now we have total control over the layout, the position and size of the boxes, the distribution of the boxes inside other boxes, and how they share and use the available space. The code satisfies the designers' needs in a natural way once and for all.

In this part of the chapter, we will see how the Flexible Box Model works, how we can apply the model to our template, and all the new possibilities that it provides.

> **IMPORTANT:** Although the Flexible Box Model presents an advantage over the previous model, it is still experimental and could not be adopted by browsers and developers for at least a few more years. At present, there are two specifications available and only one is supported by browsers based on WebKit and Gecko, such as Firefox and Google Chrome. Those are the reason why we have taught you how to use the Traditional Box Model as well.

One of the main characteristics of this model is that some features (for example, the vertical or horizontal orientation) are declared in parent boxes. This characteristic makes it imperative that boxes are inserted into other boxes to organize them. In this new model, every set of boxes has to have a parent box.

Looking at the template we have been using so far, you can see some parent boxes already defined. The `<body>` and the `<div>` wrapper are elements that can be converted into parent boxes. However, there is another part of the structure that also needs a parent box. A new `<div>` element has to be incorporated to wrap the subset of boxes that represents the two columns in the middle of the page (created by the elements `<section>` and `<aside>`).

This is how the template looks after the addition of the new wrapper:

```
<!DOCTYPE html>
<html lang="en">
<head>
  <meta charset="utf-8">
  <meta name="description" content="This is an HTML5 example">
  <meta name="keywords" content="HTML5, CSS3, JavaScript">
  <title>This text is the title of the document</title>
  <link rel="stylesheet" href="mystyles.css">
</head>
<body>
<div id="wrapper">
  <header id="main_header">
    <h1>This is the main title of the website</h1>
  </header>
  <nav id="main_menu">
    <ul>
      <li>home</li>
      <li>photos</li>
      <li>videos</li>
      <li>contact</li>
    </ul>
  </nav>
  <div id="container">
    <section id="main_section">
      <article>
        <header>
          <hgroup>
            <h1>Title of post One</h1>
            <h2>subtitle of the post One</h2>
          </hgroup>
          <time datetime="2011-12-10" pubdate>posted 12-10-
2011</time>
        </header>
        This is the text of my first post
        <figure>
          <img src="http://minkbooks.com/content/myimage.jpg">
          <figcaption>
            this is the image of the first post
          </figcaption>
        </figure>
        <footer>
          <p>comments (0)</p>
        </footer>
      </article>
      <article>
        <header>
          <hgroup>
            <h1>Title of post Two</h1>
            <h2>subtitle of the post Two</h2>
          </hgroup>
          <time datetime="2011-12-15" pubdate>posted 12-15-
2011</time>
```

```
      </header>
      This is the text of my second post
      <footer>
        <p>comments (0)</p>
      </footer>
    </article>
  </section>
  <aside id="main_aside">
    <blockquote>Article number one</blockquote>
    <blockquote>Article number two</blockquote>
  </aside>
</div>
<footer id="main_footer">
  Copyright &copy 2010-2011
</footer>
</div>
</body>
</html>
```

Listing 2-37: adding a parent box to contain `<section>` *and* `<aside>`

Do It Yourself: For the rest of the chapter, we will use the template in Listing 2-37. Replace the previous template in your HTML file with this code. You will also need to empty the file **mystyles.css** to insert the CSS rules presented next.

Before you apply the CSS properties specific to the Flexible Box Model, let's incorporate to the new styles sheet the basic rules that are common for both models:

```
* {
  margin: 0px;
  padding: 0px;
}
h1 {
  font: bold 20px verdana, sans-serif;
}
h2 {
  font: bold 14px verdana, sans-serif;
}
header, section, footer, aside, nav, article, figure, figcaption,
hgroup{
  display: block;
}
```

Listing 2-38: common CSS rules for both models

As we saw before, the first rule on Listing 2-38 sets every element's margin to 0 pixels. After that, the font properties for the texts in the H tags are specified and the

HTML5 elements are declared as block elements for browsers that don't grant that style by default.

With the basic rules ready, it is time to apply the Flexible Box Model to our template. In this model, every element that has structural elements inside has to be declared as a parent box. The first parent box of our document is the body itself:

```css
body {
  width: 100%;

  display: -moz-box;
  display: -webkit-box;

  -moz-box-pack: center;
  -webkit-box-pack: center;
}
```

Listing 2-39: declaring the <body> as a parent box

To configure an element as a parent box, we have to use the property **display** and set its value to **box**.

In Listing 2-39, in addition to declaring the body as a parent box, we also assigned another style to **<body>** that will center its content. The property **box-pack** with the value **center** will center the children of the parent box. In this case, **<body>** has only one child, the element **<div id="wrapper">**, thus the whole web page will be centered.

Another important characteristic of this model is the ability to easily expand or reduce any element of the web page according to the space available. However, for a box to be flexible, its parent must be flexible as well. No element will adjust its size if it doesn't know what the size of its parent is, so we must specify that the body will occupy the whole space in the browser's window. To achieve this purpose, the size of 100% was declared for the body.

> **IMPORTANT:** Because the CSS properties we are studying are experimental at this moment, most of them have to be declared with a specific prefix according to the rendering engine. In the future, we will be able to declare only **display: box**, but until the experimental phase is over, we have to do it as shown on Listing 2-39. The prefixes for the most common browsers are:
>
> - **-moz-** for Firefox
> - **-webkit-** for Safari and Chrome
> - **-o-** for Opera
> - **-khtml-** for Konqueror
> - **-ms-** for Internet Explorer
> - **-chrome-** specific for Google Chrome

There are different properties to specify the position of every box on the screen. We can stack the boxes one over another, put them side by side, invert their order or even declare a specific order. We will apply some of these properties to our template now and study them later in further detail.

One of these properties is **box-orient**. This property specifies a vertical or horizontal orientation for the children. The default value is **horizontal**, so we didn't need to assign this style to the **<body>**, but we do need it for the wrapper:

```
#wrapper{
  max-width: 960px;
  margin: 15px 0px;

  display: -moz-box;
  display: -webkit-box;

  -moz-box-orient: vertical;
  -webkit-box-orient: vertical;

  -moz-box-flex: 1;
  -webkit-box-flex: 1;
}
```

Listing 2-40: a parent box with a maximum size and vertical orientation

A box declared with **display: box** has the characteristics of a block element and occupies all the space available in its container. In the previous model, we used a fixed value of 960 pixels for the main box; this value fixed not only the size of this box but also the whole web page. To take advantage of the flexible properties of this new box model, we have to be less specific. However, if the **<body>** already occupies 100% of the window, the wrapper will do the same, and sometimes our page will get out of proportion. To avoid this and still have a flexible content, we used the property **max-width** with a value of **960px** in Listing 2-40. This will make the size of the wrapper (and therefore the whole web page) variable, but never bigger than 960 pixels. Now the size of the web page will get adapted to every device and environment, but it will have a maximum value to preserve a consistent design.

Because the **<div>** we are styling using the last code wraps the entire content of the web page, it also has to be declared as a parent box with **display: box**. This time its children will be positioned one over another, hence the property **box-orient** has the value **vertical**.

Given that we need this parent box to be flexible, we have to declare this condition using the property **box-flex**. Without this property, the **<div>** won't be expanded or reduced; it will be only as wide as its content. The value **1** is for flexible and **0** is for fixed, but this property can take other values that we will study later in other circumstances.

Next in our HTML document, we have the boxes created by the elements **<header>** and **<nav>**. These are the first children of the parent box **<div id="wrapper">**. On

Listing 2-41, we just have to declare some styles for visual purposes because these elements already have the properties of vertical boxes thanks to the rules previously declared for their parent:

```
#main_header {
  background: #FFFBB9;
  border: 1px solid #999999;
  padding: 20px;
}
#main_menu {
  background: #CCCCCC;
  padding: 5px 15px;
}
#main_menu li {
  display: inline-block;
  list-style: none;
  padding: 5px;
  font: bold 14px verdana, sans-serif;
}
```

Listing 2-41: simple rules to present the header and the menu on the screen

Below the box created by the **<nav>** tag, we have another box that is also a parent of two more boxes. This is the new **<div>** added on Listing 2-37 to wrap the columns in the middle of the web page. This box was identified with the attribute **id="container"**:

```
#container {
  display: -moz-box;
  display: -webkit-box;

  -moz-box-orient: horizontal;
  -webkit-box-orient: horizontal;
}
```

Listing 2-42: creating another parent box

The rule in Listing 2-42 defines the parent box for the two middle columns. The first style creates the box and the second provides horizontal orientation for its children. This container, as well as the header and menu bar, doesn't need to be declared as flexible. Their sizes are by default 100%, which mean that they will occupy all the available space provided by their container. Because their parent is flexible, they will be flexible as well; there is no need to specify that property either.

With the parent ready, now we can work on the columns. Applying the rules in Listing 2-43, the first column defined by the element **<section>** won't have any specific size. Thanks to the property **box-flex**, the column will be adapted according to the space provided by its parent. In contrast, the right column created by the element **<aside>** has been set as fixed, with a size of 220 pixels, plus 40 pixels of internal margin (padding). This was, of course, our decision for this template. We could have made both columns flexible or distributed the space proportionally using the rest of the tools provided for this model, but instead we decided to keep one column fixed so you can compare the behavior of both box models applied to the same document. Besides, the practice of keeping one column fixed is the most common. Usually in this column the designer places menus, advertisement, or important information that has to be preserved in its original size.

```
#main_section {
  -moz-box-flex: 1;
  -webkit-box-flex: 1;

  margin: 20px;
}
#main_aside {
  width: 220px;
  margin: 20px 0px;
  padding: 20px;
  background: #CCCCCC;
}
```

Listing 2-43: *creating flexible and fixed columns*

The combination of flexible and fixed columns is not unique to the Flexible Box Model, but the capacity of this model has never been equalled, and some effects that once took several lines of code to develop can now be implemented with a few simple properties.

There is another important property that we didn't need to declare because it is assigned automatically to both columns. The property **box-align**, with its default value **stretch**, extends the columns vertically to occupy all the space available. This will make the column at the right in our template expand and take the same vertical size as the left column.

The final result of applying those properties, explicitly or by default, is that some content of the web page will change its horizontal and vertical size according to the space available in the entire window. The column created with the element **<section>**, as well as its own content, will be variable horizontally. Also the header, the navigation bar and the footer of our template will change their size if we reduce or expand the browser's window. The second column, created with the element **<aside>** will also stretch all the way vertically to occupy the space available between the navigation bar and the footer. All these effects were really complicated to achieve in the previous box model. The ease in creating effects makes the Flexible Box Model a great candidate for replacing the Traditional Box Model.

With the last rules incorporated in Listing 2-43 basically we have now all the necessary styles to organize the boxes and apply the Flexible Box Model to our template. The only remaining task is to add some visual styles for the rest of the elements to get the same look that we previously had:

```
#main_footer {
  text-align: center;
  padding: 20px;
  border-top: 2px solid #999999;
}
article {
  background: #FFFBCC;
  border: 1px solid #999999;
  padding: 20px;
  margin-bottom: 15px;
}
time {
  color: #999999;
}
article footer {
  text-align: right;
}
figcaption {
  font: italic 14px verdana, sans-serif;
}
```

Listing 2-44: *finishing the styles sheet*

The last rules above are similar to those included before. The only difference is that we don't need to use the property **clear: both** for the footer anymore because there are no float elements to "clear" in this model.

> **Do It Yourself:** You should already have replaced the code of the template in the HTML file with the one shown on Listing 2-37. You should also have all the CSS styles from Listing 2-38 inside the file **mystyles.css**. The next step is to open the HTML file and check the results in your browser. Expand and contract the browser's window to check which boxes change their size to adjust it to the new space available. Check the vertical expansion of the column at the right. For a one-click access to these codes and examples go to our website: www.minkbooks.com.

In Figure 2-3 (next page), we created a visual representation of what we have done so far. The boxes number 1, 2 and 3 are parent boxes. The rest of the boxes are children ordered according to the properties provided by their parents.

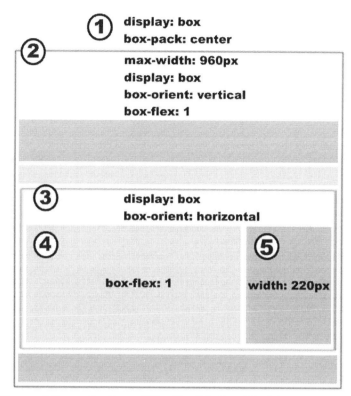

Figure 2-3: application of the Flexible Box Model to our template

Understanding the Flexible Box Model

What we have done so far is to simply apply the Flexible Box Model to our template, but in order to take full advantage of its potential, you need to know exactly how the model works and to study its properties further.

One of the main reasons for the creation of the Flexible Box Model was the need to distribute space in the window. The elements had to be reduced or increased in size according to the space available within the container. In order to know what amount of space was going to be distributed, we had to know what exactly the size of the container was, which led to the definition of parent boxes.

The parent boxes are defined by the property **display**, and may be determined as block elements with the value **box**, or inline elements with the value **inline-box**.

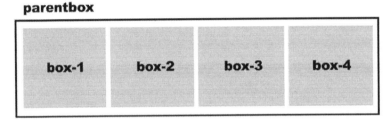

Figure 2-4: *a parent box with four children*

The HTML code to generate the boxes in Figure 2-4 could be the following:

```
<!DOCTYPE html>
<html lang="en">
<head>
  <title>Flexible Box Model sample</title>
  <link rel="stylesheet" href="test.css">
</head>
<body>
<section id="parentbox">
  <div id="box-1">Box 1</div>
  <div id="box-2">Box 2</div>
  <div id="box-3">Box 3</div>
  <div id="box-4">Box 4</div>
</section>
</body>
</html>
```

Listing 2-45: *basic HTML code to work with*

Do It Yourself: Create another empty text file with a name you like and the `.html` extension. Copy the code on Listing 2-45 into the file. This is the file we will use to experiment with the properties of the Flexible Box Model. The CSS rules will be included from an external file called `test.css`. Create this file as well and add the rules provided next. Check the results of applying every rule by opening the HTML file in your browser.

Display

As we said before, the `display` property may take two values: `box` and `inline-box`. We are going to define our parent as `box`:

```css
#parentbox {
  display: box;
}
```

Listing 2-46: declaring the element `parentbox` as a parent box

IMPORTANT: Always keep in mind that, at the moment, these properties are experimental. To use them, you have to declare every one by adding the prefixes `-moz-` or `-webkit-` according to the browser you are using. For example, `display: box` at this moment must be written as `display: -moz-box` for the Gecko engine and `display: -webkit-box` for the WebKit engine. Check the previous codes for a reference or go to our website to get the full version of these examples. We didn't include the prefixes in this part of the chapter to make the codes easy to follow.

Box-Orient

By default, a parent box will have a horizontal orientation for its children. The property `box-orient` is used to declare a specific orientation:

```css
#parentbox {
  display: box;
  box-orient: horizontal;
}
```

Listing 2-47: orienting the children

The property `box-orient` can receive four values: `horizontal`, `vertical`, `inline-axis` and `block-axis`. The value `inline-axis` is set by default, and the boxes are order horizontally (as shown on Figure 2-4). A similar effect can be achieved with the value `horizontal`, which we applied in Listing 2-47.

> **IMPORTANT:** This example and the followings will only work in your browser if you declare every new style by adding the prefixes **–moz–** or **–webkit–** according to the browser you are using (e.g., Firefox, Google Chrome).

Box-Direction

As you can see, the boxes will follow the normal document's flow and be distributed from left to right in the horizontal orientation, and from top to bottom in the vertical orientation. This normal flow can be reversed with the property `box-direction`:

```
#parentbox {
  display: box;
  box-orient: horizontal;
  box-direction: reverse;
}
```

Listing 2-48: *reverting the normal flow*

Possible values of the property `box-direction` are: `normal`, `reverse` and `inherit`. Of course, by default the value is `normal`.

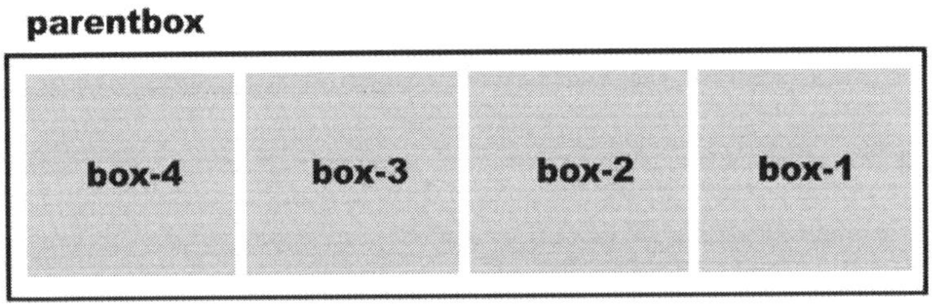

parentbox

box-4	box-3	box-2	box-1

Figure 2-5: *box's order reversed*

Box-Ordinal-Group

The order of the children boxes may be also customized. The property `box-ordinal-group` lets us define a specific place for each box:

```
#parentbox {
  display: box;
  box-orient: horizontal;
}
#box-1{
  box-ordinal-group: 2;
}
#box-2{
  box-ordinal-group: 4;
}
#box-3{
  box-ordinal-group: 3;
}
#box-4{
  box-ordinal-group: 1;
}
```

Listing 2-49: custom position for every box

When the order is customized, the property must be assigned to the children. If the value is duplicated, those boxes will follow the order they have in the HTML structure.

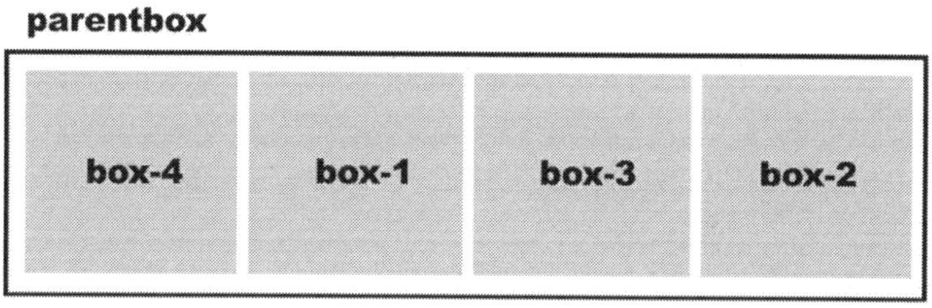

Figure 2-6: specific positions for every box according to Listing 2-49

As we already said, the most important feature of the Flexible Box Model is the capacity to distribute space. There are different situations in which the available space will be shared by the children boxes—for example, flexible parent box, flexible children with no specific size, parent box size wider than the sum of its children.

Let's check one example:

```
#parentbox {
  display: box;
  box-orient: horizontal;
  width: 600px;
}
#box-1{
  width: 100px;
}
```

```
#box-2{
   width: 100px;
}
#box-3{
   width: 100px;
}
#box-4{
   width: 100px;
}
```

Listing 2-50: assigning a fixed size to the parent box and its children

Do It Yourself: Add other properties to the children—for example, a color background, height, or a border to get a better look and to be able to identify every one of them on the screen.

In Listing 2-50, the size of our parent box has been set as 600 pixels and each child is 100 pixels wide. Therefore, there will be 200 pixels of free space available to share.

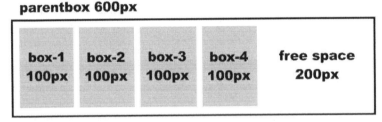

Figure 2-7: declaring sizes and providing free space to share

We can opt for different ways to distribute the free space. By default, the children will be ordered according to Figure 2-7, from left to right, side by side, leaving the free space at the end. However, let's see other alternatives.

Box-Pack

The **box-pack** property specifies how the children and the additional space will be distributed in a parent box. This property can take four values: **start, end, center** and **justify**.

```
#parentbox {
   display: box;
   box-orient: horizontal;
   width: 600px;
   box-pack: center;
}
```

```
#box-1{
   width: 100px;
}
#box-2{
   width: 100px;
}
#box-3{
   width: 100px;
}
#box-4{
   width: 100px;
}
```

Listing 2-51: *distributing free space with* box-pack

The **box-pack** property affects the boxes in certain ways depending on their orientation. If the boxes are oriented horizontally, **box-pack** will distribute the free horizontal space. The same way, in a vertical orientation, only the free vertical space will be distributed.

The following figures show the potential of this property and the competence of the Flexible Box Model.

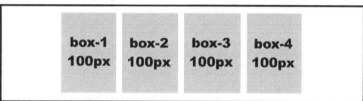

Figure 2-8: *free space distributed with* box-pack: center;

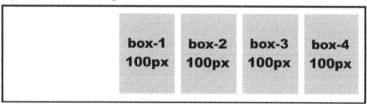

Figure 2-9: *free space distributed with* box-pack: end;

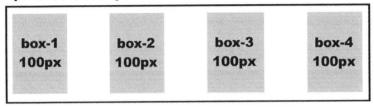

Figure 2-10: free space distributed with `box-pack: justify;`

Box-Flex

Up to now, we have done what could be considered a practice that goes against the principles of this model. We didn't take advantage of the ability to manipulate flexible elements. The **box-flex** property will let us work with this feature.

The **box-flex** property declares a box as flexible or inflexible, and it helps to distribute space. By default, the boxes are inflexible and the value of the property is 0. By giving a value of at least 1, you can declare the box as flexible. Flexible boxes will be expanded or reduced to fill the extra space; they change their horizontal or vertical size according to the orientation established by their parent.

The distribution of the space depends on the properties of the rest of the boxes. If all of the children are set as flexible, the size of each one of them will depend on the size of their parent and the value of the property **box-flex**. Let's see an example:

```
#parentbox {
   display: box;
   box-orient: horizontal;
   width: 600px;
}
#box-1{
   box-flex: 1;
}
#box-2{
   box-flex: 1;
}
#box-3{
   box-flex: 1;
}
#box-4{
   box-flex: 1;
}
```

Listing 2-52: turning the boxes flexible with `box-flex`

parentbox 600px

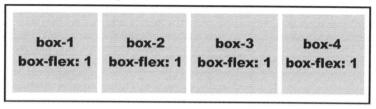

Figure 2-11: the space is distributed equally

The size of each box is calculated by multiplying the value of the size of the parent by the value of its **box-flex** property, and then divided by the sum of the **box-flex** values of all the children. In the example of Listing 2-52, the formula for the box number 1 will be: **600 × 1 / 4 = 150**. The value **600** is the size of the parent, **1** is the value of the property **box-flex** of **box-1**, and **4** is the sum of the values of the property **box-flex** of every child. Because each box in our example has the same value of **1** for the **box-flex** property, the size of every child will be 150 pixels.

The potential of this property is evident when we start providing different values, combining flexible boxes with inflexible ones, or declaring sizes in flexible boxes.

```
#parentbox {
  display: box;
  box-orient: horizontal;
  width: 600px;
}
#box-1{
  box-flex: 2;
}
#box-2{
  box-flex: 1;
}
#box-3{
  box-flex: 1;
}
#box-4{
  box-flex: 1;
}
```

Listing 2-53: uneven distribution

In Listing 2-53, we changed the value of the **box-flex** property in **box-1** to **2**. Now the formula to calculate the size of this box will be the following: **600 × 2 / 5 = 240**. Because we didn't change the size of the parent box, the first value is the same, but the second value is now **2** (the new value of the **box-flex** property for **box-1**). And, of course, now the sum of the values of the property of all the children is **5** (2 in **box-1**, and **1** in the other three boxes). Applying the same formula for the rest of the children we get their sizes: **600 × 1 / 5 = 120**.

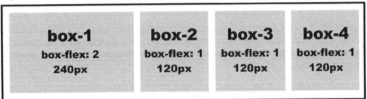

parentbox 600px

box-1	box-2	box-3	box-4
box-flex: 2	box-flex: 1	box-flex: 1	box-flex: 1
240px	120px	120px	120px

Figure 2-12: *the space is distributed according to the value of* `box-flex`

Comparing the results we can see how the space is distributed. The available space is divided into portions according to the sum of the values of the property **box-flex** in each child (the sum of which is **5** in our example). Then, the pieces are distributed between the boxes. The box number 1 will get two pieces and the rest of the children just one piece each because the value of their property **box-flex** is **1**.

The impact of applying this method is represented in Figure 2-12. The advantage is that, when you add a new child, you don't have to recalculate the size as was the case when percentages are used. The sizes are recalculated automatically.

There are other scenarios. For example, when one of the children is by default inflexible and has an explicit size, the other children will share the rest of the space available.

```
#parentbox {
  display: box;
  box-orient: horizontal;
  width: 600px;
}
#box-1{
  width: 300px;
}
#box-2{
  box-flex: 1;
}
#box-3{
  box-flex: 1;
}
#box-4{
  box-flex: 1;
}
```

Listing 2-54: *inflexible and flexible children*

The first box of the example of Listing 2-54 has a size of 300 pixels, so the available space to be distributed between the rest of the children is 300 pixels (**600 − 300 = 300**). The browser will calculate the size of every flexible box with the same formula we use before: **300 × 1 / 3 = 100.**

parentbox 600px

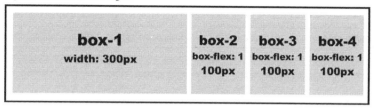

Figure 2-13: only the free space is distributed

Just as you might have one box of an explicit size, you can have several. The principle is the same: only the free space is distributed among the rest of the boxes.

We could also have flexible boxes with specific sizes:

```
#parentbox {
  display: box;
  box-orient: horizontal;
  width: 600px;
}
#box-1{
  width: 200px;
  box-flex: 1;
}
#box-2{
  width: 100px;
  box-flex: 1;
}
#box-3{
  width: 100px;
  box-flex: 1;
}
#box-4{
  width: 100px;
  box-flex: 1;
}
```

Listing 2-55: flexible boxes with a preferred size

In this case, every box has a preferred width value, but after all the boxes are positioned there will be a space of 100 pixels left. This extra space will be divided up between the flexible boxes. To calculate the portion of space assigned to every box, we use the same formula again: **100 × 1 / 4 = 25**. This means that 25 pixels of extra width will be added to the preferred size of each box.

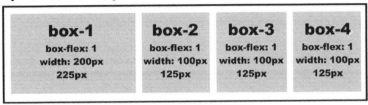

Figure 2-14: adding free space to every box's width

Box-Align

Another property that will help us distribute space is **box-align**. This property works similarly to **box-pack**, but will align the boxes following the direction that is not the boxes' orientation. In a vertical orientation of boxes, it specifies how the boxes are positioned horizontally and vice versa. This quality makes the property appropriate for vertically aligning boxes—something that has been missing since the use of tables has declined.

```
#parentbox {
  display: box;
  box-orient: horizontal;
  width: 600px;
  height: 200px;
  box-align: center;
}
#box-1{
  height: 100px;
  box-flex: 1;
}
#box-2{
  height: 100px;
  box-flex: 1;
}
#box-3{
  height: 100px;
  box-flex: 1;
}
#box-4{
  height: 100px;
  box-flex: 1;
}
```

Listing 2-56: distributing vertical space

In Listing 2-56, we provided a specific height for every box, including the parent. There will be a free space of 100 pixels that will be distributed according to the value of the **box-align** property.

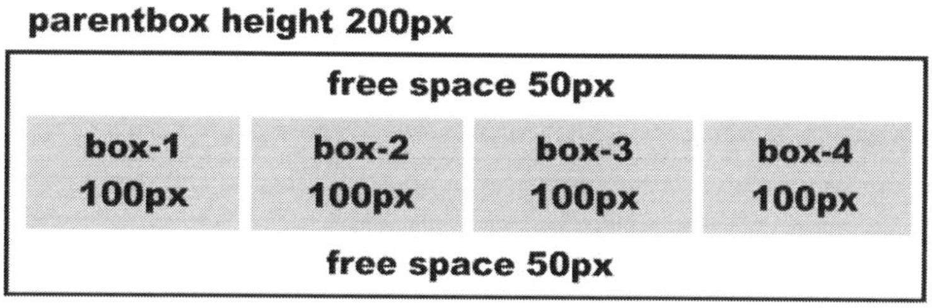

parentbox height 200px
free space 50px
box-1
100px
box-2
100px
box-3
100px
box-4
100px
free space 50px

Figure 2-15: *vertical align with* `box-align`

The possible values of the **`box-align`** property are: **`start`**, **`end`**, **`center`**, **`baseline`** and **`stretch`**. The last value will stretch the boxes from top to bottom to adjust the children to the available space. This characteristic is so important that the value **`stretch`** is set by default. The effect of the value **`stretch`** is that, independently of their own height, children automatically adopt the height of their parent:

parentbox height 200px
box-1
100px
box-2
100px
box-3
100px
box-4
100px

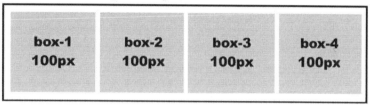

Figure 2-16: *stretching the children with* `box-align: stretch`

Probably you already noticed the application of this property in our template. The right column, generated by the **<aside>** element, was stretch all the way from top to bottom without a specific property or script assigned to it. To achieve that same effect in the Traditional Box Model could cause a nervous breakdown!

Quick Reference
CSS Styling and Box Models

With HTML5, the responsibility for the structure is more than ever before in the hands of CSS. Incorporations and improvements were made to the last version of CSS to provide better ways to organize documents and work with their elements.

Flexible Box Model

The Flexible Box Model is the new model proposed to replace the Traditional Box Model currently in use. CSS3 incorporates several properties to apply this new model to our document's structure:

> **display**—This property was already implemented, but now includes two more values: `box` and `inline-box`. These values turn an element into a box that will contain and organize other boxes.

> **box-orient**—This property has two values: `horizontal` and `vertical`. These values are related to the orientation of the boxes inside a parent box.

> **box-direction**—This property and the value `reverse` will invert the regular document's flow (from left to right and top to bottom). By default, the value is `normal`. According to this property, the box will overflow its content to the right or left when the children are occupying more space than is available.

> **box-ordinal-group**—This property selects the exact position of all children. It must be assigned to the child with an integer value that represents a position in the group. It can be used with `box-direction` to invert positions.

> **box-pack**—This property helps the browser to make the decisions about how to distribute the free space left over in the parent box when the children are inflexible or have a maximum width. By default the value is `start`, which means the boxes will be located from left to right, unless the direction is inverted with `box-direction`. Other possible values are `end`, `center` and `justify`. With the last (`justify`), the space will be divided evenly and placed between the children.

> **box-flex**—This property makes a box flexible. The size of the box will be calculated according to the space available in the parent box and the size and properties of the rest of the children. The property `box-flex` only affects the size in the axis according to the orientation. The value of this property is a floating point number, and it represents a portion of the space available according to the formula: **space × box-flex of child / sum of box-flex values of children**. A value of **0** means the box is inflexible, and a value of at least **1** makes the box flexible.

box-align—This property determines how to distribute the extra space in the axis perpendicular to the box orientation. The value by default is **stretch**. In the horizontal orientation, this means that the boxes will be stretched vertically to occupy all the space available from top to bottom. This is a property that will make the columns grow automatically according to the size of the rest of the columns in the same row on a typical web design. Other possible values are: **start**, **end**, **center** and **baseline**, providing another great capability that is vertical alignment.

Pseudo-Classes and Selectors

CSS3 also has added new mechanisms to reference and select HTML elements.

Attribute Selector—Now we can use other attributes than **id** and **class** to find elements in the document and provide styling. With the construction **keyword[attribute=value]**, we can reference an element that has a particular attribute with a particular value. For example, **p[name="text"]** will reference every element **<p>** with an attribute called **name** and the value "**text**". CSS3 also provides techniques to make this reference less specific. Using the following combination of symbols ^=, $= and *= we can find elements that start with the value provided, elements that end with the value provided, and elements that have the text provided in some part of their value. For example, **p[name^="text"]** will be used to find elements **<p>** that have an attribute called **name** and a value starting by "**text**".

Pseudo-Class :nth-child()—This pseudo-class finds a specific child in the tree structure. For example, with the style **span:nth-child(2)**, we are referencing the **<span>** element that has other **<span>** elements as siblings and is located in the position 2. This number is considered the index. Instead of a number, we can use the keywords **odd** and **even** to reference elements with an odd or an even index—for example, **span:nth-child(odd)**.

Pseudo-Class :first-child—This pseudo-class is for referencing the first child, similar to **:nth-child(1)**.

Pseudo-Class :last-child—This pseudo-class is for referencing the last child.

Pseudo-Class :only-child—This pseudo-class is for referencing an element when it's the only child of its parent.

Pseudo-Class :not()—This pseudo-class is used to reference every element except the one between parentheses.

Selector >—This selector references the second element when it has the first element as a parent. For example, **div > p** will reference every **<p>** element that is a child of a **<div>** element.

Selector +—This selector references elements that are siblings. The reference will point to the second element when it's immediately preceded by the first element. For example, `span + p` will affect the `<p>` elements that are siblings and located after a `<span>` element.

Selector ~—This selector is similar to the previous one, but in this case the second element doesn't have to be immediately preceding the first element.

Chapter 3
CSS3 Properties

The New Rules

The web changed forever when in the early 2000s new applications that were developed over Ajax implementations improved designs and users' experience. The version 2.0, assigned to the web in order to describe a new level of development, represented a change not only in the way the information was transmitted but also in how websites and applications were designed.

The codes implemented in this new generation of websites soon became the standard. The innovation turned out to be so important to the success of every work on Internet that programmers developed entire libraries to overcome limitations and satisfy designers' requirements.

The lack of browser support was evident, but the organization responsible for web standards didn't take market tendencies too seriously and tried to follow its own path. Fortunately, some bright guys were developing new standards in parallel and soon HTML5 was born. After the dust settled, the integration of HTML, CSS and Javascript under the HTML5 umbrella was like a victorious, brave knight who had led the troops towards the enemy's palace.

Despite the recent turmoil, this battle began a long time ago, with the first specification of the third version of CSS. When finally, in 2005, this technology was officially considered a standard, CSS was ready to provide the features required by developers that programmers had been creating for years using complicated and not always compatible Javascript codes.

In this chapter, we are going to study the contributions made by CSS3 to HTML5 and all the new properties that simplify the lives of designers and programmers.

CSS3 Goes Crazy

CSS was always about look and formatting, but not anymore. In an attempt to reduce the use of Javascript code and in order to standardize popular features, CSS3 not only addresses design and web styles but also form and movement. The CSS3 specification is presented in modules that allow the technology to provide a standard specification for every aspect involved in the visual presentation of the document. From round corners and shadows to transformations and rearrangement of the elements already rendered on the screen, every possible effect applied previously using Javascript was covered. This level of change turned CSS3 into almost an entirely new technology compared with previous versions.

When the HTML5 specification was written and considered CSS in charge of the design, half the battle against the rest of the proposed specifications was already won.

Template

The new CSS3 properties are extremely powerful and have to be studied one by one, but to make things easier we are going to apply all of them to the same template. So let's start with the HTML document and some basic styles:

```
<!DOCTYPE html>
<html lang="en">
<head>
  <title>New CSS3 styles</title>
  <link rel="stylesheet" href="newcss3.css">
</head>
<body>
<header id="mainbox">
  <span id="title">CSS Styles Web 2.0</span>
</header>
</body>
</html>
```

Listing 3-1: a simple template to test new properties

Our document has just one section with a short text inside. The **<header>** element used on this template could be replaced by **<div>**, **<nav>**, **<section>** or any other structural element according to the location in the design and its function. After the styling, the box in the example of Listing 3-1 will look like a header, hence the **<header>** element.

Because the **<font>** element was deprecated in HTML5, the elements used to display texts are usually **<span>** for short lines and **<p>** for paragraphs, among others. For this reason, the text in our template was inserted using **<span>** tags.

> **Do It Yourself:** Use the code provided in Listing 3-1 as the template for this chapter. You will also need to create a new CSS file called **newcss3.css** to save the CSS styles.

Next are the basic styles for our document:

```
body {
  text-align: center;
}
#mainbox {
  display: block;
  width: 500px;
  margin: 50px auto;
  padding: 15px;
  text-align: center;
  border: 1px solid #999999;
  background: #DDDDDD;
}
#title {
  font: bold 36px verdana, sans-serif;
}
```

Listing 3-2: basic CSS rules to start from

There is nothing new in the rules of Listing 3-2—just the necessary styles to shape our header and create a long box, positioned at the center of the window, with a grey background, a border and a big text inside that reads "CSS Styles Web 2.0".

One of the things you will notice about this box when it is rendered on the screen is that it has square corners. I don't like that. And, while I'm not sure if it's about human psychology or what, almost nobody in the web business likes square corners. So let's change them.

Border-Radius

For so many years I suffered trying to get round corners for the boxes on my web pages. I'm not a good graphic designer, so the process was exhausting and painful. And I know it wasn't just me. If you watch any video presentation about the features incorporated with HTML5, every time someone talks about the CSS property that makes round corners easy to generate, the audience go wild. Round corners were that kind of thing that made you think: "It should be easy to do." However, for many years, round corners weren't.

That's why, among all the new possibilities and amazing properties incorporated in CSS3, the one we will explore first is **border-radius**.

```
body {
  text-align: center;
}
```

```
#mainbox {
  display: block;
  width: 500px;
  margin: 50px auto;
  padding: 15px;
  text-align: center;
  border: 1px solid #999999;
  background: #DDDDDD;

  -moz-border-radius: 20px;
  -webkit-border-radius: 20px;
  border-radius: 20px;
}
#title {
  font: bold 36px verdana, sans-serif;
}
```

Listing 3-3: generating round corners

The property **border-radius** is experimental at this point, so we used the prefixes **−moz−** and **−webkit−** (just as we did before with the properties studied in Chapter 2). If every corner takes the same value, we can provide one value for this property. However, as with the **margin** and **padding** properties, we can select a different value for each corner:

```
body {
  text-align: center;
}
#mainbox {
  display: block;
  width: 500px;
  margin: 50px auto;
  padding: 15px;
  text-align: center;
  border: 1px solid #999999;
  background: #DDDDDD;

  -moz-border-radius: 20px 10px 30px 50px;
  -webkit-border-radius: 20px 10px 30px 50px;
  border-radius: 20px 10px 30px 50px;
}
#title {
  font: bold 36px verdana, sans-serif;
}
```

Listing 3-4: different values for every corner

As you can see in Listing 3-4, the four values assigned to the **border-radius** property represent four different locations. Going clockwise, the order of these values will be for the top-left corner, top-right corner, bottom-right corner, and bottom-left corner. The values are always given clockwise starting from the top-left corner.

As with `margin` or `padding`, `border-radius` can work with just two values. The first value will be assigned to the first and third corners (top left, bottom right), and the second one to the second and forth corners (top right, bottom left)—again, with the corners always counted clockwise, starting from the top-left corner.

We can also shape the corners by providing new values separated by a slash. The values to the left of the slash will represent the horizontal radius and the values at the right the vertical radius; the combination of these values generates an ellipsis:

```
body {
    text-align: center;
}
#mainbox {
    display: block;
    width: 500px;
    margin: 50px auto;
    padding: 15px;
    text-align: center;
    border: 1px solid #999999;
    background: #DDDDDD;

    -moz-border-radius: 20px / 10px;
    -webkit-border-radius: 20px / 10px;
    border-radius: 20px / 10px;
}
#title {
    font: bold 36px verdana, sans-serif;
}
```

Listing 3-5: elliptic corners

Do It Yourself: Copy into the CSS file called `newcss3.css` the styles you want to test and open the HTML file of Listing 3-1 in your browser.

Box-Shadow

Now that we finally have nice corners, you can try more. Another great effect, which had been extremely complicated to achieve, is shadows. For years designers have combined images, elements and some CSS properties to generate a shadow. Thanks to CSS3 and the new property `box-shadow`, we will be able to do that for our box with just one single line of code:

```
body {
    text-align: center;
}
```

```
#mainbox {
  display: block;
  width: 500px;
  margin: 50px auto;
  padding: 15px;
  text-align: center;
  border: 1px solid #999999;
  background: #DDDDDD;

  -moz-border-radius: 20px;
  -webkit-border-radius: 20px;
  border-radius: 20px;

  -moz-box-shadow: rgb(150,150,150) 5px 5px;
  -webkit-box-shadow: rgb(150,150,150) 5px 5px;
  box-shadow: rgb(150,150,150) 5px 5px;
}
#title {
  font: bold 36px verdana, sans-serif;
}
```

Listing 3-6: adding shadow to our box

The box-shadow property needs at least three values. The first one, which you can check in the rule in Listing 3-6, is the color. This value was built here using rgb() and decimal numbers, but you can write it in hexadecimal (as we did before for other parameters in this book).

The next two values, expressed in pixels, set the offset of the shadow. The offset may be positive or negative. The values indicate, respectively, the horizontal and the vertical distance from the shadow to the element. Negative values will position the shadow at the left and above the element; in contrast, positive values will create a shadow at the right and below the element. Values of 0 will place the shadow behind the element, providing the possibility of generating a blur effect all around it.

> **Do It Yourself:** To test the different parameters and possibilities to create a shadow for a box, copy the code in Listing 3-6 into the CSS file and open the HTML file with the template in Listing 3-1 in your browser. Now you can experiment with changing the values of the property box-shadow and use the same code for the new parameters that we study next.

The shadow we get so far is solid, with no gradient and transparency—not yet how a shadow really appears. There are a few more parameters and changes we can make to improve the shadow's appearance.

A fourth value to add to the property we are specifying is the blur distance. With this effect, now the shadow will look like a real shadow. You can try this parameter by declaring a value of 10 pixels in the rule in Listing 3-6—as in the following example:

```
box-shadow: rgb(150,150,150) 5px 5px 10px;
```

Listing 3-7: adding the blur value to `box-shadow`

Adding one more value in pixels at the end of the property will spread the shadow. This effect changes the nature of the shadow a little bit by expanding the area that it covers. While we don't recommend this effect in general, it could be suitable for some designs.

> **Do It Yourself:** Try to add a value of 20 pixels at the end of the style in Listing 3-7, combine that code with the code in Listing 3-6 and test it.

> **IMPORTANT:** Always keep in mind that, at the moment, these properties are experimental. To use them, you have to declare every one by adding the prefixes **-moz-** or **-webkit-** according to the browser you are using (e.g., Firefox, Google Chrome).

The last possible value for **box-shadow** is not a number, but rather the keyword **inset**. This keyword turns the external shadow into an inner shadow that provides a depth effect to the box.

```
box-shadow: rgb(150,150,150) 5px 5px 10px inset;
```

Listing 3-8: inner shadow

The style in Listing 3-8 will show an internal shadow of 5 pixels far from the border of the box and with a blur effect of 10 pixels.

> **Do It Yourself:** The styles in Listing 3-7 and 3-8 are just examples. To check the effect in your browser, you must apply those changes to the complete set of rules in Listing 3-6.

> **IMPORTANT:** Shadows don't expand the element nor increase its size so you will have to check carefully that the available space will allow the shadow to be seen.

Text-Shadow

Now that we know everything about shadows, you will probably want to generate one for every element in your document. The **box-shadow** property was designed specifically for boxes. If you try to apply this effect to a **<span>** element, for example, the invisible box occupied by this element on the screen will have a shadow, not the content of the element. So, to create shadows for the irregular shapes presented by texts, there is a special property called **text-shadow**:

```
body {
  text-align: center;
}
#mainbox {
  display: block;
  width: 500px;
  margin: 50px auto;
  padding: 15px;
  text-align: center;
  border: 1px solid #999999;
  background: #DDDDDD;

  -moz-border-radius: 20px;
  -webkit-border-radius: 20px;
  border-radius: 20px;

  -moz-box-shadow: rgb(150,150,150) 5px 5px 10px;
  -webkit-box-shadow: rgb(150,150,150) 5px 5px 10px;
  box-shadow: rgb(150,150,150) 5px 5px 10px;
}
#title {
  font: bold 36px verdana, sans-serif;
  text-shadow: rgb(0,0,150) 3px 3px 5px;
}
```

Listing 3-9: *adding shadow to the title*

The values for **text-shadow** are similar to those for **box-shadow**. We can set the color of the shadow, the horizontal distance from the shadow to the object, the vertical distance and the blur radius.

In Listing 3-9, a blue shadow was applied to the title of our template with a distance of only 3 pixels and a blur radius of 5.

@font-face

A text shadow is a pretty good trick—hard to get with previous methods—but it just provides a three-dimensional effect rather than changing the text itself. A shadow is like painting an old car; at the end it will be the same car. In this case, it will be the same font.

The problem with fonts is as old as the web. Regular web users often have a limited number of fonts installed, they don't always have the same families of fonts, and some user will have a font that others don't. For years, websites were only able to use a minimum set of reliable fonts—a basic group that most users will have—to render and show the information on the screen.

The property @font-face allows designers to provide a specific font file to display text on a web page. Now we can include any font we want in a website just by providing the file for it:

```css
body {
  text-align: center;
}
#mainbox {
  display: block;
  width: 500px;
  margin: 50px auto;
  padding: 15px;
  text-align: center;
  border: 1px solid #999999;
  background: #DDDDDD;

  -moz-border-radius: 20px;
  -webkit-border-radius: 20px;
  border-radius: 20px;

  -moz-box-shadow: rgb(150,150,150) 5px 5px 10px;
  -webkit-box-shadow: rgb(150,150,150) 5px 5px 10px;
  box-shadow: rgb(150,150,150) 5px 5px 10px;
}
#title {
  font: bold 36px MyNewFont, verdana, sans-serif;
  text-shadow: rgb(0,0,150) 3px 3px 5px;
}
@font-face {
  font-family: 'MyNewFont';
  src: url('font.ttf');
}
```

Listing 3-10: new font for the title

Do It Yourself: Download the file `font.ttf` from our website or use one of your own and copy it in the same folder or directory as your CSS file (To download the file, follow this link: minkbooks.com/content/font.ttf).
You can get more free fonts like this one on the following link: www.moorstation.org/typoasis/designers/steffmann/

IMPORTANT: The font's file must be on the same domain as the web page (or in the same computer, in this case). This is a restriction for some browsers, such as Firefox.

The property @font-face needs at least two properties to declare the font and load the file. The **font-family** property specifies the name that we want to use to reference that particular font, and the **src** property indicates the URL of the file with the codes to render the font. In Listing 3-10, the name **MyNewFont** was assigned to our font and the **font.ttf** file was indicated as the source.

Once the font is loaded, we are able to use it in any element of the document just by writing its name (**MyNewFont**). In the style **font** of the rule in Listing 3-10, we specified that the title will be rendered with the new font or with the alternatives **verdana** and **sans-serif** if the font is not loaded properly.

Linear Gradient

Gradients are one of the most attractive features among those incorporated to CSS3. They were almost impossible to implement using past techniques but are really easy to do in CSS. A **background** property with a few parameters is enough to turn your document into a web page that looks professional:

```
body {
   text-align: center;
}
#mainbox {
   display: block;
   width: 500px;
   margin: 50px auto;
   padding: 15px;
   text-align: center;
   border: 1px solid #999999;
   background: #DDDDDD;

   -moz-border-radius: 20px;
   -webkit-border-radius: 20px;
   border-radius: 20px;

   -moz-box-shadow: rgb(150,150,150) 5px 5px 10px;
   -webkit-box-shadow: rgb(150,150,150) 5px 5px 10px;
   box-shadow: rgb(150,150,150) 5px 5px 10px;

   background: -webkit-linear-gradient(top, #FFFFFF, #006699);
   background: -moz-linear-gradient(top, #FFFFFF, #006699);
}
#title {
   font: bold 36px MyNewFont, verdana, sans-serif;
   text-shadow: rgb(0,0,150) 3px 3px 5px;
}
@font-face {
   font-family: 'MyNewFont';
   src: url('font.ttf');
}
```

Listing 3-11: adding a beautiful gradient background to our box

Gradients are set as backgrounds, so we can use the **background** or **background-image** properties to apply them. The syntax for the values assigned to these properties is **linear-gradient(start position, from color, to color)**. The attributes for the **linear-gradient()** function indicate the starting point and the colors used to create the gradient. The first value can be specified in pixels, percentage or using the keywords **top**, **bottom**, **left** and **right** (as we did in our example). The starting position may be replaced by an angle to provide a specific direction for the gradient:

```
background: linear-gradient(30deg, #FFFFFF, #006699);
```

Listing 3-12: *gradient with a direction angle of 30 degrees*

We can also declare the stopping points for every color:

```
background: linear-gradient(top, #FFFFFF 50%, #006699 90%);
```

Listing 3-13: *setting stopping points*

> **IMPORTANT:** At the moment, the gradient effect can be implemented in a variety of ways. What we have learned in this chapter is the standard proposed by the W3C. Browsers such as Firefox and Google Chrome have a working implementation available for this standard, but Internet Explorer and others are still dealing with it. Microsoft announced that we have to wait for the version 10 of its browser to use it. As always, test the codes in every browser in the market to check the current state of the implementation yourself.

Radial Gradient

The standard syntax for radial gradients differs in just a few aspects from the previous one. We have to use the **radial-gradient()** function and a new attribute for the shape:

```
background: radial-gradient(center, circle, #FFFFFF 0%, #006699 200%);
```

Listing 3-14: *radial gradient*

The start position is the origin and can be declared either as pixels, a percentage or a combination of the keywords **center, top, bottom, left** and **right**). There are two values for the shape (**circle** and **ellipse**) and the color stops indicate the color and the position where transitions start.

Do It Yourself: Replace the corresponding code in Listing 3-11 with the code in Listing 3-14 to test the effect in your browser (don't forget to add the prefixes – `moz-` or `-webkit-` according to the browser you are using).

RGBA

Until this point, the colors were declared as solid, with hexadecimal numbers or the function `rgb()` for decimals. CSS3 has added a new function called `rgba()` that simplifies the assigning of colors and transparencies. This also solves a previous problem with the `opacity` property.

The `rgba()` function has four attributes. The first three values are similar to `rgb()` and simply declare the combination of colors. The last one is for the opacity. This value goes from 0 to 1, with 0 as a fully transparent and 1 fully opaque.

```
#title {
   font: bold 36px MyNewFont, verdana, sans-serif;
   text-shadow: rgba(0,0,0,0.5) 3px 3px 5px;
}
```

Listing 3-15: improving the shadow with transparency

Listing 3-15 shows a simple example to demonstrate how the effects are improved by the use of transparency. We replaced the function `rgb()` by `rgba()` in the shadow of the title to add an opacity value of `0.5`. Now the shadow of our title will be merged with the background of the box, creating a more natural effect.

In previous versions of CSS, we had to use different techniques for different browsers to make an element transparent. All of them presented the same problem: the opacity value for an element was inherited by all its children. That problem was solved by `rgba()` and now you can assign an opacity value to the background of a box and its content won't be affected.

Do It Yourself: Replace the corresponding code in Listing 3-11 with the code in Listing 3-15 in order to test the effect in your browser.

HSLA

Just as the `rgba()` function adds the opacity value for `rgb()`, the function `hsla()` does the same for the previous `hsl()` function.

The function `hsla()` is simply another function to generate the color for an element, but it is more intuitive than `rgba()`. Some designers will find it easier to create a personal set of colors using `hsla()`. The syntax is: `hsla(hue, saturation, lightness, opacity)`.

```
#title {
  font: bold 36px MyNewFont, verdana, sans-serif;
  text-shadow: rgba(0,0,0,0.5) 3px 3px 5px;
  color: hsla(120, 100%, 50%, 0.5);
}
```

Listing 3-16: new color for the title with `hsla()`

According to the syntax, hue represents the color extracted from an imaginary wheel, and it's expressed in degrees from 0 to 360. Around 0 and 360 are red colors, around 120 are greens and around 240 are blues. Saturation is represented in a percentage, from 0% (grey scale) to 100% (full color or fully saturated). Lightness is also a value in percentage from 0% (completely dark) to 100% (completely light). The value of 50% is average lightning. And the last value, as well as in **rgba()**, represents the opacity.

> **Do It Yourself:** Replace the corresponding code in Listing 3-11 with the code in Listing 3-16 to test the effect in your browser.

Outline

The property **outline** is an old CSS property that has been expanded on to include an offset in CSS3. This property is used to create a second border, and now that border can be rendered away from the edge of the element.

```
#mainbox {
  display: block;
  width: 500px;
  margin: 50px auto;
  padding: 15px;
  text-align: center;
  border: 1px solid #999999;
  background: #DDDDDD;

  outline: 2px dashed #000099;
  outline-offset: 15px;
}
```

Listing 3-17: adding an outline for the header box

In Listing 3-17, we added to the styles originally assigned to the box of our template an outline of 2 pixels with an offset of 15 pixels. The **outline** property has similar characteristics and it uses the same parameters as **border**. The **outline-offset** property only needs one value in pixel units.

Do It Yourself: Replace the corresponding code in Listing 3-11 with the code in Listing 3-17 to test the effect in your browser.

Border-Image

The possible effects achieved by the properties **border** and **outline** are limited to single lines and a few configuration options. The new **border-image** property is intended to overcome this limitations and leave in the designer's hands the quality and variety of borders providing the alternative to use custom images.

Do It Yourself: We are going to use a PNG image with diamonds to test this property. Follow the link to download the file **diamond.png** from our website and then copy the file in the same folder or directory as your CSS file: www.minkbooks.com/content/diamonds.png

The **border-image** property takes an image as a pattern. According to the provided values, the image is sliced like a cake to get the parts and then these parts are placed around the object to build the border.

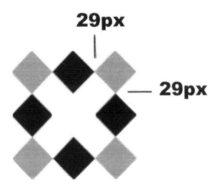

Figure 3-1: the pattern we are going to build our border from, with each piece 29 pixels wide

To get the job done, we need to specify three attributes: the name of the image file and its location, the size of the pieces we want to get from the pattern, and a few keywords to specify how those pieces will be distributed around the object.

```
#mainbox {
   display: block;
   width: 500px;
   margin: 50px auto;
   padding: 15px;
   text-align: center;
```

```
  border: 29px;
  -moz-border-image: url("diamonds.png") 29 stretch;
  -webkit-border-image: url("diamonds.png") 29 stretch;
  border-image: url("diamonds.png") 29 stretch;
}
```

Listing 3-18: a custom border for the header box

With the modifications made in Listing 3-18, we are setting a border of 29 pixels for the header box and then loading the image **diamonds.png** to build the border. The value 29 in the **border-image** property declares the size of the pieces, and **stretch** is one of the methods available to distribute these pieces around the box.

There are three possible values for the last attribute. The keyword **repeat** will repeat the pieces taken from the image all the times needed to cover the side of the element. In this case, the size of the pieces is preserved and the image will be cut if there is not enough space to place it. The keyword **round** will consider how long the side to be covered is and then stretch the pieces to make sure that none of the pieces is cut. Finally, the keyword **stretch** (used in Listing 3-18) stretches only one piece to cover the whole side.

We used the **border** property to set the size of the border, but you can also use **border-with** to specify a different size for each side of the element (The **border-with** property uses four parameters, similar to the syntax of **margin** and **padding**.). The same happens with the size of every piece; up to four values can be declared to get different images of different sizes from the pattern.

> **Do It Yourself:** Replace the corresponding code of Listing 3-11 with the code in Listing 3-18 to test the effect in your browser.

Transform and Transition

HTML elements are like solid immovable blocks when are created. They may be moved using Javascript code or by taking advantage of some popular libraries such as jQuery (www.jquery.com), for instance, but there was no standard procedure for this purpose until CSS3 arrived with the **transform** and **transition** properties.

Now we don't have to think about how to do it. Instead, we just have to know a few parameters and our website can be as dynamic as we imagined it.

The **transform** property can perform four basic transformations of an object: **scale**, **rotate**, **skew** and move or **translate**. Let's see how they work:

Transform: Scale

```
#mainbox {
  display: block;
  width: 500px;
  margin: 50px auto;
```

```
    padding: 15px;
    text-align: center;
    border: 1px solid #999999;  ·
    background: #DDDDDD;

    -moz-transform: scale(2);
    -webkit-transform: scale(2);
}
```

Listing 3-19: scaling the header box

In the example of Listing 3-19, we took the basic styles used in Listing 3-2 for the header box and transformed it by scaling the element to double its size. The **scale** function receives two parameters, the **x** value for horizontal scaling and the **y** value for vertical scaling. If only one value is given, the same value is applied to both parameters.

Integer and decimal values can be provided to perform the scaling. The scaling is calculated by a matrix. The values between 0 and 1 will reduce the element, a value of 1 will keep the original proportions, and values greater than 1 will increase the dimensions of the object incrementally.

A nice effect possible with this function can be achieved using negative values:

```
#mainbox {
    display: block;
    width: 500px;
    margin: 50px auto;
    padding: 15px;
    text-align: center;
    border: 1px solid #999999;
    background: #DDDDDD;

    -moz-transform: scale(1,-1);
    -webkit-transform: scale(1,-1);
}
```

Listing 3-20: creating a mirror image with `scale`

In Listing 3-20, two parameters have been declared to scale the **mainbox**. The first value, 1, keeps the original proportion for the horizontal dimension. The second value also keeps the original proportion, but inverts the element vertically to produce a mirror effect.

There are two more functions similar to **scale** but restricted to the horizontal or vertical dimensions: **scaleX** and **scaleY**. These functions, of course, have only one parameter.

> **Do It Yourself:** Replace the corresponding code in Listing 3-11 with the code in Listing 3-19 or 3-20 in order to test the effect in your browser.

Transform: Rotate

The function **rotate** rotates the element clockwise. The value must be specified in degrees using the "**deg**" unit:

```
#mainbox {
  display: block;
  width: 500px;
  margin: 50px auto;
  padding: 15px;
  text-align: center;
  border: 1px solid #999999;
  background: #DDDDDD;

  -moz-transform: rotate(30deg);
  -webkit-transform: rotate(30deg);
}
```

Listing 3-21: rotating the box

If a negative value is specified, it will only change the direction in which the element is rotated.

> **Do It Yourself:** Replace the corresponding code in Listing 3-11 with the code in Listing 3-21 in order to test the effect in your browser.

Transform: Skew

This function changes the symmetry of the element by degrees and in both dimensions.

```
#mainbox {
  display: block;
  width: 500px;
  margin: 50px auto;
  padding: 15px;
  text-align: center;
  border: 1px solid #999999;
  background: #DDDDDD;

  -moz-transform: skew(20deg);
  -webkit-transform: skew(20deg);
}
```

Listing 3-22: skew horizontally

The **skew** function has two parameters, but unlike with other functions, each parameter for the **skew** function only affects one dimension, thus the parameters are independent of one another. In Listing 3-22, we performed a **transform** operation to the header box in order to skew it. Only the first parameter was declared, so only the horizontal dimension will be modified. If we used both parameters, we could alter both dimensions of the object. Alternatively, we could use independent functions for this purpose: **skewX** and **skewY**.

> **Do It Yourself:** Replace the corresponding code in Listing 3-11 with the code in Listing 3-22 in order to test the effect in your browser.

Transform: Translate

Similar to the old **top** and **left** properties, the function **translate** moves the element on the screen to a new position.

```
#mainbox {
  display: block;
  width: 500px;
  margin: 50px auto;
  padding: 15px;
  text-align: center;
  border: 1px solid #999999;
  background: #DDDDDD;

  -moz-transform: translate(100px);
  -webkit-transform: translate(100px);
}
```

Listing 3-23: moving the header box to the right

The **translate** function considers the screen to be like a grid of pixels, with the original position of the element used as the reference point. The top-left corner of the element is the 0,0 position, so the negative values will move the object to the left or above the original position, and positive values will move it to the right or below.

In Listing 3-23, we moved the header box to the right 100 pixels from the original position. Two values may be declared for this function to move the element both horizontally and vertically. Or the **translateX** and **translateY** functions can be used to do it independently.

> **Do It Yourself:** Replace the corresponding code in Listing 3-11 with the code in Listing 3-23 in order to test the effect in your browser.

Transforming All at Once

Sometimes it might be useful to perform a few transformations to one element all at once. To get a compound **transform** property, we just have to separate the functions with a space:

```
#mainbox {
  display: block;
  width: 500px;
  margin: 50px auto;
  padding: 15px;
  text-align: center;
  border: 1px solid #999999;
  background: #DDDDDD;

  -moz-transform: translateY(100px) rotate(45deg) scaleX(0.3);
  -webkit-transform: translateY(100px) rotate(45deg) scaleX(0.3);
}
```

Listing 3-24: moving, scaling and rotating the element in just one line

One of the things you have to remember here is that the order is important. This is because some functions move the origin point and the center of the object, thus changing the parameters the rest of the functions will operate from.

> **Do It Yourself:** Replace the corresponding code in Listing 3-11 with the code in Listing 3-24 in order to test the effect in your browser.

Dynamic Transformations

What we have learned so far will change the web but keeps it as static as always. However, we can take advantage of the combination of transformations and pseudo-classes to turn our page into a dynamic application:

```
#mainbox {
  display: block;
  width: 500px;
  margin: 50px auto;
  padding: 15px;
  text-align: center;
  border: 1px solid #999999;
  background: #DDDDDD;
}
```

```
#mainbox:hover{
  -moz-transform: rotate(5deg);
  -webkit-transform: rotate(5deg);
}
```

Listing 3-25: responding to user's activity

In Listing 3-25, the original rule of Listing 3-2 for the header box was kept intact and a new rule was added to apply the transformation effect using the :hover pseudo-class. The result is that, every time the mouse goes over the header box, the transform property rotates it 5 degrees, and when the mouse goes outside the box, the header box is rotated back to its previous position. This achieves a basic but useful animation with no more than CSS properties.

> **Do It Yourself:** Replace the corresponding code in Listing 3-11 with the code in Listing 3-25 in order to test the effect in your browser.

Transitions

From now on, beautiful effects with dynamic transformations are accessible and easy to implement in our designs. However, a real animation requires a transition between the two steps of the process.

The transition property was created to smooth things out—to magically create the rest of the steps implicit in the movement. By just adding this property, we are forcing the browser to take care of the situation, create all those invisible steps for us, and generate a smooth transition from one status to another.

```
#mainbox {
  display: block;
  width: 500px;
  margin: 50px auto;
  padding: 15px;
  text-align: center;
  border: 1px solid #999999;
  background: #DDDDDD;

  -moz-transition: -moz-transform 1s ease-in-out 0.5s;
  -webkit-transition: -webkit-transform 1s ease-in-out 0.5s;
}
#mainbox:hover{
  -moz-transform: rotate(5deg);
  -webkit-transform: rotate(5deg);
}
```

Listing 3-26: a beautiful rotation using transition

As we can see in Listing 3-26, the transition property can take up to four parameters separated by space. The first value is the property that will be considered to create the transition. This is necessary because several properties can change at the same time and probably we will just need to create steps for one of them. The second parameter sets the time that the transition will take from the initial position to the end. The third parameter can be any of five keywords: `ease, linear, ease-in, ease-out` or `ease-in-out`. These keywords determine how the transition process will take place based on a Bézier curve. Every keyword represents a different Bézier curve, and the only way to know which one will be best for every transition is by testing them on the screen. The last parameter for the `transition` property is the delay. It indicates how long it will take for the transition to start.

To produce a transition for all the properties that are changing in an object, the `all` keyword must be specified. We can also declare every property that will be affected by listing them separated by commas.

Do It Yourself: Replace the corresponding code in Listing 3-11 with the code in Listing 3-26 in order to test the effect in your browser.

IMPORTANT: In Listing 3-26, we performed a transition with the `transform` property. Not every CSS property is supported by the `transition` property and probably the list will change over time. You will have to test them by yourself or visit the website for every browser to find more information about it.

Quick Reference
CSS3 Properties

CSS3 provides new properties to create visual and dynamic effects that are an essential part of the web these days.

border-radius—This property generates rounded corners for box elements. It has two different parameters that shape every corner of the box. The first parameter determines the horizontal curve and the second the vertical curve, providing the possibility of creating an ellipsis. Using just one value will shape the corners equally (e.g., **border-radius: 20px**). A value for each corner may be declared, clockwise, from top-left to bottom-left. To declare both parameters of the curve, the values must be separated with a slash (e.g., **border-radius: 15px / 20px**).

box-shadow—This property creates shadows for box elements. It may take five parameters: the color, the horizontal offset, the vertical offset, the blur effect, and the **inset** keyword to generate the shadow inside the element. The offsets may be negative, and the blur and inset values are optional (e.g., **box-shadow: #000000 5px 5px 10px inset**).

text-shadow—This property is similar to **box-shadow** but specific for texts. It takes four parameters: the color, the horizontal offset, the vertical offset, and the blur effect (e.g., **text-shadow: #000000 5px 5px 10px**).

@font-face—This rule will let you load and use any font you want. First you have to create the font, providing a name with the **font-family** property and the file with **src** (e.g., **@font-face{ font-family: Myfont; src: url('fontfile.ttf') }**). After this, you will be able to assign the font (in the example, **Myfont**) to any element in the document.

linear-gradient(start position, from color, to color)—This function may be applied to the **background** or **background-image** property to generate a linear gradient. The attributes indicate the starting point and the colors used to create the gradient. The first value can be specified in pixels, in a percentage or using the keywords **top, bottom, left** and **right**. The starting position may be replaced by an angle to provide a specific direction for the gradient (e.g., **linear-gradient(top, #FFFFFF 50%, #006699 90%);**).

radial-gradient(start position, shape, from color, to color)—This function may be applied to the **background** or **background-image** property to generate a radial gradient. The start position is the origin and can be declared either as pixels, as percentage or as a combination of the keywords **center, top, bottom, left** and **right**. There are two values for the shape: **circle** and **ellipse**, and the color stops indicate the color and the position where transitions start (e.g., `radial-gradient(center, circle, #FFFFFF 0%, #006699 200%);`).

rgba()—This function is an improvement of the previous `rgb()`. It will take four values: the red color (0-255), the green color (0-255), the blue color (0-255), and the opacity (a value between 0 and 1).

hsla()—This function is an improvement of the previous `hsl()`. It will take four values: the hue (a value between 0 and 360), the saturation (a percentage), the lightness (a percentage), and the opacity (a value between 0 and 1).

outline—This property has been improved by the addition of another property called `outline-offset`. Both properties combined generate a second border away from the first one (e.g., `outline: 1px solid #000000; outline-offset: 10px;`).

border-image—This property creates a border with a custom image. It needs a border set previously with the property `border` or `border-with`, and it takes at least three parameters: the URL of the image, the size of the pieces that will be taken from that image to build the border and a keyword that specifies how those pieces will be placed (e.g., `border-image: url("file.png") 15 stretch;`).

transform—This property modifies the shape of an element. It uses four basic functions: `scale`, `rotate`, `skew`, and `translate`. The function `scale` takes only one value. A negative value inverts the element, a value between 0 and 1 reduces the element, and a value greater than 1 expands the element (e.g., `transform: scale(1.5);`). The function `rotate` uses only one value expressed in degrees to rotate the image (e.g., `transform: rotate(20deg);`). The function `skew` has two values, also in degrees, for horizontal and vertical transformation (e.g., `transform: skew(20deg, 20deg);`). The function `translate` moves the object as many pixels as specified by its two parameters (e.g., transform: `translate(20px);`).

transition—This property can be applied to other properties to create a transition between two status of an element. It takes up to four parameters: the property affected, the time it takes from start to end, a keyword to declared how the transition will be made (`ease`, `linear`, `ease-in`, `ease-out`, `ease-in-out`) and a delay for the time to take the transition to start (e.g., `transition: color 2s linear 1s;`).

Chapter 4
Javascript

The Relevance of Javascript

HTML5 may be thought as a building supported by three columns: HTML, CSS and Javascript. We already studied the elements incorporated in HTML and the new properties that turn CSS into the ideal tool for designers. Now it's time to unveil what may be considered one of the strongest aspects of this specification: Javascript.

Javascript is an interpreted language used for multiple purposes but considered just as a complement so far. One of the innovations that helped change how we see Javascript was browsers' new engines, developed to accelerate script processing. The key in the most successful engines was to turn scripts into machine code in order to reach execution speeds similar to those in desktop applications. This improved capacity overcame previous Javascript performance limitations and confirmed this language as the best coding option for the web.

To be able to take advantage of this promising infrastructure, Javascript was enhanced for portability and integration. Also, full application programming interfaces (APIs) were incorporated by default in every browser to assist the language with elemental features. These new APIs (such as Web Storage, Canvas, and others) are the interfaces for libraries embedded in browsers. The idea is to make powerful features available everywhere through simple and standard programming techniques, expanding the language's scope and facilitating the creation of compelling and useful software for the web.

In this chapter, we are going to study how to incorporate Javascript into our HTML documents and introduce the recent incorporations for this language to prepare you for the rest of the book.

> **IMPORTANT:** Our approach to Javascript in this book is introductory. We work through complex issues but just using the minimum codes necessary to take advantage of new features. To expand your knowledge about this topic, visit our website and follow the links for this chapter.

Incorporating Javascript

Following the same approach as with CSS, there are three different techniques to incorporating Javascript code within HTML. However, just as with CSS, only the inclusion of external files is the one recommended to use in HTML5.

> **IMPORTANT:** In this chapter, we introduce new features and basic techniques necessary to understand the examples of the book. If you are already familiar with the basic information presented, please feel free to ignore it.

Inline

This is a simple technique to insert Javascript in our document that takes advantage of attributes available for HTML elements. These attributes are event handlers that execute code according to the user's actions.

The most commonly used event handlers are mouse-related, such as **onclick**, **onMouseOver**, or **onMouseOut**. However, you will also find websites that implement keyword and window events, performing actions after a key press or a window condition change (for example, **onload** or **onfocus**).

```
<!DOCTYPE html>
<html lang="en">
<head>
  <title>This text is the title of the document</title>
</head>
<body>
  <div id="main">
    <p onclick="alert('you clicked me!')">Click Me</p>
    <p>You Can't Click Me</p>
  </div>
</body>
</html>
```

Listing 4-1: *inline Javascript*

Using the event handler **onclick** in Listing 4-1, a code is executed every time the user clicks on the text "Click Me". What the handler **onclick** is saying is something like: "when someone clicks on this element execute this code" and the code is (in this case) a predefined Javascript function that shows a small window with the message "you clicked me!"

Try to change the **onclick** handler by **onMouseOver**, for example, and the code will be executed just by hovering over the element with the mouse pointer.

The use of Javascript inside HTML elements is allowed by HTML5, but for the same reasons as CSS, this kind of practice is not recommended. The HTML code is extended unnecessarily and is hard to maintain or update; as well, the code distributed all over the document makes it really hard to build useful applications.

New methods and techniques were developed to reference HTML elements and register event handlers without having to use inline scripting. We will go back to this and learn more about events and event handlers later in this chapter.

> **Do It Yourself:** Copy the code in Listing 4-1 and the following codes studied in this chapter into a new empty HTML file. Then open the file in your browser to test them.

Embedded

To work with extensive codes and customized functions, we have to group the scripts together between **<script>** tags. The **<script>** element acts exactly like the **<style>** element for CSS, organizing the code in one place and affecting the rest of the elements in the document using references.

Just as with the **<style>** element for HTML5, we don't have to use the **type** attribute to specify the language in the **<script>** tag. In HTML5, Javascript is assigned by default.

```
<!DOCTYPE html>
<html lang="en">
<head>
  <title>This text is the title of the document</title>
  <script>
    function showalert(){
      alert('you clicked me!');
    }
    function clickme(){
      document.getElementsByTagName('p')[0].onclick=showalert;
    }
    window.onload=clickme;
  </script>
</head>
<body>
  <div id="main">
    <p>Click Me</p>
    <p>You Can't Click Me</p>
  </div>
</body>
</html>
```

Listing 4-2: embedded Javascript

The `<script>` element and its content can be positioned in any place in the document, inside other elements or between them. For clarity, we recommend that you always allocate scripts only in the head of the document (as in the example of Listing 4-2) and then reference the elements to be affected using the proper Javascript methods provided for that purpose.

Currently, there are three methods to reference HTML elements in Javascript:

- `getElementsByTagName` (used in Listing 4-2) references an element by its keyword
- `getElementById` references an element by the value of its `id` attribute
- `getElementsByClassName` is a new incorporation that helps us reference an element using the value of the `class` attribute.

Even when you follow the recommended practice (positioning the scripts inside the head of the document), a situation must be considered: the code is read sequentially by the browser and we can't reference an element that hasn't been created yet.

In Listing 4-2, the script is positioned in the head of the document and is read prior to the creation of the `<p>` elements. If we had tried to affect the `<p>` element from this code with just a reference, we would have received an error message explaining that the element doesn't exist. To avoid this problem, the code was converted into a function called `showalert()`, and the reference to the `<p>` element and the event handler were placed on a second function called `clickme()`.

The functions are called from the last line of the script using another event handler (in this case, associated with the window) called `onload`. This handler will execute the function provided when the window is completely loaded and all the elements created.

So let's take a look at the execution of the whole document in Listing 4-2. First the functions are loaded but not executed. Then the HTML elements, including the `<p>` elements, are created. And finally, when the whole document is loaded, the `load` event is fired and the `clickme()` function is called.

In this function, the method `getElementsByTagName` is referencing the `<p>` elements. This method returns an array containing a list of the elements found in the document. However, by using the index `[0]` at the end of the method, we indicated that only the first element should be selected. Once this element is identified, the code registers the `onclick` event handler for it. The `showalert()` function will be executed when the event is fired and show a small window with the message "you clicked me!".

It might look like a lot of code and work to reproduce the effect achieved by a single line in the example in Listing 4-1. However, considering the potential of HTML5 and the complexity achieved by Javascript, the concentration of code in one place and a proper organization represent a great advantage for our future implementations and make our websites and applications easy to develop and maintain.

> **Review the Basics:** A function is a group of code that is executed only when the function is invoked (activitated or called) by its name. Usually a function is called using the name and some values enclosed by parentheses—for example, `clickme(1,2)`. An exception to this syntax is used in Listing 4-2. In this code

we are not using parentheses because we are passing the reference of the function to the event handler, not the result of the execution of the function. To learn more about Javascript functions, go to our website and visit the links for this chapter.

External File

Javascript codes grow exponentially according to the addition of new functions and the application of some of the APIs mentioned above. Embedded codes make our documents bigger and repetitive. To reduce downloading times, increase our productivity, and be able to distribute and reuse our codes in every document without compromising efficiency, we recommend you to save the Javascript codes in one or more external files and call them using the **src** attribute:

```
<!DOCTYPE html>
<html lang="en">
<head>
  <title>This text is the title of the document</title>
  <script src="mycode.js"></script>
</head>
<body>
  <div id="main">
    <p>Click Me</p>
    <p>You Can't Click Me</p>
  </div>
</body>
</html>
```

Listing 4-3: *getting the code from external files*

The **<script>** element in Listing 4-3 loads the Javascript code from an external file called **mycode.js**. From now on we are able to insert this file in every document of our website and reuse the code any time we want. From the user's perspective, this practice reduces the time to download and access our website; for us, this practice simplifies organization and maintenance.

> **Do It Yourself:** Copy the code in Listing 4-3 inside the HTML file previously created. Create a new empty file called **mycode.js** and copy the Javascript code from Listing 4-2. Note that only the code between **<script>** tags has to be copied, not including the tags.

New Selectors

As we saw before, the HTML elements have to be referenced from Javascript in order to be affected by the code. If you remember from previous chapters, CSS, and specially CSS3, has a powerful system for reference and selection that is beyond comparison with the few methods provided by Javascript. The **getElementById**, **getElementsByTagName** and **getElementsByClassName** methods are not enough to support the integration this language needs and the relevance it has in the HTML5 specification. To get Javascript to the level that circumstances require, better alternatives have been incorporated. From now on, we can select HTML elements applying all kind of CSS selectors using the new methods **querySelector()** and **querySelectorAll()**.

querySelector()

This method returns the first element that matches the specified group of selectors within the parentheses. The selectors are declared using quotes and CSS syntax, as in the following example:

```
function clickme(){
  document.querySelector("#main p:first-
child").onclick=showalert;
}
function showalert(){
  alert('you clicked me!');
}
window.onload=clickme;
```

Listing 4-4: using querySelector()

In Listing 4-4, the method **getElementsByTagName** used before has been replaced by **querySelector()**. The selectors for this particular query are referencing the first <p> element that is a child of the element identified with the **id** attribute and the value **main**.

Because we already explained that this method only returns the first element found, you have probably noticed that the **first-child** pseudo-class is redundant. The method **querySelector()** in our example will return the first <p> element inside the <div> that is, of course, its first child. The purpose of this example is to show you that **querySelector()** accepts all kind of valid CSS selectors and now, as well as CSS, Javascript also provides important tools to reference every element in the document.

Several groups of selectors may be declared separated by comma. The **querySelector()** method will return the first element that matches any one of them.

> **Do It Yourself:** Replace the code in the **mycode.js** file for the one provided in Listing 4-4 and open the HTML file with the code in Listing 4-3 in your browser to see the **querySelector()** method in action.

querySelectorAll()

Instead of one, **querySelectorAll()** returns *every* element that matches the specified group of selectors within the parentheses. The value returned is an array containing every element found in document order.

```
function clickme(){
  var list=document.querySelectorAll("#main p");
  list[0].onclick=showalert;
}
function showalert(){
  alert('you clicked me!');
}
window.onload=clickme;
```

Listing 4-5: using querySelectorAll()

The group of selectors provided in the **querySelectorAll()** method in Listing 4-5 will find every **<p>** element in the HTML document in Listing 4-3 that is the child of the **<div>** element. After the execution of that first line, the array **list** will have two values: a reference to the first **<p>** element and a reference to the second **<p>** element. Because the keywords of every array created automatically starts from 0, in the next line the first element found is referenced using square brackets with the value 0.

Note that this example doesn't show the potential of **querySelectorAll()**. Usually this method will be used to affect several elements and not only one, as in our case. To iterate through the list of elements returned by the method, we can use a **for** loop:

```
function clickme(){
  var list=document.querySelectorAll("#main p");
  for(var f=0; f<list.length; f++){
    list[f].onclick=showalert;
  }
}
function showalert(){
  alert('you clicked me!');
}
window.onload=clickme;
```

Listing 4-6: affecting all the elements found by querySelectorAll()

In Listing 4-6, instead of selecting only the first element found, we registered the **onclick** event handler for every one of them using a **for** loop. Now, all the **<p>** elements inside the **<div>** will pop-up a small window when the user clicks on them.

The **querySelectorAll()** method, as well as **querySelector()**, may contain one or more groups of selectors separated by a comma. These and previous methods may be combined to reach the elements we want. For example, in Listing 4-7, the same result of the code for Listing 4-6 is achieved using **querySelectorAll()** and **getElementById()** together.

```
function clickme(){
  var list=document.getElementById('main').querySelectorAll("p");
  list[0].onclick=showalert;
}
function showalert(){
  alert('you clicked me!');
}
window.onload=clickme;
```

Listing 4-7: combining methods

Using this technique, we can see how precise these methods can be. We are able to combine methods in the same line or select a group of elements and then perform a second selection with another method to reach elements inside the first ones. Later in this book, we will study more examples.

Event Handlers

As we said before, Javascript code is usually executed after the user performs actions. These actions and other events are processed by event handlers and Javascript functions associated with them.

There are three different ways to register an event handler for an HTML element: we can add a new attribute to the element, register an event handler as a property of the element, or use the new standard `addEventListener()` method.

> **Review the Basics:** In Javascript user's actions are called events. When the user performs an action, such as click the mouse or press a key, an event specific for each action is fired. Besides the events produced by users there are also events fired by the system—for example, the `load` event that fires when the document is fully loaded. These events are handled by codes or entire functions. The code that responds to the event is called handler. When we register a handler what we are doing is defining how our application will respond to a particular event. After the standardization of the `addEventListener()` method, this procedure is usually called "listen to the event", and what we do to prepare the code that will respond to the event is "add an event listener" to a particular element.

Inline Event Handlers

We already used this technique in the code in Listing 4-1 including the `onclick` attribute in the `<p>` element. This is a deprecated technique but still extremely useful and practical in some circumstances.

Event Handlers as Properties

To avoid the complications of the inline technique, we must register the events from Javascript code. Using Javascript selectors, we can reference an HTML element and assign to that element the event handler we want as a property.

On the code in Listing 4-2 you will find this technique put into practice. Two event handlers were assigned as properties to different elements. The event handler `onload` was registered for the window using the construction `window.onload`, and the event handler `onclick` was registered for the first `<p>` element found in the document using the selector `getElementsByTagName` in the line of code `document.getElementsByTagName('p')[0].onclick`.

Review the Basics: The names of the event handlers are made by adding the prefix **on** to the name of the event. For example, the name of the event handler for the `click` event is `onclick`. When we talk about `onclick` we are making reference to the code that will be executed after a `click` event takes place.

Previously to HTML5, this was the only cross-browser technique available to use event handlers from Javascript code. Some browser vendors were developing their own systems but nothing caught up until the new standard was adopted. Therefore, we recommend this technique for compatibility with old browsers, but recommend against it in HTML5 applications.

The addEventListener() Method

The `addEventListener()` method is the ideal technique and the one implemented as standard for the HTML5 specification. This method has three arguments: the event type, the function to be executed, and a boolean value.

```
<!DOCTYPE html>
<html lang="en">
<head>
  <title>This text is the title of the document</title>
  <script>
    function showalert(){
      alert('you clicked me!');
    }
    function clickme(){
      var pelement=document.getElementsByTagName('p')[0];
      pelement.addEventListener('click', showalert, false);
    }
    window.addEventListener('load', clickme, false);
  </script>
</head>
<body>
  <div id="main">
    <p>Click Me</p>
    <p>You Can't Click Me</p>
  </div>
</body>
</html>
```

Listing 4-8: adding event listeners with `addEventListener()`

Listing 4-8 shows the same code from Listing 4-2 but now a listener is added for every event by the `addEventListener()` method. To organize the code in the `clickme()` function, we assigned the element's reference to a variable named `pelement` and then added the listener for the `click` event using that variable.

The syntax of the **addEventListener()** method is shown in Listing 4-8. The first attribute is the event's name. The second is the function to be executed, which could be a function's reference (as in this case) or an entire anonymous function. The third attribute will set, by using **true** or **false**, how multiple events will be fired. For example, if we are listening to the **click** event in two elements that are nested (one inside another), when the user clicks over those elements, two **click** events are fired in an order according to this value. If this attribute is set as **true** for one of the elements, then that event will be considered first, and the other next. Usually the value **false** is enough for most situations.

> **Review the Basics:** Anonymous functions are functions that are dynamically declared and don't have a name (hence "anonymous"). These kinds of functions are extremely useful in Javascript; they help us to organize the code and not overpopulate the global scope with independent functions. We will use anonymous functions several times in the following chapters.

Even when the results of applying this technique and the previous one are similar, **addEventListener()** lets us add as many event listeners as we want for the same element. This distinction gives **addEventListener()** an advantage over the rest, making it the ideal implementation for HTML5 applications.

Because events are the key for interactive websites and web applications, several were added in the HTML5 specification. We will study each one of them in their own environment later on this book.

APIs

If you have any previous experience programming, or just simply followed the chapter to this point, it will be easy to notice the amount of code necessary to perform simple tasks. Now imagine all the work you would have to do to build a database system from scratch, to generate complex graphics on the screen or to create an application for photo manipulation.

Javascript is as powerful as any other developing language at this moment. For the same reason that professional programming languages have libraries to create graphic elements, 3D engines for video games, or interfaces to access databases, to name a few, Javascript has APIs to help programmers deal with complex issues.

HTML5 introduces several APIs to provide access to powerful libraries from simple Javascript code. The potential of these additions is so important that they will turn soon into our main subject of study. Let's take a look at these features and get a perspective on what we are going to see in the rest of the book.

Canvas API

The **Canvas** API is a drawing API that provides a basic but powerful drawing surface. This is the most amazing and promising API of all. The possibility to dynamically generate and render graphics, create animations or manipulate images and videos—combined with the rest of the HTML5 functionality—opens the door for everything you can imagine.

The Canvas API generates a bitmap, an image with pixels that is created and manipulated by a set of functions and methods specific for this purpose.

Drag and Drop API

The **Drag and Drop** API was developed to make simple for the web a common action in desktop applications. Now, with short lines of codes, we can make an element available to be dragged and then dropped into another element. These elements can include not only graphics but also text, links, files or data.

Geolocation API

The **Geolocation** API is used to establish the physical location of the device used to access the application. There are several methods to get this information—from network signals as IP address to Global Positioning System (GPS). The values returned include latitude and longitude, making possible to integrate this API with external map APIs (for example, GoogleMaps) or to access very specific local information to build practical applications.

Storage APIs

Two APIs were created for storage purposes: **Web Storage** and **Indexed Database**. Mainly these APIs take the responsibility for data handling from servers to the user's computer, but in the case of Web Storage and the attribute sessionStorage, this incorporation also increases the level of control and efficiency for web applications.

The **Web Storage** API has two important attributes that are sometimes considered to be APIs by themselves: sessionStorage and localStorage.

The attribute **sessionStorage** is responsible for maintaining consistency over the duration of a page session and keeping temporary information such as the content of a shopping cart safe in case of accident or wrong use (for example, when a second window is open).

In contrast, the **localStorage** attribute for this API lets us save large files in the user's computer. The information saved is persistent and never expires except for security reasons.

Both, sessionStorage and localStorage are replacing the function of cookies and overcome their limitations.

The second API, grouped under the storage APIs but independent from the rest, is the **Indexed Database** API. The database capability is intended to store indexed information. The previously mentioned API was working over the storage of large files or temporary data, but not structured data. This is a possibility only available for database systems and the reason for the existence of this database API.

The Indexed Database API is a substitution for the Web SQL Database API. Due to disagreements about the proper standard, neither of the two APIs had been fully accepted. In fact, at the moment of this writing, the Web SQL Database API (which was received with open arms in the early days), has already been cancelled.

Because the Indexed Database API, also known as **IndexedDB**, looks more promising and has the support of Microsoft, the Firefox developers and Google, it will be our choice for this book. However, keep in mind that, at this moment, new implementations of SQL are still under consideration.

File APIs

Under the title of File API the specification offers several APIs to manage files. At this moment, there are three APIs available for this purpose: File API, File API: Directories & System, and File API: Writer.

Thanks to this group of APIs, we are now able to read, process and create files in the user's computer.

Communication APIs

Some APIs have a common denominator that lets us group them together. That's the case for the XMLHttpRequest API Level 2, the Cross Document Messaging API, and the Web Sockets API.

The Internet has been always about communication, of course, but a few unsolved issues have made the process complicated or sometimes even impossible. Three particular problems had to be addressed: the API for Ajax applications was incomplete and complicated to implement across different browsers, the communication between unrelated applications was nonexistent, and there was no way to have effective two-way communication to access information on a server in real-time.

The first issue listed above was solved with the development of **XMLHttpRequest API Level 2**. XMLHttpRequest was the API used to create Ajax applications, applications that access the server without refreshing the page. The level 2 of this API incorporates new events, provides more functionality (with events to keep track of progress), portability (the API now is standard), and accessibility (using cross-origin requests).

The approach to the second issue was the creation of the **Cross Document Messaging** API. This API helps developers overcome the limitations for communication between different frames and windows. Now a secure communication across several locations is possible through this feature using messages.

The last communication API incorporated in HTML5 is **Web Sockets**. Its purpose is to provide tools necessary for real-time applications (for example, chat rooms). The API enables applications to get and send information to a server in short periods of time, making real-time applications possible.

Web Workers API

This is a unique API that expands Javascript to a new level. Javascript is not a multithread language, which means that it can take care of only one task at a time. Web Workers API provides the capability to process code in the background, on separate threads, without interfering with the activity on the page. Thanks to this API, Javascript is now able to perform multitasking.

History API

Ajax changed the way users interact with websites and web applications. Browsers were not prepared for these situations. The History API was implemented to adapt modern applications to the way browsers keep track of the user's activity. The API incorporates techniques to artificially generate URLs for every step in the process, providing the possibility of returning to previous states using standard navigation procedures.

Offline API

Even now, with Internet access in almost every place we go, getting offline is still possible. Portable devices are everywhere, but not the signal necessary to establish communication. And desktop computers can also send us offline at the most critical moments. With the combination of HTML attributes, events controlled by Javascript and text files, the Offline API will make our applications work online or offline according to the user's situation.

External Libraries

HTML5 was developed to expand the web with a standard set of technologies that every browser would support. And it was created to provide everything a developer needs. In fact, HTML5 was conceptualized to depend on no third-party technology, but for one reason or another we will always have to get extra help.

Before the appearance of HTML5, several Javascript libraries were developed to overcome the limitations of the technologies available at that time. Some of those libraries were created with specific purposes—from processing and validation of forms, to generation and manipulation of graphics. These libraries have become extremely popular, and some of them are almost impossible for independent developers to imitate (for example, Google Maps).

Even when future implementations provide better methods or improve pre-programmed applications, programmers will always find an easier way to deal with different issues. Libraries that simplify complicated tasks will always be alive and growing in number.

These libraries are not part of HTML5, but are an important part of the web, and some of them are already used in the most successful websites and applications nowadays. They, along with the rest of the features incorporated by this specification, enhance Javascript and help to put cutting edge technology in everyone's hands.

jQuery

This is the most popular library available today. The library jQuery is free and was designed to simplify the creation of modern applications with Javascript. It makes HTML elements easier to select, animations easy to generate, and it also handles events and help to implement Ajax in our applications.

The library jQuery is just a small file that you can download from **www.jquery.com** and then include in your documents using `<script>` tags. It provides a simple API that anyone can learn and immediately apply.

Once jQuery is included in our document, we are able to take advantage of simple methods added by the library and turn our static web into a modern and practical application.

jQuery has the advantage of providing support for old browsers and makes normal tasks simpler and accessible for any developer. It can be used along with HTML5 or as a simple way to replace some basic HTML5 features in browsers not ready for this technology.

Google Maps

Accessible by a Javascript API (and other technologies), Google Maps is a unique, complex set of tools that let us develop any mapping service for the web we can imagine. Google has become the leader in this type of service and through the Google Maps technology they provide access to an extremely accurate and detailed map of the world. We can search for specific locations, calculate distances, find popular spots, or even get a look at the selected place as if we were there.

The Google Maps API is free and available for every developer. Different versions of the API are ready to use from here: code.google.com/apis/maps/

Quick Reference
Javascript

In HTML5, Javascript was enhanced by the addition of new features and improved native methods.

Elements

<script>—This element now has Javascript as the default scripting language; no `type` attribute is longer necessary.

Selectors

The possibility of selecting a document's elements dynamically from Javascript code has turned out to be essential for any web application. New methods have been incorporated for this purpose.

getElementsByClassName—This selector allows us to find elements in the document by the value of their `class` attribute. It's an addition of the already available `getElementsByTagName` and `getElementById`.

querySelector(selectors)—This method uses CSS selectors to reference elements in the document. The selectors are declared within the parentheses and the method can be combined with others to build a more specific reference. It returns the first element found.

querySelectorAll(selectors)—This method is similar to `querySelector()` but returns all the elements that match the specified selectors.

Events

The relevance of events in web applications motivated the standardization of methods already used for leading browsers.

addEventListener(type, listener, useCapture)—This method is used to add an event listener. The method receives three values: the name of the event, the function to handle the event, and a boolean value that indicates order of execution for several events fired at the same time. Usually the third attribute is set to `false`.

removeEventListener(type, listener, useCapture) —This method is used to remove event listeners, deactivating the event handler. The values we must provide are the same of `addEventListener()`.

APIs

The scope of Javascript has been expanded with a set of powerful embedded applications accessible through APIs.

Canvas API—This API is a drawing API, to create and manipulate bitmap graphics. It uses predefined Javascript methods to work.

Drag and Drop API—This API makes a common action in desktop applications available for the web. It lets users drag and drop any element in a web document.

Geolocation API—This API is intended to provide access to the physical location of the device that is running the application. It can retrieve data such as latitude and longitude using different mechanisms (such as network information and GPS).

Web Storage API—This API introduces two attributes to save persistent data in the user's computer: `sessionStorage` and `localStorage`. The attribute `sessionStorage` allows developers to keep track of the user's activity by storing information that is available in every window during the current session. The attribute `localStorage`, on the other hand, lets developers use a private storage area created for every application that can store several megabytes, thus preserving the information and data in user's computer.

Indexed Database API—This API adds database capability to web applications on the user side. The system was developed independently of previous technologies and provides a simple database implementation aimed at web applications. The database is stored in the user's computer, it's persistent, and of course, it's exclusive for the application that created it.

File APIs—This is a group of APIs provided to read, write and process the user's files.

XMLHttpRequest API Level 2—This API is an improvement on the old XMLHttpRequest API for the construction of Ajax applications. It includes new methods to control progress and perform cross-origin requests.

Cross Document Messaging API—This API introduces a new communication technology that allows applications to communicate with each other across different frames and windows.

WebSockets API—This API provides a mechanism for two-way communication between clients and servers for real-time applications such as chat rooms or online video gaming.

Web Workers API—This API enhances Javascript allowing scripts to run in the background without interrupting the activity on the current page.

History API—This API provides the alternative to incorporate every step in an application's processing into the browser's history.

Offline API—This API aims to preserve applications running when users go offline.

Chapter 5
Video and Audio

Playing Video with HTML5

One of the most mentioned features of HTML5 was video processing. The excitement had nothing to do with the new tools provided by HTML5 for this purpose, but with the fact that because video became the centerpiece of Internet, everybody expected native support from browsers. It was like everybody knew the importance of videos except those developing technologies for the web.

But now that we already have native support—and even a standard that will let us build cross-browser applications for video processing—we realized that it was more complicated that we had imagined. From codecs to resource consumption issues, the reasons to not implement video before were far more complex than the codes necessary to do it.

Despite the complications, HTML5 finally introduced an element to insert and play video files in an HTML document. The **<video>** element uses opening and closing tags and just a few parameters to accomplish its function. The syntax is extremely simple and only the **src** attribute is mandatory:

```
<!DOCTYPE html>
<html lang="en">
<head>
  <title>Video Player</title>
</head>
<body>
<section id="player">
  <video src="http://minkbooks.com/content/trailer.mp4" controls>
  </video>
</section>
</body>
</html>
```

Listing 5-1: *basic syntax for the* <video> *element*

In theory, the code in Listing 5-1 should be more than enough—I repeat, ... in theory. But as we explained before, things get a little bit complicated than that in real life. First, we have to provide at least two files for different video formats: OGG and MP4. This is because even when the <video> element and its attributes are standard, there is no standard video format. First, some browsers support a group of codecs that others don't, and the other way around. And second, the codec used in the MP4 format (the only one supported by important browsers such as Safari and Internet Explorer) has a commercial license.

The formats OGG and MP4 are containers for video and audio. OGG contains Theora video and Vorbis audio codecs, and the ones for the MP4 container are H.264 for video and AAC for audio. At this moment OGG is supported by Firefox, Google Chrome and Opera; in contrast, MP4 works on Safari, Internet Explorer and Google Chrome.

The <video> Element

Let's try to avoid those complications and enjoy the simplicity of the <video> element for a moment. This element has several attributes to set its properties and default configuration. The attributes width and height, like any other known HTML element, declare the dimensions for the element or window's player. The size of the video will be automatically adjusted to fit into these values, but they are not intended to stretch the video, so we have to use them in order to limit the area occupied by the media and preserve consistency in our design, not to customize video dimensions. The attribute src, as we said before, specifies the source for the video. This attribute can be replaced by the <source> element and its own src attribute in order to declare several sources for different video formats (as in the following example).

```
<!DOCTYPE html>
<html lang="en">
<head>
  <title>Video Player</title>
</head>
<body>
<section id="player">
  <video id="media" width="720" height="400" controls>
    <source src="http://minkbooks.com/content/trailer.mp4">
    <source src="http://minkbooks.com/content/trailer.ogg">
  </video>
</section>
</body>
</html>
```

Listing 5-2: a working cross-browser video player with default controls

In Listing 5-2, the <video> element was expanded. Now, within the element's tags, there are two <source> elements. These elements are providing different video sources for the browser to choose from. The browser will read the **<source>** tags and decide which file should be played according to the supported formats (MP4 or OGG).

> **Do It Yourself:** Create a new empty HTML file with the name **video.html** (or whatever you want), copy the code in Listing 5-2, and open the file in different browsers to check the **<video>** element at work.

<video> Attributes

There is an attribute in the **<video>** tag used in Listings 5-1 and 5-2 that probably caught your attention. The **controls** attribute is one of several specific attributes available for this element. This, in particular, shows video controls provided by browsers. Every browser will activate its own interface, allowing the user to start the video, pause it or jump to a specific frame, among other features.

Along with **controls**, you can also use the following:

> **autoplay**—When this attribute is present, the browser will automatically play the video as soon as it can.
>
> **loop**—If this attribute is specified, the browser will restart the video upon reaching the end.
>
> **poster**—This attribute provides a URL of an image that will be shown while waiting for the video to be played.
>
> **preload** —This attribute can take three values: **none**, **metadata** or **auto**. The first one indicates that the video shouldn't be cached, usually with the purpose of minimizing unnecessary traffic. The second value, **metadata**, will recommend that the browser fetch some information about the resource—for example, dimensions, duration, first frame. The third value, **auto**, is the value set by default and will prompt the browser to download the file as soon as possible.

```
<!DOCTYPE html>
<html lang="en">
<head>
  <title>Video Player</title>
</head>
<body>
  <section id="player">
    <video id="media" width="720" height="400" preload controls
loop poster="http://minkbooks.com/content/poster.jpg">
      <source src="http://minkbooks.com/content/trailer.mp4">
      <source src="http://minkbooks.com/content/trailer.ogg">
    </video>
  </section>
```

```
</body>
</html>
```

In Listing 5-3, the **<video>** element was populated with attributes. Because of changes in behavior from one browser to another, some attributes will be enabled or disabled by default, and a few of them won't even work in some browsers and under variable circumstances. To have absolute control over the **<video>** element and the media being played, we will have to program our own video player with Javascript, taking advantage of the new methods, properties and events incorporated by the HTML5 specification.

Programming a Video Player

If you have tested the previous codes in different browsers, you will have noticed that the graphic design for the player controls differs in each case. Each browser has its own buttons and progress bars, and even its own features. This situation might be acceptable in some circumstances, but in a professional environment, where every detail counts, it's absolutely necessary that a consistent design is preserved across all devices and applications, and that we have absolute control over the whole process.

HTML5 provides new events, properties and methods to manipulate video and integrate it with the document. From now on, we can create our own video player and provide the features we want using HTML, CSS and Javascript. The video is now part of the document.

The Design

Every video player needs a control panel with at least some basic features. In the new template in Listing 5-4, a **<nav>** element was added after **<video>**. This **<nav>** element contains two **<div>** elements, **buttons** and **bar**, to provide a "play" button and a progress bar.

```
<!DOCTYPE html>
<html lang="en">
<head>
  <title>Video Player</title>
  <link rel="stylesheet" href="player.css">
  <script src="player.js"></script>
</head>
<body>
<section id="player">
  <video id="media" width="720" height="400">
    <source src="http://minkbooks.com/content/trailer.mp4">
    <source src="http://minkbooks.com/content/trailer.ogg">
  </video>
  <nav>
    <div id="buttons">
      <button type="button" id="play">Play</button>
    </div>
    <div id="bar">
      <div id="progress"></div>
    </div>
    <div style="clear: both"></div>
  </nav>
```

```
</section>
</body>
</html>
```

Listing 5-4: HTML template for our video player

This template also includes two files to access external codes. One of the files is **player.css** for the following CSS styles:

```css
body{
   text-align: center;
}
header, section, footer, aside, nav, article, figure, figcaption,
hgroup{
   display : block;
}
#player{
   width: 720px;
   margin: 20px auto;
   padding: 5px;
   background: #999999;
   border: 1px solid #666666;

   -moz-border-radius: 5px;
   -webkit-border-radius: 5px;
   border-radius: 5px;
}
nav{
   margin: 5px 0px;
}
#buttons{
   float: left;
   width: 85px;
   height: 20px;
}
#bar{
   position: relative;
   float: left;
   width: 600px;
   height: 16px;
   padding: 2px;
   border: 1px solid #CCCCCC;
   background: #EEEEEE;
}
#progress{
   position: absolute;
   width: 0px;
   height: 16px;
   background: rgba(0,0,150,.2);
}
```

Listing 5-5: CSS styles for the player

The code in Listing 5-5 uses techniques from the Traditional Box Model to create a box that contains every part of the video player. The box is centered in the window using this model. Notice that we also added a third `<div>` at the end of the `<nav>` element in the template with an inline style to recover the normal flow of the document.

There are no new properties or surprises in the last code; it's just a group of CSS properties (which you already studied) to provide styles to the player's elements. However, there is one style that could be considered unusual: the `width` for the `<div>` element `progress` was initialized to 0. This is because we are going to use this element to simulate a progress bar that will change while the video is being played.

> **Do It Yourself:** Copy the new template in Listing 5-4 in the HTML file (`video.html`). Create two new empty files for the CSS styles and Javascript codes. These files should be named `player.css` and `player.js` respectively. Copy the code in Listing 5-5 into the CSS file and then copy every Javascript code listing next into the Javascript file.

The Code

Now it's time to write the Javascript code for our player. There are different ways to program a video player, but we will show you just how to apply the necessary events, methods and properties for basic video processing. The rest is up to you and where your imagination takes you.

For our purposes, we will work with a few simple functions that will play and pause the video, show a progress bar when the video is played and give the option clicking over this bar to move forward and backwards in the timeline.

The Events

HTML5 incorporates new events that are API specific. For video and audio processing, events were incorporated to inform the media situation—such as the downloading progress, whether the video has reached the end, or whether the video is paused or playing, among others. We are not going to use them for our example, but they will be necessary to build more complex applications. Here are the most common:

> **progress**—This event is fired periodically to update about the progress in downloading the media. The information will be accessible through the `buffered` attribute, as we will see later.
>
> **canplaythrough**—This event is fired when the entire media can be played without interruption. The status is established considering the current download rate and assuming that will be the same for the rest of the process. There is another event for this purpose, `canplay`, but it doesn't consider the whole situation and it's fired when there are just a couple of frames available.

ended—It's fired when the media reaches the end.

pause—It's fired when the playback is paused.

play—It's fired when the media starts playing.

error—This event is fired when an error occurs. It's delivered to the `<source>` element corresponding to the media source that produces the error.

We are going to listen only to the usual `click` and `load` events for our player.

> **IMPORTANT:** Events, methods and properties for APIs are still under development at this moment. In this book, we are going to review only those that we consider relevant and indispensable for our applications. To see how the specification is progressing in this regard, please visit our website and follow the links for each chapter.

```
function initiate() {
  maxim=600;
  mmedia=document.getElementById('media');
  play=document.getElementById('play');
  bar=document.getElementById('bar');
  progress=document.getElementById('progress');

  play.addEventListener('click', push, false);
  bar.addEventListener('click', move, false);
}
```

Listing 5-6: initial function

Listing 5-6 presents the first function for our video player. The function was called **initiate** because it is the function that will run the application once the window is loaded.

Because this is the first function to be executed, we need to set global variables to configure the player. Using the selector **getElementById** we created a reference to every player's element to be able to access them later throughout the code. We also set the variable **maxim** to always know the maximum size of the progress bar (600 pixels).

There are two actions we have to pay attention to for our player: when the user clicks on the button "play" and when the user clicks on the progress bar to go forward or backward in the timeline. Two event listeners were added for this purpose. First, a listener for the **click** event was added to the element **play**. This listener will execute the **push()** function every time the user clicks on the element (the "play" button). The other listener is for the element **bar**. In this case, the **move()** function will be executed every time the user clicks on the progress bar.

The Methods

The **push()** function incorporated in Listing 5-7 is the first function that already performs an action. It will execute the special methods **pause()** and **play()** according to the situation:

```
function push(){
  if(!mmedia.paused && !mmedia.ended) {
    mmedia.pause();
    play.innerHTML='Play';
    window.clearInterval(loop);
  }else{
    mmedia.play();
    play.innerHTML='Pause';
    loop=setInterval(status, 1000);
  }
}
```

Listing 5-7: *this function plays and pauses the video*

The special methods **play()** and **pause()** are part of a list of methods incorporated by HTML5 for media processing. Here are the most common:

> **play()**—This method will play the media file from the beginning unless the media was previously paused.
> **pause()**—This method will pause playback.
> **load()**—This method loads the media file. It's useful to load the media in advance for dynamic applications.
> **canPlayType(type)**—With this method, we are able to know whether a file format is supported by the browser or not.

The Properties

The **push()** function also uses a few properties to retrieve information about the media. Here are the most common:

> **paused**—This property returns **true** if the media is currently paused or it hasn't started playing.
> **ended**—This property returns **true** if the media has finished playing.
> **duration**—This property returns the duration of the media in seconds.
> **currentTime**—This is a property that can return and receive a value to inform the position in which the media is being played or it sets a new position to start playing.
> **error**—This returns the error value if an error has occurred.

buffered—This property offers information about how much the file has loaded so far into the buffer. It let us create an indicator to show the downloading progress. The property is usually read when the **progress** event is fired. Because users may force the browser to download the media from different positions on the timeline, the information returned by **buffered** is an array containing every part of the media that was downloaded, not just the one that starts from the beginning. The elements of the array are accessible by the attributes **end()** and **start()**. For example, the code **buffered.end(0)** will return the duration in seconds of the first portion of the media in the buffer. The support for this feature is under development at this moment.

The Code at Work

Now that we know all the elements involved in video processing, let's take a look at how the **push()** function works.

The function is executed when the user clicks the "play" button. This button will have two purposes: it will show the text "Play" to play the video or "Pause" to pause the video, according to the circumstances. So, when the video is paused or it wasn't started, pressing the button will play the video. The opposite will happen if the video is already being played, then pressing the button will pause the video.

To accomplish this, the code will detect the situation of the media checking the properties **paused** and **ended**. So, in the first line of the function we have a conditional **if** to check this situation. If the value of **mmedia.paused** and **mmedia.ended** is **false**, it will mean that the video is playing, then the **pause()** method is executed to pause the video and the text for the button is changed to "Play" using **innerHTML**.

If the opposite happens, the video is paused or has finished playing, then the condition will be **false** and the **play()** method will be executed to start or resume the video. In this case, we are also performing an important action which is that we start executing the **status()** function each second with **setInterval()**.

```
function status(){
  if(!mmedia.ended){
    var size=parseInt(mmedia.currentTime*maxim/mmedia.duration);
    progress.style.width=size+'px';
  }else{
    progress.style.width='0px';
    play.innerHTML='Play';
    window.clearInterval(loop);
  }
}
```

Listing 5-8: this function updates the progress bar

The **status()** function in Listing 5-8 is executed each second while the video is playing. We also have a conditional **if** in this function to test the video status. If the property **ended** returns **false**, we calculate how long the progress bar should be in pixels and set the size of the **<div>** that is representing it. In case the property is **true** (which means the video is finished), we set the size of the progress bar back to 0 pixels, change the text for the button to "Play", and cancel the loop with **clearInterval**. In this case, the **status()** function won't be executed anymore.

Let's go back to how we calculated the size of the progress bar. Because the **status()** function will be executed each second while the video is playing, the current time that is being played will change constantly. This value in seconds is retrieved using the property **currentTime**. We also have the value for the duration of the video in the property **duration**, and the maximum size of the progress bar in the variable **maxim**. With those three values, we can calculate how many pixels long the bar should be to represent the seconds already played. The formula **current time × maximum / total duration** will transform the seconds into pixels to change the size of the **<div>** that represents the progress bar.

The function to handle the **click** event for the element **play** (the button) was already created. Now it's time to do the same for the progress bar:

```
function move(e){
  if(!mmedia.paused && !mmedia.ended){
    var mouseX=e.pageX-bar.offsetLeft;
    var newtime=mouseX*mmedia.duration/maxim;
    mmedia.currentTime=newtime;
    progress.style.width=mouseX+'px';
  }
}
```

Listing 5-9: start playing from the position selected by the user

A listener for the **click** event was added to the **bar** element to check every time the user wants to start playing the video from a new position. The listener uses the **move()** function to handle the event when it's fired. You can see this function in Listing 5-9. It starts with an **if**, as well as the previous functions, but this time the goal is to perform the action only when the video is being played. If the properties **paused** and **ended** are **false** it means that the video is playing and the code has to be executed.

We have to do several things to calculate the time in which the video should start playing. We have to determine what exactly was the position of the mouse when the **click** event took place, what is the distance in pixels from that position to the beginning of the progress bar, and how many seconds that distance represents in the timeline.

The processes to register an event handler (of event listener)—such as **addEventListener()** — always sends a reference to the event. This reference is sent to the handler function as an attribute. Traditionally the variable **e** is used to keep this value. In the function in Listing 5-9 we used this variable and the property **pageX** to capture the exact position of the mouse at the moment the event took place. The value returned by **pageX** is relative to the page, not to the progress bar or the window. To know how many pixels there are from the beginning of the progress bar to the position of the mouse, we have to subtract the space between the left side of the page and the beginning of the bar. Remember that the progress bar is located inside a box that is centered on the screen. So lets say that the bar is located 421 pixels from the left side of the page, and the click was made in the middle of the bar. Because the bar is 600 pixels long, the click was made at 300 pixels. However, the property **pageX** won't return 300; it will return the value 721. To get exactly the position in the bar where the click was made, we have to subtract the distance from the left side of the page to the beginning of the bar (in this example, 421 pixels). This distance can be retrieved using the property **offsetLeft**. So, with the formula **e.pageX - bar.offsetLeft** we are getting exactly the position of the mouse relative to the bar. In this example, the end formula will be: **721 - 421 = 300**.

Once we have this value, it has to be converted into seconds. Using the property **duration**, the exact position of the mouse in the bar, and the maximum size of the bar, we built the formula **mouseX × video.duration / maxim** to get the value and save it in the variable **newtime**. The result is the time in seconds that the position of the mouse represents in the time line.

Now we have to start playing the video from the new position. The property **currentTime**, as was mentioned before, returns the time of the video that is being played but it also moves the video to a specific time if it's set to a new value. Setting this property using the variable **newtime** moves the video to the desired position.

The only thing left is to change the size of the **progress** element to reflect the new situation on the screen. Using the value in the variable **mouseX** we can change the size of the element to reach exactly the position where the click was made.

The code for the video player is almost ready. We have all the events, methods, properties and functions we need for our application. There is only one more line, one more event that has to be listened to get this running:

```
window.addEventListener('load', initiate, false);
```

Listing 5-10: *listening to the* `load` *event*

We could have used the old standard **window.onload** technique to register the event handler, and in fact this would have been the best choice to make our code compatible with old browsers. However, because this book is all about HTML5, we decided to use the HTML5 standard **addEventListener()**.

> **Do It Yourself:** Copy all the Javascript codes since Listing 5-6 into the `player.js` file. Open the file **video.html** with the template in Listing 5-4 in the browser and click the "Play" button. Try the application in different browsers.

Video Formats

For the time being, there is no standard video and audio format for the web. There are several containers and different codecs available, but no one has been widely adopted, and there is no consensus from browser vendors to do it in the near future.

The most common containers are OGG, MP4, FLV and the new container proposed by Google, WEBM. These containers usually have video coded with Theora, H.264, VP6 and VP8 codecs respectively. Here is the list:

- **OGG**—Theora video codec and Vorbis audio codec
- **MP4**—H.264 video codec and AAC audio codec
- **FLV**—VP6 video codec and MP3 audio codec. It also supports H.264 and AAC
- **WEBM**—VP8 video codec and Vorbis audio codec

The codecs used for OGG and WEBM are free, but the codecs used for MP4 and FLV are restricted by patents, which means that, if you want to use MP4 and FLV for your applications, you will have to pay. Some restrictions are revoked for free applications.

The thing is that, at this moment, Safari and Internet Explorer are not supporting free technology. Both are only working with MP4, and only Internet Explorer has announced the inclusion of VP8 video codec in the future (Nothing has been announced yet about audio.). Here is the list:

- **Firefox**—Theora video codec and Vorbis audio codec
- **Google Chrome**—Theora video codec and Vorbis audio codec. It also supports H.264 video codec and AAC audio codec
- **Opera**—Theora video codec and Vorbis audio codec
- **Safari**—H.264 video codec and AAC audio codec
- **Internet Explorer**—H.264 video codec and AAC audio codec

Future support for open formats such as WEBM will make things easier, but probably for the next two or three years there won't be a standard format available and we will have to consider different alternatives according to the nature of our application and business.

Playing Audio with HTML5

Audio is not as popular as video on the Internet. We can shoot a video with a personal camera that will generate millions of views on websites such as www.youtube.com, but creating an audio file to accomplish the same result will be almost impossible. However, audio is still there, getting its own market in radio shows and podcasts around the net.

HTML5 provides a new element to play audio in an HTML document. The element, of course, is **<audio>** and it shares almost the same characteristics of the **<video>** element.

```
<!DOCTYPE html>
<html lang="en">
<head>
  <title>Audio Player</title>
</head>
<body>
<section id="player">
  <audio src="http://minkbooks.com/content/beach.mp3" controls>
  </audio>
</section>
</body>
</html>
```

Listing 5-11: basic HTML for audio

The <audio> Element

The **<audio>** element works in the same way and shares several attributes with the **<video>** element:

> **src**—This specifies the URL of the file to be played. This attribute, as well as in the **<video>** element, will usually be replaced by the **<source>** element to provide different audio formats for the browser to choose from.
> **controls**—This activates the interface provided by default for every browser.
> **autoplay**—When this attribute is present, the browser will automatically play the audio as soon as it can.
> **loop**—If this attribute is specified, the browser will restart the audio upon reaching the end.

preload—This attribute can take three values: `none`, `metadata` or `auto`. The first one indicates that the audio shouldn't be cached, usually with the goal of minimizing unnecessary traffic. The second value, `metadata`, will recommend the browser to fetch some information about the resource (for example, duration). The third value, `auto`, is the value set by default and it prompts the browser to download the file as soon as possible.

Again, we have to talk about codecs, and again, the code in Listing 5-11 should be more than enough, but it's not. MP3 is under commercial license, therefore it is not supported by browsers such as Firefox or Opera. Vorbis (the audio codec in the OGG container) is supported by those browsers, but not by Safari and Internet Explorer. So, once again, we have to use the `<source>` element to provide at least two formats for the browser to choose from:

```
<!DOCTYPE html>
<html lang="en">
<head>
  <title>Audio Player</title>
</head>
<body>
<section id="player">
  <audio id="media" controls>
    <source src="http://minkbooks.com/content/beach.mp3">
    <source src="http://minkbooks.com/content/beach.ogg">
  </audio>
</section>
</body>
</html>
```

Listing 5-12: two sources for the same audio

The code in Listing 5-12 will play music in every browser with controls by default. Those that can't play MP3 will play OGG and the other way around. Just remember that MP3, as well as MP4 for video, are restricted by commercial licenses, so we can use them only in specific circumstances according to what is determined by each license.

The support for free audio codecs (such as Vorbis) is expanding, but it will take time to turn an unknown format into a standard.

Programming an Audio Player

The media API was developed for video and audio. Every event, method and property incorporated for video will work with audio as well. So we only have to replace the `<video>` element by the `<audio>` element in our template and instantly we will get an audio player:

```
<!DOCTYPE html>
<html lang="en">
<head>
  <title>Audio Player</title>
  <link rel="stylesheet" href="player.css">
  <script src="player.js"></script>
</head>
<body>
<section id="player">
  <audio id="media">
    <source src="http://minkbooks.com/content/beach.mp3">
    <source src="http://minkbooks.com/content/beach.ogg">
  </audio>
  <nav>
    <div id="buttons">
      <button type="button" id="play">Play</button>
    </div>
    <div id="bar">
      <div id="progress"></div>
    </div>
    <div style="clear: both"></div>
  </nav>
</section>
</body>
</html>
```

Listing 5-13: *template for the audio player*

In the new template of Listing 5-13, we just incorporated the `<audio>` element and its sources, keeping the rest of the code intact, including the external files. We don't need to change anything else; the events, methods and properties are the same for both media.

> **Do It Yourself:** Create a new file called `audio.html`, copy the code in Listing 5-13 into this file and open it in your browser. Use the same `player.css` and `player.js` files created before to run your audio player.

Video and audio are an essential part of the web. HTML5 incorporates all the elements necessary to take advantage of these features in web applications.

Elements

HTML5 provides two new HTML elements to process media and a specific API to access the media library.

> **<video>**—This element allows us to insert a video file into an HTML document.
>
> **<audio>**—This element allows us to insert an audio file into an HTML document.

Attributes

The specification also provides attributes for the **<video>** and **<audio>** elements:

> **src**—This attribute declares the URL of the media to be embedded. You may use the **<source>** element within the media element to provide more than one source and to let the browser choose the format to play.
>
> **controls**—This attribute, if present, will activate the media controls by default. Every browser will provide its own features such as a "play" and "pause" button or a progress bar.
>
> **autoplay**—This attribute, if present, will prompt the browser to start playing the media as soon as possible.
>
> **loop**—This attribute will make the browser play the media indefinitely.
>
> **preload**—This attribute gives a hint to the browser about what to do. There are three possible values for this attribute: **none**, **metadata** and **auto**. The value **none** tells the browser to not download the file until the user orders to do it. The value **metadata** will prompt the browser to download just basic information about the media. The value **auto** tells the browser to download the file as soon as possible.

Video Attributes

There are a few attributes that are specific for the `<video>` element:

> **poster**—This provides an image to show instead of the video until the user plays it.
>
> **width**—This determines the size of the video display in pixels.
>
> **height**—This determines the size of the video display in pixels.

Events

The most common events for this API are:

> **progress**—This event is fired periodically to inform of the progress downloading the media.
>
> **canplaythrough**—This event is fired when the entire media can be played without interruption.
>
> **canplay**—This event is fired when the media can be played. Unlike the previous, it's fired when there are just a couple of frames available.
>
> **ended**—This event is fired when the media reaches the end.
>
> **pause**—This event is fired when the playback is paused.
>
> **play**—This event is fired when the media starts playing.
>
> **error**—This event is fired when an error occurs. The event is delivered to the `<source>` element, if present, corresponding to the media source that produces the error.

Methods

The most common methods for this API are:

> **play()**—This method will play or resume the media file.
>
> **pause()**—This method will pause playback.
>
> **load()**—This method loads the media file for dynamic applications.
>
> **canPlayType(type)**—This method will indicate whether a file format is supported by the browser or not. It returns an empty string if the browser can't play the media, and the strings "maybe" or "probably" based on how confident it is that it can be played.

Properties

The most common properties for this API are:

paused—It returns `true` if the media is currently paused or it hasn't started playing.

ended—It returns `true` if the media has reached the end.

duration—It returns the duration of the media in seconds.

currentTime—This is a property that can return and receive a value to inform the position in which the media is being played or sets a new position to start playing.

error—This returns the error value if an error has occurred.

buffered—This offers information about how much the file has loaded so far into the buffer. It returns an array containing data about every portion of the media that has been downloaded. If the user jumps to a part of the media that hasn't been loaded yet, the browser will start downloading the media from that point. The elements of the array are accessible by the attributes `end()` and `start()`. For example, the code `buffered.end(0)` will return the duration in seconds of the first portion of the media in the buffer.

Chapter 6
Forms and Forms API

HTML Web Forms

The Web 2.0 is all about the user. And when the user is the center of attention, it's all about interfaces—how to make them more intuitive, more natural, more practical, and of course, more beautiful. Forms are the most important interface of all; they allow users to insert data, make decisions, communicate information and change an application's behavior. During the last few years customized codes and libraries were created to process forms in user's computer. HTML5 makes these features standard, providing new attributes, elements and an entire API. Now the capacity to process information inserted in forms in real time has been incorporated in browsers and completely standardized.

The <form> Element

Forms haven't changed so much. The structure is still the same but HTML5 has added new elements, input types and attributes to expand them as far as necessary to provide the features currently implemented in web applications.

```
<!DOCTYPE html>
<html lang="en">
<head>
  <title>Forms</title>
</head>
<body>
  <section id="form">
    <form name="myform" id="myform" method="get">
      <input type="text" name="name" id="name">
      <input type="submit" value="Send">
    </form>
  </section>
</body>
</html>
```

Listing 6-1: a regular form structure

In Listing 6-1, we created a template for a basic form. As you can see, the structure of the form and the attributes hasn't changed from previous specifications. However, there are new attributes we can use for the `<form>` element:

> **autocomplete**—This is an old attribute that has become a standard. The attribute can take two values: **on** and **off**. The value by default is **on**. When it is set to **off** the `<input>` elements belonging to the form will have the autocomplete feature disabled, not showing texts from previous entries as possible values. It can be implemented in the `<form>` element or in any `<input>` element independently.
>
> **novalidate**—One of the characteristics of forms in HTML5 is the built-in capability for validation. The forms are automatically validated. To avoid this behavior, you can use the attribute **novalidate**. To achieve the same in a specific `<input>` element, there is another attribute called **formnovalidate**. Both attributes are boolean; no value has to be specified.

The `<input>` Element

The most important element in a form is `<input>`. This element can change its characteristics thanks to the attribute **type**. This attribute determines what kind of input is expected from users. The types available were a multipurpose **text** and just a few more specific, such as **password** or **submit**. HTML5 has expanded the number of options available thus increasing the possibilities for this element.

In HTML5 these new types are not only specifying what kind of input is expected, but also telling the browser what to do with the information received. The browser will process the input data according to the value of the **type** attribute and validate the entry or not.

The **type** attribute works along with additional attributes to help the browser limit and control the user's input in real time.

> **Do It Yourself:** Create a new HTML file with the template in Listing 6-1. To check how each new input type works, replace the `<input>` elements in the template for the one you want to test and open the file in your browser. At this point, the way the input types are processed varies, so we recommend checking the code in every available browser.

Email Type

Almost every form in the world has an input field to insert an email address. But so far, the only type available for this kind of data was **text**. The type **text** represents a general text, not specific data, so we had to control the input with Javascript code to know for sure that the text inserted was a valid email address. Now the browser is taking care of that thanks to the new **email** type:

```
<input type="email" name="myemail" id="myemail">
```

Listing 6-2: the email type

The text inserted in the field generated by the code in Listing 6-2 will be checked by the browser and validated as an email. If the validation fails, the form won't be sent.

How every browser will respond to an invalid input is not determined by the HTML5 specification. For example, some browsers will show a red border around the **<input>** element that produces the error, and others will show a blue one. There are ways to customize this procedure, but we will see them later.

Search Type

The **search** type doesn't control the entry; it's just an indication for browsers. Some browsers will change the design of this element by default to provide a hint to the user about the purpose of the field.

```
<input type="search" name="mysearch" id="mysearch">
```

Listing 6-3: the search type

URL Type

This type works exactly like **email**, but for web addresses. It's destined to receive only absolute URLs and return an error if the value is invalid.

```
<input type="url" name="myurl" id="myurl">
```

Listing 6-4: the url type

Tel Type

This type is for telephone numbers. Unlike the **email** and **url** types, the **tel** type doesn't force any particular syntax. It's an indication for the browser in case the application needs to make adjustments according to the device in which it's being executed.

```
<input type="tel" name="myphone" id="myphone">
```

Listing 6-5: the tel type

Number Type

As indicated by its name, the **number** type is only valid when it receives a numeric input. There are a few new attributes that might be useful for this field:

> **min**—The value of this attribute determines the minimum acceptable value for the field.
>
> **max**—The value of this attribute determines the maximum acceptable value for the field.
>
> **step**—The value of this attribute determines the size of the steps by which the value of the field will be increased or decreased. For example, if you set a step of 5, with a minimum value of 0 and a maximum of 10, the browser won't let you specify a value between 0 and 5 or 5 and 10.

```
<input type="number" name="mynumber" id="mynumber" min="0"
max="10" step="5">
```

Listing 6-6: *the* number *type*

It's not necessary to specify both, **min** and **max** attributes, and the default value for **step** is 1.

Range Type

This type makes the browser build a new kind of control that didn't exist before. As its name indicates, this new control lets users pick a value from a range of numbers. Usually it is rendered with a slider or arrows to move the value up and down, but there is no standard design so far.

The **range** type uses the attributes **min** and **max** to set the limits of the range. As well, it can have the attribute **step** to declare the set value by which it should be increased or decreased in each step.

```
<input type="range" name="mynumbers" id="mynumbers" min="0"
max="10" step="5">
```

Listing 6-7: *the* range *type*

You can set the initial value with the old **value** attribute, and use Javascript to show numbers on screen for a reference. We will experiment with this and the new **<output>** element later.

Date Type

This is another type that will generate a new kind of control. In this case, it was included to provide a better way for date entry. Browsers are implementing this feature with a calendar that shows up every time the user clicks on the field. The calendar lets users select a day that will be inserted in the input field along with the rest of the date. An example of usage is when a user tries to pick a date for a flight or a ticket; in this case, with the **date** type, the browser will build the calendar for us and we just have to insert the **<input>** element in the document to make it available for our users.

```
<input type="date" name="mydate" id="mydate">
```

Listing 6-8: *the* date *type*

The interface is not declared in the specification. Every browser is providing its own interface and sometimes adapting the design according to the device in which the application is being run. Usually, the value generated and expected has the syntax **year-month-day**.

Week Type

This type provides a similar interface to **date**, but only for picking entire weeks. Usually the value expected has the syntax **2011-W50**, where **2011** is the year and **50** is the number of the week.

```
<input type="week" name="myweek" id="myweek">
```

Listing 6-9: *the* week *type*

Month Type

Similar to the previous type, this one is for an entire month. Usually, the value expected has the syntax **year-month**.

```
<input type="month" name="mymonth" id="mymonth">
```

Listing 6-10: *the* month *type*

Time Type

The **time** type is similar to **date**, but only for the time. It takes the format of hours and minutes, but its behavior also depends on each browser at this moment. Usually, the value expected has the syntax **hour:minutes:seconds**, but also can be just **hour:minutes**.

```
<input type="time" name="mytime" id="mytime">
```

Listing 6-11: the time *type*

Datetime Type

The **datetime** type is for full date and time input, including a time zone.

```
<input type="datetime" name="mydatetime" id="mydatetime">
```

Listing 6-12: the datetime *type*

Datetime-local Type

The **datetime-local** type is just a **datetime** type without a time zone.

```
<input type="datetime-local" name="mylocaldatetime"
id="mylocaldatetime">
```

Listing 6-13: the datetime-local *type*

Color Type

In addition to types for dates and times, there is also a type that provides a predefined interface so that users can pick a color. Usually, the value expected for this field is a hexadecimal number, such as #00FF00.

```
<input type="color" name="mycolor" id="mycolor">
```

Listing 6-14: the color *type*

There is no standard interface specified by HTML5 for **color**, but it is possible that a regular grid with a set of basic colors will be adopted by browsers.

New Attributes

Some input types require the help of attributes—such as **min**, **max** and **step**, studied before—to perform their tasks. Other input types require the assistance of attributes to improve their performance or to determine their importance in the validation process. We already saw some of them—for example, **novalidate** to avoid validation in the entire form or **formnovalidate** for individual elements. The **autocomplete** attribute, also studied before, provides additional security measures for the entire form or individual elements as well. Now it's time to take a look at the rest of the attributes incorporated by HTML5.

placeholder Attribute

Usually for **search** type inputs, but also used in text entries, the **placeholder** attribute represents a short hint, a word or phrase, provided to help the user produce the right entry. The value of this attribute is rendered by browsers inside the field, like preview text that disappears when the element is focused.

```
<input type="search" name="mysearch" id="mysearch"
placeholder="type your seach">
```

Listing 6-15: the `placeholder` attribute

required Attribute

This boolean attribute won't let the form be submitted if the field is empty. For example, when we used the **email** type previously to receive an email address, the browser would check whether the entry is a valid email or not, but would validate the input field even if it's empty. When the **required** attribute is included, the input will be valid if the field is filled in and if it complies with the requisites of its type.

```
<input type="email" name="myemail" id="myemail" required>
```

Listing 6-16: the `email` input now is a required field

multiple Attribute

The `multiple` attribute is another boolean attribute that can be used in some input types (for example, `email` or `file`) to allow multiple entries in the same field. The inserted values must be separated by a comma to be valid.

```
<input type="email" name="myemail" id="myemail" multiple>
```

Listing 6-17: the `email` input allows multiple values separated by a comma

The code in Listing 6-17 allows the insertion of multiple values separated by comma, and each one of them will be validated by the browser as an email address.

autofocus Attribute

This is a feature that most developers were applying using the Javascript method `focus()`. This method was effective, but was forcing the focus over the selected element, even when the user was already using another one. This behavior was irritating but impossible to avoid until now. The `autofocus` attribute will focus the web page over the selected element but considering the current situation; it will not move the focus when it has already been set in another element by the user.

```
<input type="search" name="mysearch" id="mysearch" autofocus>
```

Listing 6-18: the `autofocus` attribute on a search field

pattern Attribute

The `pattern` attribute is for validation purposes. It uses regular expressions to customize validation rules. Some of the input types already studied validate specific kinds of strings, but suppose, for example, that you want to validate a zip code that consists of 5 numbers. There is no predetermined input type for this kind of entry. The `pattern` attribute will let you create your own to check values like that. You can also include a `title` attribute to customize the error message.

```
<input pattern="[0-9]{5}" name="pcode" id="pcode" title="insert
the 5 numbers of your postal code">
```

Listing 6-19: customized types with the `pattern` attribute

IMPORTANT: Regular expressions are a complicated subject. To learn more about them, go to our website and follow the links for this chapter.

form Attribute

The **form** attribute is a useful addition that lets us declare elements for a form outside the **<form>** tags. Until now, to build a form, you had to write the opening and closing **<form>** tags and then declare every form's element in between. In HTML5, we can insert the elements any place we want in the document and then reference the form they belong to by its name using the **form** attribute:

```
<!DOCTYPE html>
<html lang="en">
<head>
  <title>Forms</title>
</head>
<body>
  <nav>
    <input type="search" name="mysearch" id="mysearch"
form="myform">
  </nav>
  <section id="form">
    <form name="myform" id="myform" method="get">
      <input type="text" name="name" id="name">
      <input type="submit" value="Send">
    </form>
  </section>
</body>
</html>
```

Listing 6-20: declaring form elements anywhere

New Form Elements

We already studied the new input types available in HTML5, and so now it's time to learn about new HTML elements that are intended to improve or expand the possibilities of forms.

The <datalist> Element

The element **<datalist>** is a form-specific element that prebuilds a list of items that, with the help of the **list** attribute, will be used as a suggestion by an input field later.

```
<datalist id="mydata">
  <option value="123123123" label="Phone 1">
  <option value="456456456" label="Phone 2">
</datalist>
```

Listing 6-21: building the list

With the **<datalist>** already declared, the only thing left to do is to reference the list of items from an **<input>** element using the **list** attribute.

```
<input type="tel" name="myphone" id="myphone" list="mydata">
```

Listing 6-22: offering a list of values with the `list` attribute

The element in Listing 6-22 shows possible values for the user to choose from.

> **IMPORTANT:** The **<datalist>** element was only implemented in Opera and Firefox Beta at this moment.

The <progress> Element

This element is not a form-specific element, but because it represents the completion progress of a task, and usually tasks are started and processed through forms, it can be included in the form elements group.

The element **<progress>** uses two attributes to set its status and limits. The **value** attribute indicates how much the task has been processed, and **max** declares the value to reach for the task to be completed.

The <meter> Element

Similar to `<progress>`, the `<meter>` element is used to show a scale, but not for progression. It's intended to be a representation of a known range—for example, bandwidth usage.

The element `<meter>` has several attributes associated: `min` and `max` set the bounds of the range, `value` determines the measured value, and `low`, `high` and `optimum` are used to segment the range into differentiated sections and set the position that is optimum.

The <output> Element

This element represents the result of a calculation. Usually it will help to show the result of values processed by form elements. The `for` attribute will let us associate `<output>` with the source elements that participate in the calculation, but the element is usually referenced and modified from Javascript code. The syntax for this element is `<output>value</output>`.

Forms API

It won't surprise you to learn that, as well as any other aspect of HTML5, forms have their own Javascript API to customize any aspect of a form's processing and validation.

There are different ways to take advantage of the validation process in HTML5. You can use input types that require validation by default (for example, **email**) or turn a regular **text** type into a required field with the **required** attribute. You can also use special types like **pattern** to customize the validation requisites. However, when it comes to more complex validation mechanisms (for example, combining fields or checking for the results of a calculation), you will have to resort to the new resources provided by this API.

setCustomValidity()

Browsers that support HTML5 show an error message when the user tries to submit a form that has an invalid field. We can create messages for our own validation requirements using the **setCustomValidity(message)** method.

With this method, we set a custom error that will display a message when the form is submitted. When a null message is provided, the error is cleared.

```
<!DOCTYPE html>
<html lang="en">
<head>
  <title>Forms</title>
  <script>
    function initiate(){
      name1=document.getElementById("firstname");
      name2=document.getElementById("lastname");
      name1.addEventListener("input", validation, false);
      name2.addEventListener("input", validation, false);
      validation();
    }
    function validation(){
      if(name1.value=='' && name2.value==''){
        name1.setCustomValidity('insert at least one name');
        name1.style.background='#FFDDDD';
      }else{
        name1.setCustomValidity('');
        name1.style.background='#FFFFFF';
      }
    }
    window.addEventListener("load", initiate, false);
  </script>
</head>
```

```
<body>
  <section id="form">
    <form name="registration" method="get">
      First Name:
      <input type="text" name="firstname" id="firstname">
      Last Name:
      <input type="text" name="lastname" id="lastname">
      <input type="submit" id="send" value="sign up">
    </form>
  </section>
</body>
</html>
```

Listing 6-23: setting custom errors

The code in Listing 6-23 presents a situation of complex validation. Two input fields were created to receive the user's first and last name. However, the form will only be invalid when both fields are empty. The user has to insert either a first or last name to validate the entry.

In a case like this, it is not possible to use the **required** attribute, because we don't know which input the user will choose to fill. Only with Javascript code and customized errors, will we be able to create an effective validation mechanism for this scenario.

Our code starts running when the **load** event is fired. The **initiate()** function is called to handle the event. This function creates references for the two **<input>** elements and adds listeners for the **input** event to both. These listeners will execute the **validation()** function every time the user types into the fields.

Because the **<input>** elements are empty when the document is loaded, we have to set an invalid condition to stop the user from submitting the form before at least one name is typed. For this reason the **validation()** function is called at the beginning to check this condition. If both names are empty strings, the error is set and the color for the background of **firstname** is changed to light red. However, if that condition later does not hold true because at least one of the names was inserted, the error is cleared and the background of **firstname** is set back to white.

It's important to remember that the only change produced during the processing is the modification of the background color. The message declared for the error with **setCustomValidity()** will be visible only when the user tries to submit the form.

> **Do It Yourself:** For testing purposes, we included the Javascript code in the document. As a result, the only things you have to do to test this example is copy the code in Listing 6-23 into an empty HTML file and open the file in your browser.

> **IMPORTANT:** The Forms API is being developed at this moment, so depending on how much the technology is adopted by the time you read this book, you will likely need to perform several tests to check the codes in this chapter and see how they work in every browser.

The Invalid Event

Every time the user submits the form, an event is fired if an invalid field is detected. The event is called **invalid** and is focused on the element that produces the error. We can register an event handler to customize the response as in the following example:

```
<!DOCTYPE html>
<html lang="en">
<head>
  <title>Forms</title>
  <script>
    function initiate(){
       age=document.getElementById("myage");
       age.addEventListener("change", changerange, false);

       document.information.addEventListener("invalid",
validation, true);
       document.getElementById("send").addEventListener("click",
sendit, false);
    }
    function changerange(){
      var output=document.getElementById("range");
      var calc=age.value-20;
      if(calc<20){
        calc=0;
        age.value=20;
      }
      output.innerHTML=calc+' to '+age.value;
    }
    function validation(e){
      var elem=e.target;
      elem.style.background='#FFDDDD';
    }
    function sendit(){
      var valid=document.information.checkValidity();
      if(valid){
        document.information.submit();
      }
    }
    window.addEventListener("load", initiate, false);
  </script>
</head>
<body>
  <section id="form">
    <form name="information" method="get">
      Nickname:
      <input pattern="[A-Za-z]{3,}" name="nickname" id="nickname"
maxlength="10" required>
      Email:
      <input type="email" name="myemail" id="myemail" required>
      Age Range:
```

```
      <input type="range" name="myage" id="myage" min="0"
max="80" step="20" value="20">
      <output id="range">0 to 20</output>
      <input type="button" id="send" value="sign up">
   </form>
  </section>
</body>
</html>
```

Listing 6-24: our own validation system

In Listing 6-24, we created a new form with three input fields to ask for a nickname, an email, and a 20-year age range.

The **nickname** input has three validation attributes: the **pattern** attribute that only admits a minimum of 3 characters from A to Z (upper and lower case), the **maxlength** attribute that limits the input to 10 characters maximum and the **required** attribute that invalidates the field if it's empty. The **email** input has its natural limitation due to its type and a **required** attribute. The **range** input uses the **min, max, step** and **value** attributes to set the conditions for the range.

We are also declaring an **<output>** element to show the selected range on the screen as a reference.

What the Javascript code does with this form is simple: when the user clicks on the "submit" button, an **invalid** event will be fired for every invalid field, and the background color of those fields will be changed to light red by the **validation()** function.

Let's take a closer look. The code starts running when the typical **load** event is fired after the document is completely loaded. The **initiate()** function is executed and three listeners are added for the events **change, invalid** and **click**.

Every time a form element changes for some reason, the **change** event is fired for that particular element. We captured this event for the **range** input and call the **changerange()** function when it takes place. So when the user moves the slider of this control to change the age range, the new values will be calculated by the **changerange()** function. The values admitted for this input are a 20-year period—for example, 0 to 20 or 20 to 40. However, the input returns only one value, such as 20, 40, 60 or 80. To calculate the starting value, we subtract 20 from the current range value with the formula **age.value - 20**, and save the result in the **calc** variable. The minimum period admitted is 0 to 20; therefore with a conditional **if**, we check this condition and do not allow a smaller period (Check the **changerange()** function to understand how this works.).

The second listener added in the **initiate()** function is for the **invalid** event. The **validation()** function is called when the event is fired to change the background color for the invalid fields. Remember that this event will be fired for an invalid input when the "submit" button is clicked. The event is not referencing the form or the "submit" button, but is referencing the input that generated the error. In the **validation()** function, this reference is captured and saved in the **elem** variable using the **e** variable and the **target** property. Therefore the **e.target** construction is returning a reference to the invalid input. In the following line of the **validation()** function the background color for that element is changed.

Going back to the **initiate()** function, we still have one more listener to analyze. To have absolute control over the form submission and the moment of validation, we created a regular button instead of a **submit** button. When this button is clicked, the form is submitted, but only if all its elements are valid. The listener for the **click** event added to this element in the **initiate()** function will execute the **sendit()** function when the button is clicked. Using the **checkValidity()** method, we force browser validation and only submit the form using the traditional **submit()** method when there are no more invalid conditions.

What we did with the Javascript code in this document was to take control over the entire process of validation, customizing every aspect and the browser's behavior.

Real-Time Validation

When you open the file with the template in Listing 6-24 in the browser, you will notice that there is no real-time validation. The fields are validated only when the "submit" button is pressed. To make our customized validation process more practical, we can take advantage of the several attributes provided by the **ValidityState** object.

```
<!DOCTYPE html>
<html lang="en">
<head>
  <title>Forms</title>
  <script>
    function initiate(){
      age=document.getElementById("myage");
      age.addEventListener("change", changerange, false);

      document.information.addEventListener("invalid",
validation, true);
      document.getElementById("send").addEventListener("click",
sendit, false);
      document.information.addEventListener("input", checkval,
false);
    }
    function changerange(){
      var output=document.getElementById("range");
      var calc=age.value-20;
      if(calc<20){
        calc=0;
        age.value=20;
      }
      output.innerHTML=calc+' to '+age.value;
    }
```

```
    function validation(e){
      var elem=e.target;
      elem.style.background='#FFDDDD';
    }
    function sendit(){
      var valid=document.information.checkValidity();
      if(valid){
        document.information.submit();
      }
    }
    function checkval(e){
      var elem=e.target;
      if(elem.validity.valid){
        elem.style.background='#FFFFFF';
      }else{
        elem.style.background='#FFDDDD';
      }
    }
    window.addEventListener("load", initiate, false);
  </script>
</head>
<body>
  <section id="form">
    <form name="information" method="get">
      Nickname:
      <input pattern="[A-Za-z]{3,}" name="nickname" id="nickname"
maxlength="10" required>
      Email:
      <input type="email" name="myemail" id="myemail" required>
      Age Range:
      <input type="range" name="myage" id="myage" min="0"
max="80" step="20" value="20">
      <output id="range">0 to 20</output>
      <input type="button" id="send" value="sign up">
    </form>
  </section>
</body>
</html>
```

Listing 6-25: checking for validation in real time

In Listing 6-25, a new listener for the **input** event was added to the form. Every time the user modifies a field, writing or changing its content, the **checkval()** function is executed to handle the event.

The **checkval()** function also takes advantage of the **target** property to create a reference to the element that fired the event. And it controls its validity by checking the **valid** state with the **validity** attribute in the construction **elem.validity.valid**.

The **valid** state will be **true** if the element is valid and **false** if not. Using this information, we changed the color of the background for the element that fired the **input** event. The color will be white for valid and light red for invalid.

With that simple addition, now every time the user modifies the value of any element of the form, the element will be validated and its condition will be shown on the screen in real time.

Validity Constraints

In the example in Listing 6-25, we checked the `valid` state. This particular state is an attribute of the `ValidityState` object that will return the validity state of an element considering every other possible validity status. If every condition is valid, then the `valid` attribute will return `true`.

There are eight possible validity statuses for different conditions:

> **valueMissing**—This status is `true` when the `required` attribute was declared and the input field is empty.
>
> **typeMismatch**—This status is `true` when the entry's syntax doesn't comply with the type specified—for example, if the text inserted for an `email` type input is not an email address.
>
> **patternMismatch**—This status is `true` when the entry doesn't match the provided pattern.
>
> **tooLong**—This status is `true` when the `maxlength` attribute was declared and the entry is longer than the value specified for the attribute.
>
> **rangeUnderflow**—This status is `true` when the `min` attribute was declared and the entry is lower than the value specified for the attribute.
>
> **rangeOverflow**—This status is `true` when the `max` attribute was declared and the entry is higher than the value specified for the attribute.
>
> **stepMismatch**—This status is `true` when the `step` attribute was declared and its value doesn't correspond with the value of attributes such as `min`, `max` and `value`.
>
> **customError**—This status is `true` when we set a custom error—for example, when we use the `setCustomValidity()` method studied earlier.

To check for these validity statuses, we have to use the syntax `element.validity.status` (where `status` is any of the values listed before). We can take advantage of these attributes to know exactly what triggered the error on the form, as in the following example:

```
function sendit(){
  var elem=document.getElementById("nickname");
  var valid=document.information.checkValidity();
```

```
   if(valid){
     document.information.submit();
   }else if(elem.validity.patternMismatch ||
elem.validity.valueMissing){
     alert('nickname must have a minimum of 3 characters');
   }
}
```

Listing 6-26: using validity status to display a customized error message

In Listing 6-26 the `sendit()` function was modified to include this kind of control. The form is validated by the `checkValidity()` method, and if it's valid, it is submitted with `submit()`. Otherwise the validity statuses `patternMismatch` and `valueMissing` for the `nickname` input are checked and an error message is shown when one or both of them return `true`.

> **Do It Yourself:** Replace the `sendit()` function in the template in Listing 6-25 with the new function in Listing 6-26 and open the HTML file in your browser.

willValidate

In dynamic applications, it is possible that the element involved doesn't have to be validated. This might be the case, for example, with a button, a hidden input or an `<output>` element. We can detect this condition using the `willValidate` attribute and the syntax `element.willValidate`.

Quick Reference
Forms and Forms API

Forms are the main means of communication between users and web applications. HTML5 incorporates new types for `<input>` elements, an entire API to validate and process forms, and attributes to improve this interface.

Types

Some of the new input types introduced by HTML5 have implicit conditions for validation. Others just declare a purpose for the field that will help browsers to render the form.

email—This input type validates the entry as an email address.

search—This input type gives information to the browser about the purpose of the field to help render the form.

url—This input type validates the entry as a web address.

tel—This input type gives information to the browser about the purpose of the field (telephone number) to help render the form.

number—This input type validates the entry as a number. It can be combined with other attributes (like `min`, `max` and `step)` to limit the numbers allowed.

range—This input type generates a slider for the insertion of a number. The input is limited by the `min`, `max` and `step` attributes. The `value` attribute sets the initial value for the element.

date—This input type validates the entry as a date in the format `year-month-day`.

month—This input type validates the entry as a date in the format `year-month`.

week—This input type validates the entry as a date in the format `year-week` where the second value is represented by a W letter and the number of the week.

time—This input type validates the entry as time in the format `hour:minutes:seconds`. It also can take other syntaxes, such as `hour:minutes`.

datetime—This input type validates the entry as a full date and time, including a time zone.

datetime-local—This input type validates the entry as a full date and time, without a time zone.

color—This input type validates the entry as a string representing a single color.

Attributes

New attributes were also added to HTML5 as new form features and for validation control.

autocomplete—This attribute specifies whether the values inserted will be saved for future references. It can take two values: `on` and `off`.

autofocus—This is a boolean attribute that focuses the element when the page is loaded.

novalidate—This attribute is only for `<form>` elements. It's a boolean attribute that establishes whether the form will be validated or not.

formnovalidate—This attribute is for individual form elements. It's a boolean attribute that establishes whether the element will be validated or not.

placeholder—This attribute offers a hint to aid the user when inserting the data. Its value can be a single word or a short text, and it will be shown inside the input field until the element is focused.

required—This attribute declares the element as required for validation. It's a boolean attribute that won't let the form be submitted until an entry for the field is provided.

pattern—This attribute specifies a regular expression against which the entry will be validated.

multiple—This attribute is a boolean attribute that allows multiple entries in the same field. Multiple email accounts separated by commas are an example.

form—This attribute associates the element with a form. The value provided must be the `id` attribute of the form.

list—This attribute associates the element with a `<datalist>` element to show a list of possible values for the field. The value provided must be the `id` attribute of the `<datalist>` element.

Elements

HTML5 also provides new elements to improve and expand forms.

<datalist>—This element makes it possible to provide a list of predefined options that will be shown in an `<input>` element as alternative values. The list is constructed with the `<option>` element, and every option is declared with the `value` and `label` attributes. This list of options is related to an `<input>` element with the `list` attribute.

<progress>—This element represents a completion of a task—for example, a download.

<meter>—This element represents a measurement, such as bandwidth usage.

<output>—This element represents an output for dynamic applications.

Methods

HTML5 includes a specific API for forms that provides new methods, events and properties. Some of the methods are:

> **setCustomValidity(message)**—This method allows us to declare an error and provide an error message for a customized validation process. To clear the error, we must call the method with an empty string as attribute.
> **checkValidity()**—This method forces validation from the script. It activates the validation process provided by browsers without submitting the form. This method returns `true` if the element is valid.

Events

The events incorporated for this API are as follows:

> **invalid**—This event is fired when an invalid element is detected during the validation process.
> **forminput**—This event is fired when a form gets the user's input.
> **formchange**—This event is fired when a change occurs in the form.

Status

The Forms API provides a set of status checks for a customized validation process.

> **valid**—This status is a general validity status. It returns `true` when none of the rest of the status is `true`, which means the element is valid.
> **valueMissing**—This status is `true` when the `required` attribute was included in the element and the field is empty.
> **typeMismatch**—This status is `true` when the entry is not the value expected—for example, in the case of an email or URL.
> **patternMismatch**—This status is `true` when the entry is not a value admitted by the regular expression specified by the `pattern` attribute.
> **tooLong**—This status is `true` when the entry's length is higher than the value specified in the `maxlength` attribute.
> **rangeUnderflow**—This status is `true` when the entry is lower than the value declared for the `min` attribute.
> **rangeOverflow**—This status is `true` when the entry is higher than the value declared for the `max` attribute.
> **stepMismatch**—This status is `true` when the value declared for the `step` attribute doesn't correspond with the values in the `min`, `max` and `value` attributes.

customError—This status is `true` when a custom error was set for the element.

Chapter 7
Canvas API

Preparing the Canvas

This API is one of the most powerful features of HTML5. It allows developers to work with a dynamic and interactive visual medium to provide desktop applications capabilities for the web.

At the beginning of the book, we talked about how HTML5 is replacing previous plug-ins, such as Flash or Java applets, for example. There were two important things to consider in order to make the web independent of third-party technologies: video processing and graphic applications. The **<video>** element and the media API cover that first aspect very well, but they do nothing about graphics. The canvas API is what takes care of the graphics aspect and does so in an extremely efficient way. Canvas lets you draw, render graphics, animate and process images and text, and it works along with the rest of the specification to create full applications and even 2D and 3D games for the web.

The <canvas> Element

This element generates an empty rectangular space in the web page in which the results of methods provided by the API will be shown. It produces just a white space, like an empty **<div>** element, but for an entirely different purpose.

```
<!DOCTYPE html>
<html lang="en">
<head>
  <title>Canvas API</title>
  <script src="canvas.js"></script>
</head>
```

```
<body>
  <section id="canvasbox">
    <canvas id="canvas" width="500" height="300">
      Your browser doesn't support the canvas element
    </canvas>
  </section>
</body>
</html>
```

Listing 7-1: syntax of the `<canvas>` *element*

There are just a few attributes we need to provide for this element, as you can see in Listing 7-1. The **width** and **height** attributes declare the size of the box; these are necessary for the reason that everything rendered over the element will have these values as reference. The **id** attribute gives us an easy way to access the element from Javascript code.

That's basically what the **<canvas>** element does: it simply creates an empty box on the screen. It is only through Javascript and the new methods and properties introduced by the API that this surface becomes a practical feature.

> **IMPORTANT:** For compatibility purposes, in case the Canvas API is not available in the browser, the content between **<canvas>** tags is shown on the screen.

getContext()

The **getContext()** method is the first method we have to call for the **<canvas>** element to be ready to work. It generates a drawing context that will be assigned to the canvas. Through its reference, we will be able to apply the rest of the API.

```
function initiate(){
  var elem=document.getElementById('canvas');
  canvas=elem.getContext('2d');
}
window.addEventListener("load", initiate, false);
```

Listing 7-2: creating the drawing context for the canvas

In Listing 7-2, a reference to the **<canvas>** element was saved into the **elem** variable and the context was created by **getContext('2d')**. The method can take two values: **2d** and **3d**. This is, of course, for a 2-dimensional or 3-dimensional environment. For now, only the **2d** is available, but serious efforts are being put into developing a 3-dimensional API for canvas.

The canvas drawing context will be a grid of pixels listed in rows and columns from top to bottom and left to right, with its origin (the pixel 0,0) located at the top-left of the square.

> **Do It Yourself:** Copy the HTML document in Listing 7-1 into a new empty file. You will also have to create a file named **canvas.js** and copy every code from Listing 7-2 into this file. Each of the codes presented in this chapter is independent and replaces the previous one.

> **Review the Basics:** When a variable is declared inside a function without the **var** keyword, it will be global. This means that the variable will be accessible from other parts of the code, including inside other functions. In the code in Listing 7-2, we declared the variable **canvas** as global in order to always have access to the canvas context.

Drawing on Canvas

After the `<canvas>` element and its context are ready, we can finally start creating and manipulating actual graphics. The list of tools provided by this API for this purpose is extensive, from simple shapes and drawing methods to text, shadows or complex transformations. We are going to study them one by one.

Drawing Rectangles

Usually the developer must prepare the figure to be drawn before sending it to the context (as we will see soon), but there are a few methods that let us draw directly on the canvas. These methods are specific for a rectangular shape and they are the only ones that generate a primitive shape (To get other shapes, we will have to combine other drawing techniques and complex paths.). The methods available are the following:

> **fillRect(x, y, width, height)**—This method draws a solid rectangle. The top-left corner will be located at the position specified by the **x** and **y** attributes. The **width** and **height** declares its size.
>
> **strokeRect(x, y, width, height)**—Similar to the previous method, this will draw an empty rectangle—in other words, just the outlines.
>
> **clearRect(x, y, width, height)**—This method is used to subtract pixels from the area specified by its attributes. It's like a rectangular eraser.

```
function initiate(){
   var elem=document.getElementById('canvas');
   canvas=elem.getContext('2d');

   canvas.strokeRect(100,100,120,120);
   canvas.fillRect(110,110,100,100);
   canvas.clearRect(120,120,80,80);
}
window.addEventListener("load", initiate, false);
```

Listing 7-3: drawing rectangles

This is the same function in Listing 7-2 but with a new few methods that will actually draw something on the canvas. As you can see, the context was assigned to the variable **canvas**, and now this variable is used for referencing the context in every method.

The first method, **strokeRect(100,100,120,120)** draws an empty rectangle with the top-left corner at the position **100,100** and a size of 120 pixels (This is a square of 120 pixels.). The second method, `fillRect(110,110,100,100)` draws a solid rectangle, this time starting from the position `110,110` of the canvas. And finally, with the last method `clearRect(120,120,80,80)` a square space of 80 pixels is subtracted from the middle of the previous rectangle.

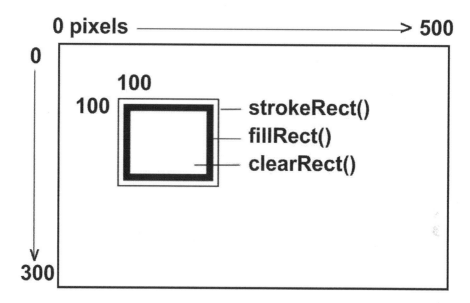

Figure 7-1: *canvas representation and rectangles drawn by the code in Listing 7-3*

Figure 7-1 is just a representation of what you are going to see after the execution of the code in Listing 7-3. The **<canvas>** element is rendered as a grid with its origin at the top-left corner and the size specified in its attributes. The rectangles are drawn on the canvas at the position declared by the attributes **x** and **y**, and one over another according to the order in the code (The first to appear in the code will be drawn first, the second will be drawn over the first one, and so on.). There is a method for customizing how the shapes are drawn, but we will see that later.

Colors

So far we have been using the color by default, a solid black. We can specify the color we want using CSS syntax with the following properties:

strokeStyle—This declares the color for the lines of the shape.
fillStyle—This declares the color for the interior of the shape.
globalAlpha—This property is not for color but for transparency. It sets the transparency for all the shapes drawn on the canvas.

```
function initiate(){
   var elem=document.getElementById('canvas');
   canvas=elem.getContext('2d');

   canvas.fillStyle="#000099";
   canvas.strokeStyle="#990000";

   canvas.strokeRect(100,100,120,120);
   canvas.fillRect(110,110,100,100);
   canvas.clearRect(120,120,80,80);
}
window.addEventListener("load", initiate, false);
```

Listing 7-4: adding color

The colors in Listing 7-4 were declared using hexadecimal numbers. We can also use functions such as **rgb()** or even specify transparency for the shape by taking advantage of the **rgba()** function. The value for these methods has to be always quoted—for example, **strokeStyle="rgba(255,165,0,1)"**.

When a color is specified using these methods, it becomes the default color for the rest of the drawings.

Even when the use of the **rgba()** function is possible, there is another property that can be used to set the level of transparency: **globalAlpha**. Its syntax is **globalAlpha=value**, where **value** is a number between 0.0 (fully opaque) and 1.0 (fully transparent).

Gradients

Gradients are an essential part of every drawing program these days, and canvas is no exception. As well as in CSS3, the gradients in canvas may be linear or radial, and we can provide a stop point to combine colors.

createLinearGradient(x1, y1, x2, y2)—This creates a gradient object to apply to the canvas.

createRadialGradient(x1, y1, r1, x2, y2, r2)—This creates a gradient object to apply to the canvas using two circles. The values represent the position of the center of each circle and its radius.

addColorStop(position, color)—This specifies the colors to create the gradient. The position is a value between 0.0 and 1.0 to determine where the degradation will start for that particular color.

```
function initiate(){
   var elem=document.getElementById('canvas');
   canvas=elem.getContext('2d');

   var grad=canvas.createLinearGradient(0,0,10,100);
   grad.addColorStop(0.5, '#0000FF');
   grad.addColorStop(1, '#000000');
   canvas.fillStyle=grad;

   canvas.fillRect(10,10,100,100);
   canvas.fillRect(150,10,200,100);
}
window.addEventListener("load", initiate, false);
```

Listing 7-5: applying a linear gradient to the canvas

In Listing 7-5, we created the gradient object from the position `0,0` to `10,100`, providing a slight inclination to the left. The colors were set by the `addColorStop()` methods, and the final gradient was applied to the `fillStyle` property, like a regular color.

Notice that the gradient positions are relative to the canvas, not to the shapes we want to affect. The result is that, if you move the rectangles at the end of the code to a new position on the screen, then the gradient for these rectangles will change.

> **Do It Yourself:** The radial gradient is similar to CSS3. Try to replace the linear gradient on the code in Listing 7-5 for a radial gradient using an expression such as `createRadialGradient(0,0,30,0,0,300)`. You can also experiment with moving the rectangles to see how the gradient is applied.

Creating Paths

The methods studied so far draw directly on the canvas, but that's not always the case. Usually we will have to process shapes and images in the background, and once that work is done, the result is sent to the context and gets drawn. For this purpose, the Canvas API introduces several methods to generate paths.

A path is like a map for a pen to follow. Once we set a path, then it's sent to the context and drawn permanently on the canvas. The path may include different kinds of strokes such as straight lines, arcs, rectangles, among others, to create complex shapes.

There are two methods to start and close a path:

> **beginPath()**—This method starts a new shape description. It's called first, before to start creating the path.
>
> **closePath()**—This method closes the path, generating a straight line from the last point to the point of origin. It can be avoided when you want an open path or when you use the `fill()` method to draw the path.

We also have three methods to draw the path on the canvas:

stroke()—This method draws the path as an outline shape.

fill()—This method draws the path as a solid shape. When you use this method you don't need to close the path with `closePath()`. The path is automatically closed with a straight line from the last point to the first.

clip()—This sets a new clipping area for the context. When the context is initialized, the clipping area is the entire area occupied by the canvas. The `clip()` method will change the clipping area to a new shape thus creating a mask. Everything that falls outside that mask won't be drawn.

```
function initiate(){
  var elem=document.getElementById('canvas');
  canvas=elem.getContext('2d');

  canvas.beginPath();
  // here goes the path
  canvas.stroke();
}
window.addEventListener("load", initiate, false);
```

Listing 7-6: basic rules for a path

The code in Listing 7-6 does not create anything, it's just starting the path for the canvas context and drawing it with `stroke()` to get later an outline shape on the screen. To set the path and create the real shape, we have several methods available:

moveTo(x, y)—This moves the pen to a specific position. This method lets us start or continue the path from different points on the grid, avoiding continuous lines.

lineTo(x, y)—This generates a straight line from the current pen's position to the new one declared by the **x** and **y** attributes.

rect(x, y, width, height)—This generates a rectangle. Unlike the methods studied before, this will generate a rectangle that is part of the path (not directly drawn onto the canvas). The attributes have the same function.

arc(x, y, radius, startAngle, endAngle, direction)—This method generates an arc or a circle in the position **x** and **y**, with the radius and from the angles declared in its attributes. The last value is a boolean value for clockwise or anticlockwise direction.

quadraticCurveTo(cpx, cpy, x, y)—This method generates a quadratic Bézier curve starting from the current position of the pen and ending at the position declared by the **x** and **y** attributes. The **cpx** and **cpy** attributes are a control point that shapes the curve.

bezierCurveTo(cp1x, cp1y, cp2x, cp2y, x, y)—This is similar to the previous method but adds two more attributes to generate a cubic Bézier curve. Now we have two control points in the grid declared by the values **cp1x, cp1y, cp2x** and **cp2y** to shape the curve.

Let's go with a simple path to understand how they work:

```
function initiate(){
  var elem=document.getElementById('canvas');
  canvas=elem.getContext('2d');

  canvas.beginPath();
  canvas.moveTo(100,100);
  canvas.lineTo(200,200);
  canvas.lineTo(100,200);
  canvas.stroke();
}
window.addEventListener("load", initiate, false);
```

Listing 7-7: our first path

We recommend that you always set the initial position of the pen immediately after starting the path. In the code in Listing 7-7, we first moved the pen to the position `100,100` and then generated a line from this point to `200,200`. Now the current position of the pen is `200,200`, and the next line will be drawn from here to the point `100,200`. Finally, the path is drawn as an outline shape by the **stroke()** method.

If you test the code in your browser, you will see an open triangle on the screen. This triangle may be closed or even filled using different methods, as in the following examples:

```
function initiate(){
  var elem=document.getElementById('canvas');
  canvas=elem.getContext('2d');

  canvas.beginPath();
  canvas.moveTo(100,100);
  canvas.lineTo(200,200);
  canvas.lineTo(100,200);
  canvas.closePath();
  canvas.stroke();
}
window.addEventListener("load", initiate, false);
```

Listing 7-8: completing the triangle

The `closePath()` method simply adds a straight line to the path, from the last to the starting point, closing the shape.

Using the `stroke()` method at the end of our path, we drew an empty triangle on the canvas. For a solid triangle, the `fill()` method is required:

```
function initiate(){
    var elem=document.getElementById('canvas');
    canvas=elem.getContext('2d');

    canvas.beginPath();
    canvas.moveTo(100,100);
    canvas.lineTo(200,200);
    canvas.lineTo(100,200);
    canvas.fill();
}
window.addEventListener("load", initiate, false);
```

Listing 7-9: solid triangle

Now the figure on the screen is a solid triangle. The `fill()` method closes the path automatically, so we don't have to use `closePath()` anymore.

One of the methods mentioned before to draw a path onto the canvas was `clip()`. This method does not draw anything, but creates a mask with the shape of the path to select what will be drawn and what won't be drawn. Everything that falls out of the mask is not drawn.

```
function initiate(){
    var elem=document.getElementById('canvas');
    canvas=elem.getContext('2d');

    canvas.beginPath();
    canvas.moveTo(100,100);
    canvas.lineTo(200,200);
    canvas.lineTo(100,200);
    canvas.clip();

    canvas.beginPath();
    for(f=0; f<300; f=f+10){
        canvas.moveTo(0,f);
        canvas.lineTo(500,f);
    }
    canvas.stroke();
}
window.addEventListener("load", initiate, false);
```

Listing 7-10: using the triangle as a mask

To show how the `clip()` method works, in Listing 7-10, we created a `for` loop to generate horizontal lines every 10 pixels. The lines goes from the left to the right side of the canvas, but only the parts of the lines that fall inside the triangle mask will be shown.

Now that we know how to draw paths, it is time to study the rest of the alternatives we have to create them. So far we have been studying how to generate straight lines and square shapes. For circular shapes, the API provides three new methods: `arc()`, `quadraticCurveTo()` and `bezierCurveTo()`. The first one is relatively simple and can generate partial or full circles, as shown in the following example:

```
function initiate(){
  var elem=document.getElementById('canvas');
  canvas=elem.getContext('2d');

  canvas.beginPath();
  canvas.arc(100,100,50,0,Math.PI*2, false);
  canvas.stroke();
}
window.addEventListener("load", initiate, false);
```

Listing 7-11: circles with `arc()`

The first thing you probably notice in the `arc()` method is the use of the value `PI`. This method uses radians instead of degrees for the angle's values. In radians, the value of `PI` represents 180 degrees, so the `PI*2` formula will multiply `PI` times 2 getting an angle of 360 degrees.

The code in Listing 7-11 generates an arc with a center in the point of 100,100, and a radius of 50 pixels, starting at 0 degrees and ending at `Math.PI*2` degrees, which represents a full circle. The use of the property `PI` from the `Math` object lets us get the precise value of PI.

If you need to calculate the value in radians from degrees, use the formula: `Math.PI / 180 × degrees`, as in the next example:

```
function initiate(){
  var elem=document.getElementById('canvas');
  canvas=elem.getContext('2d');

  canvas.beginPath();
  var radians=Math.PI/180*45;
  canvas.arc(100,100,50,0,radians, false);
  canvas.stroke();
}
window.addEventListener("load", initiate, false);
```

Listing 7-12: an arc of 45 degrees

With the code in Listing 7-12, we get an arc that covers 45 degrees of a circle. Try to change the direction value of the method to **true**. In that case, the arc is generated from 0 degrees to 315, creating an open circle.

An important thing to consider is that if you continue working the path after the arc, the current starting point will be the end of the arc. If you don't want this to happen, you will have to use the **moveTo()** method to change the pen's position. However, if the next shape is another arc—for example, a full circle—always remember that the **moveTo()** method moves the virtual pen to the point in which the circle will start to be drawn, not to the center of the circle. So let's say that the center of the circle is at the point 300,150, and its radius is 50. Then **moveTo()** should move the pen to the position 350,150 to start drawing the circle.

Besides **arc()**, we have two more methods for drawing more complex curves. The **quadraticCurveTo()** method generates a quadratic Bézier curve, and the **bezierCurveTo()** method is for cubic Bézier curves. The difference between the methods is that the first one has only one point of control and the second one has two, thus creating different types of curves.

```
function initiate(){
    var elem=document.getElementById('canvas');
    canvas=elem.getContext('2d');

    canvas.beginPath();
    canvas.moveTo(50,50);
    canvas.quadraticCurveTo(100,125, 50,200);
    canvas.moveTo(250,50);
    canvas.bezierCurveTo(200,125, 300,125, 250,200);
    canvas.stroke();
}
window.addEventListener("load", initiate, false);
```

Listing 7-13: complex curves

For the quadratic curve, we moved the virtual pen to the position 50,50 and finished the curve at the point 50,200. The control point for this curve is at the position 100,125.

The cubic curve generated by the **bezierCurveTo()** method is a little bit more complicated. There are two control points for this curve, the first one at the position 200,125 and the second at the position 300,125.

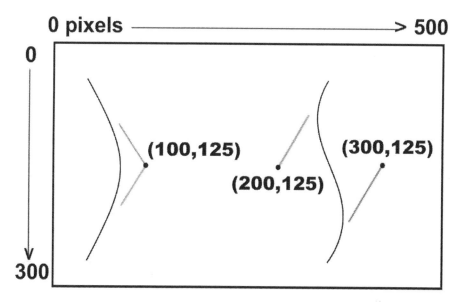

Figure 7-2: representation of Bézier curves and their control points on the canvas

The values on Figure 7-2 indicate the position of the control points for the curves. Moving those points changes the shape of the curve.

> **Do It Yourself:** You can add as many curves as you need to build your shape. Try to change the values of the control points in Listing 7-13 to see how they affect the curves. Build more complex shapes combining curves and lines to understand how the construction of the path is made.

Line Styles

Until this moment we have been using the same style for every line drawn on the canvas. The width, ending and other aspects of the line can be manipulated to get exactly the type of lines we need for our drawings.

There are four properties specific for this purpose:

> **lineWidth**—This property determines the line thickness. By default the value is 1.0 units.
> **lineCap**—This property determines the shape of the end of the lines. There are three possible values: **butt, round** and **square**.
> **lineJoin**—This property determines the shape of the connection between two lines. The possible values are: **round, bevel** and **miter**.
> **miterLimit**—Working along with **lineJoin**, this property determines how far the connections between lines will be extended when the **lineJoin** property is set to **miter**.

These properties will affect the entire path. Every time we have to change the characteristics of the lines we have to create a new path with new property values.

```
function initiate(){
    var elem=document.getElementById('canvas');
    canvas=elem.getContext('2d');
    canvas.beginPath();
    canvas.arc(200,150,50,0,Math.PI*2, false);
    canvas.stroke();

    canvas.lineWidth=10;
    canvas.lineCap="round";
    canvas.beginPath();
    canvas.moveTo(230,150);
    canvas.arc(200,150,30,0,Math.PI, false);
    canvas.stroke();
    canvas.lineWidth=5;
    canvas.lineJoin="miter";
    canvas.beginPath();
    canvas.moveTo(195,135);
    canvas.lineTo(215,155);
    canvas.lineTo(195,155);
    canvas.stroke();
}
window.addEventListener("load", initiate, false);
```

Listing 7-14: testing properties for lines

We started the drawing in the code in Listing 7-14 by creating a path for a full circle with default properties. Then, using **lineWith**, we changed the width of the line to 10 and set the **lineCap** to **round**. This will make the following path thick with rounded endings. To create the path, we moved the pen to the position **230,150** and then generated a semicircle. The round endings will help us simulate a smiling mouth.

Finally, we added to the canvas a path created by two lines to form a shape similar to a nose. Notice that the lines for this path will have a width of **5** and will be joined with the property **lineJoin** set to the value **miter**. This property will make the nose pointy, expanding the outside edges of the corner until they reach a single point.

> **Do It Yourself:** Experiment with changing the lines for the nose modifying the property **miterLimit**—for example, with the instruction **miterLimit=2**. Change the value for the property **lineJoin** to **round** or **bevel**. You can also modify the shape of the mouth by trying different values for the property **lineCap**.

Text

Writing text on the canvas is as simple as defining a few properties and calling the appropriate method. There are three properties to configure text:

> **font**—This property has a similar syntax as the **font** property from CSS, and takes the same values.
>
> **textAlign**—There are several possible values for this property. The alignment can be made to the **start, end, left, right** and **center**.
>
> **textBaseline**—This property is for vertical alignment. It sets different positions for the text (including Unicode text). The possible values are **top, hanging, middle, alphabetic, ideographic** and **bottom**.

Two methods are available to draw text onto the canvas:

> **strokeText(text, x, y)**—As well as the method for path, this will draw the specified text at the positions **x,y**, as an outline shape. It can also include a fourth value to declare the maximum size. If the text is longer than this value, it will be shrunk to fit into that space.
>
> **fillText(text, x, y)**—This is similar to the previous method except this one will draw a solid text.

```
function initiate(){
  var elem=document.getElementById('canvas');
  canvas=elem.getContext('2d');

  canvas.font="bold 24px verdana, sans-serif";
  canvas.textAlign="start";
  canvas.fillText("my message", 100,100);
}
window.addEventListener("load", initiate, false);
```

Listing 7-15: drawing text

As you can see in Listing 7-15, the **font** property can take several values at once using exactly the same syntax as CSS. The **textAling** property forces the text to be drawn starting at the position **100,100** (If the value of this property were **end**, for example, the text would be ending at the position **100,100**.). Finally, the **fillText** method draws a solid text on the canvas.

Besides the ones mentioned before, the API provides another important method to work with text:

measureText()—This method returns information about the size of a specific text. It can be useful to combine text with other shapes on the canvas and calculate positions and even collisions in animation.

```
function initiate(){
   var elem=document.getElementById('canvas');
   canvas=elem.getContext('2d');

   canvas.font="bold 24px verdana, sans-serif";
   canvas.textAlign="start";
   canvas.textBaseline="bottom";
   canvas.fillText("My message", 100,124);

   var size=canvas.measureText("My message");
   canvas.strokeRect(100,100,size.width,24);
}
window.addEventListener("load", initiate, false);
```

Listing 7-16: measuring text

Here we start from the same code in Listing 7-15, but we add a vertical alignment. The **textBaseline** was set to **bottom**, which means that the bottom of the text will be at the position **124**. This will help us know the exact vertical position of the text on the canvas.

Using the **measureText()** method and the **width** property, we get the horizontal size of the text. With all the measurements taken, we are now able to draw a rectangle that surrounds the text.

> **Do It Yourself:** Using the code in Listing 7-16, test different values for the **textAlign** and **textBaseline** properties. Use the rectangle as a reference to check how they work. Write a different text to see how the rectangle is adapted to every size automatically.

Shadows

Of course, shadows are also an important part of the Canvas API. We can generate shadows for every path and even for texts. The API provides four properties to do it:

> **shadowColor**—This property declares the color for the shadow using CSS syntax.
> **shadowOffsetX**—This property receives a number to determine how far the shadow will be from the object in the horizontal direction.
> **shadowOffsetY**—This property receives a number to determine how far the shadow will be from the object in the vertical direction.
> **shadowBlur**—This property produces a blurring effect for the shadow.

```
function initiate(){
   var elem=document.getElementById('canvas');
   canvas=elem.getContext('2d');

   canvas.shadowColor="rgba(0,0,0,0.5)";
   canvas.shadowOffsetX=4;
   canvas.shadowOffsetY=4;
   canvas.shadowBlur=5;

   canvas.font="bold 50px verdana, sans-serif";
   canvas.fillText("my message", 100,100);
}
window.addEventListener("load", initiate, false);
```

Listing 7-17: applying shadows

The shadow created in Listing 7-17 is using the **rgba()** function to get a semi-transparent black color. It is displaced 4 pixels from the object and has a blur value of **5**.

> **Do It Yourself:** Apply shadows to another shape instead of text. For example, try shadows on strokes or solid shapes, using rectangles or circles.

Transformations

Canvas allows complex operations over the graphics and the canvas itself. These operations are made using five different transformation methods, each one with a specific purpose.

> **translate(x, y)**—This transformation method is used to move the origin of the canvas. Every canvas has the point 0,0 located at the top-left corner, and the values goes up in any direction inside the canvas. Negative values will fall outside the canvas. Sometimes it is good to be able to use negative values to create complex shapes. The **translate()** method lets us move the point 0,0 to a specific position to use the origin as a reference for our drawings.
>
> **rotate(angle)**—This transformation method will rotate the canvas around the origin as many angles as specified.
>
> **scale(x, y)**—This transformation method increases or decreases the units in the canvas to reduce or enlarge everything drawn on it. The scale can be changed independently for horizontal or vertical values using **x** and **y**. The values may be negative, producing a mirror effect. By default the values are 1.0.
>
> **transform(m1, m2, m3, m4, dx, dy)**—The canvas has a matrix of values that specify its properties. The **transform()** method applies a new matrix over the current one to modify the canvas.
>
> **setTransform(m1, m2, m3, m4, dx, dy)**—This resets the current transformation and sets a new one from the values provided by its attributes.

```
function initiate(){
    var elem=document.getElementById('canvas');
    canvas=elem.getContext('2d');

    canvas.font="bold 20px verdana, sans-serif";
    canvas.fillText("TEST",50,20);

    canvas.translate(50,70);
    canvas.rotate(Math.PI/180*45);
    canvas.fillText("TEST",0,0);

    canvas.rotate(-Math.PI/180*45);
    canvas.translate(0,100);
    canvas.scale(2,2);
    canvas.fillText("TEST",0,0);
}
window.addEventListener("load", initiate, false);
```

Listing 7-18: translating, rotating and scaling

There is no better way to understand how transformations work than to use them in a code. In Listing 7-18, we applied the **translate()**, **rotate()** and **scale()** methods to the same text. First, we draw a text on the canvas with the default canvas state. The text will appear in the position **50,20** with a size of 20 pixels. After that, using **translate()**, the canvas origin was moved to the position **50,70** and the entire canvas was rotated 45 degrees with the **rotate()** method. Then another text is drawn at the new origin, with an inclination of 45 degrees. The transformations applied becomes the default values, so to test the **scale()** method, next we moved the rotation value 45 degrees back to its default position and translate again the origin to another 100 pixels down. Finally, the canvas' scale was duplicated and another text was drawn, this time with a size double the original.

Every transformation is cumulative. If we perform two transformations using **scale()**, for example, the second method will perform the scaling considering the current status. A **scale(2,2)** after another **scale(2,2)** will quadruple the scale of the canvas. And for the matrix transformation method this is not an exception. That's why we have two methods to perform transformations directly to the matrix: **transform()** and **setTransform()**.

```
function initiate(){
    var elem=document.getElementById('canvas');
    canvas=elem.getContext('2d');

    canvas.transform(3,0,0,1,0,0);

    canvas.font="bold 20px verdana, sans-serif";
    canvas.fillText("TEST",20,20);
```

```
canvas.transform(1,0,0,10,0,0);

    canvas.font="bold 20px verdana, sans-serif";
    canvas.fillText("TEST",100,20);
}
window.addEventListener("load", initiate, false);
```

Listing 7-19: accumulative transformation over the matrix

As well as the previous code, in Listing 7-19 we applied transformation methods to the same text in order to compare effects. The values by default of the canvas matrix are 1,0,0,1,0,0. Changing the first value to 3, in the first transformation of our example above, we stretched the matrix horizontally. The text drawn after this transformation will be wider than in normal conditions.

With the next transformation in the code, the matrix was stretched vertically by changing the fourth value to 10, and preserving the rest as default.

One important thing to remember is that the transformations are applied over the matrix set by a previous transformation, so the second text shown by the code in Listing 7-19 will be stretched horizontally and vertically. To reset the matrix and set brand new transformation values, we can use the setTransform() method.

> **Do It Yourself:** Try to replace the last transform() method in the example by setTransform() and check the results. Using only one text, change every value in the transform() method to see the kind of transformation performed over the canvas by every one of them.

Restoring Status

The accumulation of transformations makes it really difficult to return to previous states. In the code in Listing 7-18, for example, we had to remember the value of the rotation to be able to perform a new rotation to return to the default situation. Considering this, the Canvas API provides two methods to save and retrieve the canvas state.

> **save()**—This saves the canvas state including transformations already applied, values of styling properties and the current clipping path (the area created by the clip() method, if any).
> **restore()**—This restores the last state saved.

```
function initiate(){
    var elem=document.getElementById('canvas');
    canvas=elem.getContext('2d');
```

```
  canvas.save();
  canvas.translate(50,70);
  canvas.font="bold 20px verdana, sans-serif";
  canvas.fillText("TEST1",0,30);
  canvas.restore();

  canvas.fillText("TEST2",0,30);
}
window.addEventListener("load", initiate, false);
```

Listing 7-20: saving canvas state

If you execute the code in Listing 7-20 in your browser, you will see the text "TEST1" in big letters at the center of the canvas, and "TEST2" in smaller text, close to the origin. What we did was save the canvas state by default and then set a new position for the origin and styles for the text. Before drawing the second text on the canvas, the state was restored; thus this second text is shown with default styles, not with those declared for the first text.

It doesn't matter how many transformations you perform, the state will return exactly to the previous status when the **restore()** method is called.

globalCompositeOperation

When we were talking about paths, we said that there is a property to determine how a shape is positioned and combined with previous shapes on the canvas. The property is **globalCompositeOperation** and its value by default is **source-over**, which means that the new shape will be drawn over the ones already drawn on the canvas. There are 11 more values available:

source-in—Only the part of the new shape that overlaps the previous shape is drawn. The rest of the shape and even the rest of the previous shape are made transparent.

source-out—Only the part of the new shape that doesn't overlap the previous shape is drawn. The rest of the shape and even the rest of the previous shape are made transparent.

source-atop—Only the part of the new shape that overlaps the previous shape is drawn. The previous shape is preserved, but the rest of the new shape is made transparent.

lighter—Both shapes are drawn, but the color of the parts that overlap is determined by adding the color values.

xor—Both shapes are drawn, but the parts that overlap are made transparent.

destination-over—This is the opposite of the value by default. The new shapes are drawn behind the previous shapes on the canvas.

destination-in—The parts of the existing shapes on the canvas that are overlapped by the new shape are preserved. The rest, including the new shape, are made transparent.

destination-out—The parts of the existing shapes on the canvas that are not overlapped by the new shape are preserved. The rest, including the new shape, are made transparent.

destination-atop—The existing shapes and the new shape are preserved only in the part where they overlap.

darker—Both shapes are drawn, but the color of the parts that overlap is determined by subtracting the color values.

copy—Only the new shape is drawn and the previous are made transparent.

```
function initiate(){
  var elem=document.getElementById('canvas');
  canvas=elem.getContext('2d');

  canvas.fillStyle="#990000";
  canvas.fillRect(100,100,300,100);

  canvas.globalCompositeOperation="destination-atop";

  canvas.fillStyle="#AAAAFF";
  canvas.font="bold 80px verdana, sans-serif";
  canvas.textAlign="center";
  canvas.textBaseline="middle";
  canvas.fillText("TEST",250,110);
}
window.addEventListener("load", initiate, false);
```

Listing 7-21: *testing* `globalCompositeOperation`

Only visual representations of every possible value for the `globalCompositeOperation` property will help you understand how they work. For this purpose we prepared the code in Listing 7-21. When this code is executed, a red rectangle is drawn in the middle of the canvas, but thanks to the value **destination-atop**, only the part of the rectangle that is overlapped by the text is drawn.

> **Do It Yourself:** Replace the value **destination-atop** with any of the other possible values for this property and check the result in your browser. Test your code in different browsers.

Processing Images

The Canvas API would be nothing without the capacity for image processing. However, even though images are so important, only one native method was provided for this purpose.

drawImage()

The **drawImage()** method is the only one in charge of drawing images onto the canvas. However, this method can take a number of values that produce different results. Let's check all the possibilities:

> **drawImage(image, x, y)**—This syntax is for drawing an image on the canvas in the position declared by **x** and **y**. The first value is a reference to the image.
>
> **drawImage(image, x, y, width, height)**—This syntax lets us scale the image before drawing it on the canvas, changing its size by the values **width** and **height**.
>
> **drawImage(image, x1, y1, width1, height1, x2, y2, width2, height2)**—This is the most complex syntax. There are two values for every parameter. The purpose is to be able to slice parts of an image and then draw them onto the canvas with a customized size and position. The values **x1**, and **y1** set the top-left corner of the part of the image that will be sliced. The values **width1** and **height1** indicate the size of this piece of image. The rest of the values (**x2, y2, width2** and **height2**) declare the place where the piece will be drawn on the canvas and its size (which can be different from the original).

In every case, the first attribute can be a reference to an image in the same document generated by methods such as **getElementById()**, or by creating a new image object using regular Javascript's methods. It's not possible to use an URL or load files from external sources directly with this method.

```
function initiate(){
  var elem=document.getElementById('canvas');
  canvas=elem.getContext('2d');

  var img=new Image();
  img.src="http://www.minkbooks.com/content/snow.jpg";
```

```
    img.addEventListener("load", function(){
        canvas.drawImage(img,20,20)
    }, false);
}
window.addEventListener("load", initiate, false);
```

Listing 7-22: working with images

Let's start with a simple example. The code in Listing 7-22 is just loading the image and drawing it on the canvas. Because the canvas can only receive images that are already loaded, we need to control this situation checking the **load** event. We added the listener and declared an anonymous function to handle the event. The **drawImage()** method inside the function will draw the image when it's already loaded.

> **Review the Basics:** In Listing 7-22, we used an anonymous function instead of a reference to a function in the **addEventListener()** method. In cases like this, when the function is small, this technique makes the code simpler and easier to understand. To learn more about this topic, go to our website and visit the links for this chapter.

```
function initiate(){
    var elem=document.getElementById('canvas');
    canvas=elem.getContext('2d');

    var img=new Image();
    img.src="http://www.minkbooks.com/content/snow.jpg";
    img.addEventListener("load", function(){
        canvas.drawImage(img,0,0,elem.width,elem.height)
    }, false);
}
window.addEventListener("load", initiate, false);
```

Listing 7-23: adjusting the image to canvas size

In Listing 7-23, we added two values to the previous **drawImage()** method to resize the image. The properties **width** and **height** return the canvas measures, so the image will be stretched by this code to cover the entire canvas.

```
function initiate(){
    var elem=document.getElementById('canvas');
    canvas=elem.getContext('2d');

    var img=new Image();
    img.src="http://www.minkbooks.com/content/snow.jpg";
    img.addEventListener("load", function(){
        canvas.drawImage(img,135,30,50,50,0,0,200,200)
    }, false);
}
```

```
window.addEventListener("load", initiate, false);
```

Listing 7-24: extracting, resizing and drawing

In Listing 7-24, the code presents the most complex syntax of **drawImage()**. Nine values were provided to get a part of the source image, resize it, and then draw it on the canvas. We took a square of the source image starting from the position **135,50**, with the size of **50,50** pixels. The block is resized to **200,200** pixels and finally drawn onto the canvas in the position **0,0**.

Images Data

When we said that **drawImage()** was the only method available to draw images on the canvas, we lied. There are a few powerful methods to process images that can also draw them onto the canvas. Because they don't work with images but with data, our earlier statement is still legit. But, why would we want to process data instead of images?

Every image can be represented by a succession of integers representing rgba values (four values for each pixel). A group of values with this information will result in a one-dimensional array that can be used to generate an image. The Canvas API offers three methods to manipulate this data and process images this way:

> **getImageData(x, y, width, height)**—This method takes a rectangle of the canvas of the size declared by its properties and converts it to data. This method returns an object that can be later accessed by its properties **width**, **height** and **data**.
>
> **putImageData(imagedata, x, y)**—This method turns the data on **imagedata** into an image and draws the image onto the canvas in the position specified by **x** and **y**. This is the opposite of **getImageData()**.
>
> **createImageData(width, height)**—This method creates data for an empty image. All the pixels will be transparent black. It can also receive data as an attribute (instead of the **width** and **height** attributes) and return the image dimensions taken from that data.

The position of every value in the array is calculated with the formula **(width×4×y)+(x×4)**. This will be the first value of the pixel (red); for the rest we have to add 1 to the result—for example, **(width×4×y)+(x×4)+1** for green, **(width×4×y)+(x×4)+2** for blue, and **(width×4×y)+(x×4)+3** for the alpha value. Let's see it in an example:

> **IMPORTANT:** Due to security restrictions, no information can be retrieved from a canvas element after an image from an external source has been drawn onto the element. Only when the document and the image came from the same source (URL), will the **getImageData()** method work properly. Therefore, to test this example you will have to download the image from our server at www.minkbooks.com/content/snow.jpg (or use an image of your own), and

then upload the image, the HTML file and the Javascript file to your own server. If you just save the file in your computer and try to open it from the browser, **it won't work.**

```
function initiate(){
  var elem=document.getElementById('canvas');
  canvas=elem.getContext('2d');

  var img=new Image();
  img.src="snow.jpg";
  img.addEventListener("load", modimage, false);
}
function modimage(e){
  img=e.target;
  canvas.drawImage(img,0,0);
  var info=canvas.getImageData(0,0,175,262);

  var pos;
  for(x=0;x<=175;x++){
    for(y=0;y<=262;y++){
      pos=(info.width*4*y)+(x*4);
      info.data[pos]=255-info.data[pos];
      info.data[pos+1]=255-info.data[pos+1];
      info.data[pos+2]=255-info.data[pos+2];
    }
  }
  canvas.putImageData(info,0,0);
}
window.addEventListener("load", initiate, false);
```

Listing 7-25: generating a negative for the image

This time we had to create a new function (instead of using an anonymous function) to process the image after it is loaded. First, the **modimage()** function generates a reference to the image taking advantage of the **target** property used in previous examples. Then, using this reference and the **drawImage()** method, the image is drawn on the canvas at the position 0,0. There is nothing unusual in this part of the code, but that's going to change.

> **IMPORTANT:** The files for this example have to be uploaded to your server in order to work properly. After uploading the image you have to specify the entire path for the **src** property in the code in Listing 7-25 (e.g., **img.src="http://www.minkbooks.com/content/snow.jpg"**).

The image from our example has the size of 350 pixels wide by 262 pixels tall, so using the **getImageData()** method with the values 0,0 for the top-left corner and 175,262 for the horizontal and vertical offsets we are taking only the left half of the original image. This data is saved into the variable **info**.

After this information is collected, it is time to manipulate every pixel to get the result we want (In our example it will be a negative of this piece of image.).

Because every color is declared by a value between 0 and 255, the negative value is obtained by subtracting the real value from 255 with the formula `color=255-color`. To do it with every pixel of our image, we have to create two `for` loops, one for columns and other for rows, to get every color and calculate the value of the corresponding negative. Notice that the `for` loop for **x** values goes from 0 to 175 (the width of the part of the image we took from the canvas) and the `for` loop for **y** values goes from 0 to 262 (the total vertical size of the image and also the vertical size of the part of the image we are processing).

After every pixel has been processed, the `info` variable with the image data is sent as an image to the canvas using the `putImageData()` method. The image is located at the same position as the original, replacing the left half of our original image with the negative we just created.

The `getImageData()` method returns an object that can be processed through its properties (`width`, `height` and `data`) or can be used as-is by the `putImageData()` method. There is another way to get data from canvas that returns the canvas content as a base64 encoded string. This string can be used later as the source for another canvas, a source for an HTML element like `<img>`, sent to a server, or saved in a file, for example. This is the method included for this purpose:

> **toDataURL(type)**—The `<canvas>` element has two properties, `width` and `height`, and two methods: `getContext()` and `toDataURL()`. This last method returns a data:url containing a representation of the canvas content in a PNG format (or the image's format specified by the `type` attribute).

We will see some examples of `toDataURL()` and how can it help to integrate Canvas with other APIs later in this book.

Patterns

Patterns are a simple addition that can improve our paths. Patterns let us add a texture to the shapes we created using an image. The procedure is similar to gradients; the pattern is created by the `createPattern()` method and then applied to the path as a color.

> **createPattern(image, type)**—The `image` attribute is a reference to the image, and `type` can take four values: **repeat**, **repeat-x**, **repeat-y** and **no-repeat**.

```
function initiate(){
  var elem=document.getElementById('canvas');
  canvas=elem.getContext('2d');
```

```
  var img=new Image();
  img.src="http://www.minkbooks.com/content/bricks.jpg";
  img.addEventListener("load", modimage, false);
}
function modimage(e){
  img=e.target;
  var pattern=canvas.createPattern(img,'repeat');
  canvas.fillStyle=pattern;
  canvas.fillRect(0,0,500,300);
}
window.addEventListener("load", initiate, false);
```

Listing 7-26: *adding a pattern for our paths*

Do It Yourself: Experiment with the different values available for
createPattern() and other shapes.

Animations on Canvas

Animations are created by regular Javascript code. There is no method to help animate things on the canvas, and there is no predetermined procedure for doing it. We basically have to erase the area of the canvas we want to animate, draw the shapes on it and repeat the process again and again. Once the shapes are drawn, they can't be moved. Only by erasing the area and drawing the shapes again are we able to construct an animation. For this reason, in games or applications that requires a large amount of objects to be animated, it is better to use images instead of shapes built by complex paths (For example, games usually use PNG images.).

There are multiple techniques for animation in the programming world. Some are simple, and others are as complex as the application the animations were created for. We are going to make a simple example using the **clearRect()** method to clear the canvas and draw again, generating an animation with just one function, but keep in mind that if your intention is to create elaborate effects, you should probably grab a book about advance Javascript programming first.

```
function initiate(){
  var elem=document.getElementById('canvas');
  canvas=elem.getContext('2d');

  window.addEventListener('mousemove', animation, false);
}
function animation(e){
  canvas.clearRect(0,0,300,500);

  var xmouse=e.clientX;
  var ymouse=e.clientY;
  var xcenter=220;
  var ycenter=150;
  var ang=Math.atan2(xmouse-xcenter,ymouse-ycenter);
  var x=xcenter+Math.round(Math.sin(ang)*10);
  var y=ycenter+Math.round(Math.cos(ang)*10);

  canvas.beginPath();
  canvas.arc(xcenter,ycenter,20,0,Math.PI*2, false);
  canvas.moveTo(xcenter+70,150);
  canvas.arc(xcenter+50,150,20,0,Math.PI*2, false);
  canvas.stroke();

  canvas.beginPath();
  canvas.moveTo(x+10,y);
  canvas.arc(x,y,10,0,Math.PI*2, false);
```

```
        canvas.moveTo(x+60,y);
        canvas.arc(x+50,y,10,0,Math.PI*2, false);
        canvas.fill();
    }
window.addEventListener("load", initiate, false);
```

Listing 7-27: our first animation

The code in Listing 7-27 will show two eyes that look at the mouse pointer all the time. To move the eyes, we have to update their position every time the mouse is moved. For this purpose, a listener for the **mousemove** event was added in the **initiate()** function. Now when the event is fired the **animation()** function is called.

The function starts clearing the canvas first with the instruction **clearRect(0,0,300,500)**. Then the position of the mouse is captured and the position of the first eye is saved in the variables **xcenter** and **ycenter**.

After the variables are initialized, it is time to do the math. Using the values of the position of the mouse and the center of the left eye, we calculate the angle of the invisible line that goes from one point to another using the predefined Javascript method **atan2**. This angle is used next to calculate the exact point of the center of the iris with the formula **xcenter + Math.round(Math.sin(ang) × 10)**. The number 10 in the formula represents the distance from the center of the eye to the center of the iris (because the iris is not at the center of the eye, it's always at the edge).

With all these values, we can finally start drawing the eyes onto the canvas. The first path is two circles representing the eyes. The first **arc()** method for the first eye is positioned at the values of **xcenter** and **ycenter**, and the circle for the second eye is generated 50 pixels to the right using the instruction **arc(xcenter+50, 150, 20, 0, Math.PI*2, false)**.

The animated part of the graphic is created next with the second path. This path is using the **x** and **y** variables with the position calculated previously from the angle. Both iris are drawn as solid black circles using **fill()**.

The process will be repeated and the values recalculated every time the **mousemove** event is fired.

> **Do It Yourself:** Copy the code in Listing 7-27 in the Javascript file called **canvas.js** and open the HTML file with the template of Listing 7-1 in your browser.

Processing Video on Canvas

As with animations, there is no special method to show video on a canvas element. The only way to do it is by taking every frame from the **<video>** element and drawing it as an image onto canvas using **drawImage()**. So basically, processing video on the canvas is done just by combining techniques already studied.

Let's build a new template first and then the codes to see what we are talking about.

```
<!DOCTYPE html>
<html lang="en">
<head>
  <title>Video on Canvas</title>
  <style>
    .boxes{
      display: inline-block;
      margin: 10px;
      padding: 5px;
      border: 1px solid #999999;
    }
  </style>
  <script src="canvasvideo.js"></script>
</head>
<body>
  <section class="boxes">
    <video id="media" width="483" height="272">
      <source
src="http://www.minkbooks.com/content/trailer2.mp4">
      <source
src="http://www.minkbooks.com/content/trailer2.ogg">
    </video>
  </section>
  <section class="boxes">
    <canvas id="canvas" width="483" height="272">
      Your browser doesn't support the canvas element
    </canvas>
  </section>
</body>
</html>
```

Listing 7-28: template for video on canvas

The template in Listing 7-28 includes two specific components: the **<video>** element and the **<canvas>** element. With the combination of both, we are going to process and show video on the canvas.

The template also includes embedded CSS styles for the boxes and a Javascript file called **canvasvideo.js** for the following code:

```
function initiate(){
  var elem=document.getElementById('canvas');
  canvas=elem.getContext('2d');
  video=document.getElementById('media');

  video.addEventListener('click', push, false);
}
function push(){
  if(!video.paused && !video.ended){
    video.pause();
    window.clearInterval(loop);
  }else{
    video.play();
    loop=setInterval(processFrames, 33);
  }
}
function processFrames(){
  canvas.drawImage(video,0,0);

  var info=canvas.getImageData(0,0,483,272);
  var pos;
  var gray;
  for(x=0;x<=483;x++){
    for(y=0;y<=272;y++){
      pos=(info.width*4*y)+(x*4);
      gray=parseInt(info.data[pos]*0.2989 +
info.data[pos+1]*0.5870 + info.data[pos+2]*0.1140);
      info.data[pos]=gray;
      info.data[pos+1]=gray;
      info.data[pos+2]=gray;
    }
  }
  canvas.putImageData(info,0,0);
}
window.addEventListener("load", initiate, false);
```

Listing 7-29: converting color video to black and white video

Do It Yourself: Create a new HTML file with the code in Listing 7-28 and a Javascript file called **canvasvideo.js** with the code in Listing 7-29. To start the video click the left box on the screen.

IMPORTANT: This example uses the **getImageData()** and **putImageData()** methods to process the image data. As we explained before, these methods extract information from the canvas. Due to security reasons, the extraction of information from canvas is deactivated after the element receives content from an origin that is not the document's origin (The document belongs to one domain and the videos to another.). Therefore, to test this example, you will have to download the videos from our website and then upload every file to your own server.

Let's take a look at the code in Listing 7-29. As we said before, to process video on the canvas, we just have to resort to previous codes and techniques. In this code, we are using the **push()** function taken from Chapter 5 to start and stop the video clicking over it. We also created a function called **processFrames** that is using the same code of Listing 7-25 from this chapter, except this time (instead of inverting the image) we are using a formula to turn every color in each frame of the video into a gray color. This will turn a color video into a black and white video.

The **push()** function serves two purposes: to start or stop the video and to initiate an interval that will execute the **processFrames()** function every 33 milliseconds. This function is taking a frame from the **<video>** element and drawing it onto the canvas with the instruction **drawImage(video,0,0)**. Then the data is extracted from the canvas with the **getImageData()** method and every pixel of that frame is processed with two **for** loops.

The process used to turn every color into the corresponding gray is one of the most popular and easy to find on Internet. The formula is as follows: **red × 0.2989 + green × 0.5870 + blue × 0.1140**. After the formula is calculated the result must be assigned to every color of the pixel (red, green and blue), as we did in the code using the variable **gray**.

The process finishes with drawing the frame back onto the canvas with the **putImageData()** method.

> **IMPORTANT:** This example is for instructional purposes. Processing video in real-time is not a recommended practice. Depending on your computer's configuration and the browser used to run the application, you will probably notice some delays in the processing. To create useful Javascript applications, you always have to consider performance.

Quick Reference
Canvas API

The Canvas API is probably the most complex and extensive of the HTML5 specifications. It provides several methods and properties to create graphic applications over the `<canvas>` element.

Methods

These methods are specific for the Canvas API:

getContext(context)—This method creates the context for the canvas in which the drawings will be made. It can take two values: **2d** and **3d** for 2-dimensional or 3-dimensional graphics.

fillRect(x, y, width, height)—This method will draw a solid rectangle directly to the canvas in the position `x,y` and the size `width,height`.

strokeRect(x, y, width, height)—This method will draw an outline rectangle directly to the canvas in the position `x,y` and the size `width,height`.

clearRect(x, y, width, height)—This method clears the area in the canvas using a rectangular shape declared by the value of its attributes.

createLinearGradient(x1, y1, x2, y2)—This method creates a linear gradient to be assigned to a shape as a color using the `fillStyle` property. Its attributes only specify the start and end positions (relative to the canvas). To declare the colors involved in the gradient, this method must be used in conjunction with `addColorStop()`.

createRadialGradient(x1, y1, r1, x2, y2, r2)—This method creates a radial gradient to be assigned to a shape as a color using the `fillStyle` property. The gradient is built from two circles. The attributes only specify the position and radius of the circles (relative to the canvas). To declare the colors involved in the gradient, this method must be used in conjunction with `addColorStop()`.

addColorStop(position, color)—This method is used to declare the colors for gradients. The attribute `position` is a value between 0.0 and 1.0, used to determine where the color will start degrading.

beginPath()—This method is required to start a new path.

closePath()—This method can be used at the end of a path to close it. It will generate a straight line from the last position of the pen to the point from which the path started. It's not necessary to use this method when the path must remain open or it is drawn onto the canvas using `fill()`.

stroke()—This method is used to draw the path as an outline shape.

fill()—This method is used to draw the path as a solid shape.

clip()—This method is used to create a new clipping area defined by the path. Everything sent to the canvas after this method is declared will be drawn only if it falls inside the shape.

moveTo(x, y)—This method moves the virtual pen to a new position. The next method will continue the path from that point.

lineTo(x, y)—This method adds a straight line to the path from the current pen's position to the point indicated by the attributes **x** and **y**.

rect(x, y, width, height)—This method adds a rectangle to the path in the position **x,y** and with the size **width,height**.

arc(x, y, radius, startAngle, endAngle, direction)—This method adds an arc to the path. The center of the arc is determined by **x** and **y**, the angles are declared in radians and **direction** is a boolean value for clockwise or anticlockwise direction. To convert degrees into radians, use the formula: **Math.PI/180×degrees**.

quadraticCurveTo(cpx, cpy, x, y)—This method adds a quadratic Bézier curve to the path. It starts from the current pen's position and ends at **x,y**. The **cpx** and **cpy** attributes specify the position of the control point that will shape the curve.

bezierCurveTo(cp1x, cp1y, cp2x, cp2y, x, y)—This method adds a cubic Bézier curve to the path. It starts from the current pen's position and ends at **x,y**. The **cp1x, cp1y, cp2x,** and **cp2y** attributes specify the position of the two control points that will shape the curve.

strokeText(text, x, y, max)—This method draws an outline text directly to the canvas. The **max** attribute is optional and declares the maximum size of the text.

fillText(text, x, y, max)—This method draws a solid text directly to the canvas. The **max** attribute is optional and declares the maximum size of the text.

measureText(text)—This method calculates the size of the area that the text will occupy on the canvas using the current styles. The property **width** is used to retrieve the value.

translate(x, y)—This method moves the canvas origin to the point **x,y**. The initial position of the origin (0,0) is the top-left corner of the area generated by the **<canvas>** element.

rotate(angle)—This method is used to rotate the canvas over the origin. The angle must be declared in radians. To convert degrees into radians, use the formula: **Math.PI/180×degrees**.

scale(x, y)—This method changes the scale of the canvas. The values by default are (1.0,1.0). The values can be negative.

transform(m1, m2, m3, m4, dx, dy)—This method modifies the transformation matrix of the canvas. The new matrix is calculated over the previous one.

setTransform(m1, m2, m3, m4, dx, dy)—This method modifies the transformation matrix of the canvas. It resets the previous values and declares the new ones.

save()—This method saves the canvas state, including the transformation matrix, styling properties and the clipping mask.

restore()—This method restores the last state saved, including the transformation matrix, styling properties and the clipping mask.

drawImage()—This method will draw an image on the canvas. There are three possible syntaxes. The `drawImage(image,x,y)` syntax draws the image in the position `x,y`. The `drawImage(image,x,y,width,height)` syntax draws the image in the position `x,y` with a new size of `width,height`. And the `drawImage(image, x1, y1, width1, height1, x2, y2, width2, height2)` syntax takes a portion of the original image determined by `x1,y1,width1,height1` and draws it on the canvas in the position `x2,y2` and the new size `width2,height2`.

getImageData(x, y, width, height)—This method gets a portion of canvas and saves it as an object. The values of the object are accessible through the properties `width`, `height` and `data`. The first two properties return the size of the portion of the image taken, and `data` returns the information as an array with values representing the colors of the pixels. This values can be accessed using the formula `(width×4×y)+(x×4)`.

putImageData(imagedata, x, y)—This method draws the image represented by the information in `imagedata` onto the canvas.

createImageData(width, height)—This method creates a new image in data format. All the pixels are initially transparent black. It can take image data as an attribute instead of `width` and `height`. In this case the new image will have the size determined by the data provided.

createPattern(image, type)—This method creates a pattern from an image that later can be assigned to a shape as a color using the `fillStyle` property. The possible values for the `type` attribute are `repeat`, `repeat-x`, `repeat-y` and `no-repeat`.

Properties

The following list of properties is specific for the Canvas API:

strokeStyle—This property declares the color for the lines of the shapes. It can take any CSS value, including functions such as `rgb()` and `rgba()`.

fillStyle—This property declares the color for the interior of solid shapes. It can take any CSS value, including the functions `rgb()` and `rgba()`. It's also used to assign gradients and patterns to shapes (These styles are first assigned to a variable and then the variable is assigned as a color to this property.).

globalAlpha—This property is used to set the level of transparency for every shape. It takes values from 0.0 (fully opaque) to 1.0 (fully transparent).

lineWidth—This property sets the line thickness. By default, the value is 1.0.

lineCap—This property determines the shape of the ending of the lines. There are three possible values: `butt` (normal ending), `round` (ending the line with a semicircle) and `square` (ending the line with a square).

lineJoin—This property determines the shape of the connection between two lines. It takes three values: `round` (where the join is rounded), `bevel` (where the join is cut) and `miter` (where the join is extended until both lines reach a single point).

miterLimit—This property takes a number to determine how long the lines will be extended when the `lineJoin` property is set to `miter`.

font—This property is similar to the `font` property of CSS and takes the same values to declare the text's styles.

textAlign—This property determines how the text will be aligned. The possible values are `start`, `end`, `left`, `right` and `center`.

textBaseline—This property determines the vertical alignment for the text. The possible values are `top`, `hanging`, `middle`, `alphabetic`, `ideographic` and `bottom`.

shadowColor—This property sets the color for a shadow. It takes CSS values.

shadowOffsetX—This property declares how many units far the shadow will be from the object in the horizontal direction.

shadowOffsetY—This property declares how many units far the shadow will be from the object in the vertical direction.

shadowBlur—This property takes a number to produce a blurring effect for a shadow.

globalCompositeOperation—This property determines how the new shapes will be drawn on the canvas considering the shapes already drawn. It takes several values: `source-over`, `source-in`, `source-out`, `source-atop`, `lighter`, `xor`, `destination-over`, `destination-in`, `destination-out`, `destination-atop`, `darker` and `copy`. The value by default is `source-over`, which means that the new shapes will be drawn over the previous shapes.

Chapter 8
Drag and Drop API

Drag and Drop for the Web

Dragging an element from one place and then dropping it somewhere else is something that we do all the time in desktop applications, but we don't expect to do it on the web. This is not because web applications are different, but because developers never had a standard technology available to offer this feature.

Now, with the Drag and Drop API introduced by the HTML5 specification we finally have the opportunity to create software for the web that will behave exactly like desktop applications.

New Events

One of the most important aspects of this API is a set of seven new specific events introduced for different situations. Some of these events are fired by the source (the element to be dragged) and other events are fired by the target (the element into which the source will be dropped). For example, when a user performs a drag and drop operation, the source fires these three events:

dragstart—This event is fired the moment the drag operation starts. The data associated with the source element is set at this moment in the system.

drag—This event is similar to the `mousemove` event, except that it's fired during a drag operation by the source element.

dragend—When the drag operation is over, whether it was successful or not, this event is fired from the source.

And here are the events fired by the target during the same operation:

dragenter—When the mouse's pointer enters inside the area of a possible target element during a drag operation, this event is fired.

dragover—This event is similar to the `mousemove` event, except that it's fired during a drag operation by possible target elements.

drop—When the drop occurs during a drag operation, this event is fired by the target.

dragleave—This event is fired when the mouse leaves an element during a drag operation. This event is used along with **dragenter** to provide feedback and help users identify the target element.

Before you work with this feature, there is an important aspect that has to be considered. Browsers perform actions by default during a drag and drop operation. To get the results you want, you might need to prevent the default behavior and customize actions. For some events, like **dragenter, dragover** and **drop**, the prevention is necessary, even when a customized action was specified. With a simple example, let's see how we must proceed.

```html
<!DOCTYPE html>
<html lang="en">
<head>
  <title>Drag and Drop</title>
  <link rel="stylesheet" href="dragdrop.css">
  <script src="dragdrop.js"></script>
</head>
<body>
  <section id="dropbox">
    Drag and drop the image here
  </section>
  <section id="picturesbox">
    <img id="image"
src="http://www.minkbooks.com/content/monster1.gif">
  </section>
</body>
</html>
```

Listing 8-1: template for drag and drop

The HTML document of Listing 8-1 includes a **<section>** element identified as **dropbox** to be used as a target and an image to be used as the source. It also includes two files for CSS styles and the Javascript code that will take charge of the operation.

```css
#dropbox{
  float: left;
  width: 500px;
  height: 300px;
  margin: 10px;
  border: 1px solid #999999;
}
```

```css
#picturesbox{
    float: left;
    width: 320px;
    margin: 10px;
    border: 1px solid #999999;
}
#picturesbox > img{
    float: left;
    padding: 5px;
}
```

Listing 8-2: *styles for the template (*`dragdrop.css`*)*

The rules in Listing 8-2 simply style the boxes that will let us identify the source and the drop box.

```javascript
function initiate(){
    source1=document.getElementById('image');
    source1.addEventListener('dragstart', dragged, false);

    drop=document.getElementById('dropbox');
    drop.addEventListener('dragenter', function(e){
e.preventDefault(); }, false);
    drop.addEventListener('dragover', function(e){
e.preventDefault(); }, false);
    drop.addEventListener('drop', dropped, false);
}
function dragged(e){
    var code='<img src="'+source1.getAttribute('src')+'">';
    e.dataTransfer.setData('Text', code);
}
function dropped(e){
    e.preventDefault();
    drop.innerHTML=e.dataTransfer.getData('Text');
}
window.addEventListener('load', initiate, false);
```

Listing 8-3: *elemental code for a drag and drop operation*

There are a few attributes we can use in HTML elements to configure the procedure for a drag and drop operation, but basically everything is done by the Javascript code. In Listing 8-3, we have three functions: the **initiate()** function adds the event listeners for this operation, and the **dragged()** and **dropped()** functions generate and receive the information that is transmitted in the process.

For a regular drag and drop operation to take place, we must prepare the information that will be shared between the source and the target elements. To get this done, a listener for the **dragstart** event was added. This listener calls the **dragged()** function when the event is fired and the information is prepared in this function using **setData()**.

The drop action is usually not allowed in most elements of the document by default. Therefore, to make this operation available for our drop box, we must prevent against the default behaviour. This was done by adding a listener for the **dragenter** and **dragover** events and executing the **preventDefault()** method with an anonymous function.

And finally, a listener for the **drop** event was added to call the **dropped()** function that will receive and process the data sent by the source.

> **Review the Basics:** For the **dragenter** and **dragover** events, we used an anonymous function to apply the **preventDefault()** method and cancel them. The variable **event** was sent to reference the event inside the function. To get more information about anonymous functions, go to our website and follow the links for this chapter.

When the drag starts, the **dragstart** event is fired and the **dragged()** function is called. In this function, we get the value of the **src** attribute of the element being dragged, and set the data to be transferred using the **setData()** method of the **dataTransfer** object. From the other side, when an element is dropped over our drop box, the **drop** event is fired and the **dropped()** function is called. This function just modifies the content of the drop box with the information gotten with the **getData()** method. Browsers also perform actions by default when this event takes place (for example, open a link or refresh the window to show the image that was dropped) so we have to prevent this behavior using the **preventDefault()** method, as we did for the other events before.

> **Do It Yourself:** Create an HTML file with the template in Listing 8-1, a CSS file called **dragdrop.css** with the styles Listing 8-2, and a Javascript file called **dragdrop.js** with the code in Listing 8-3. To test the example, just open the HTML file in your browser.

dataTransfer

This is the object that will hold the information in a drag and drop operation. The **dataTransfer** object has several methods and properties associated. We already used **setData()** and **getData()** in our example in Listing 8-3. Along with **clearData()**, these are the methods in charge of the information being transferred:

> **setData(type, data)**—This method is used to declare the data to be sent and its type. The method receives regular data types (like **text/plain**, **text/html** or **text/uri-list**), special types (like **URL** or **Text**) or even personalized types. A **setData()** method must be called for every type of data that we want to send in the same operation.

getData(type)—This method returns the data of the specified type sent by the source element.

clearData()—This method removes the data of the specified type.

In the **dragged()** function in Listing 8-3, we created HTML code including the value of the **src** attribute of the element that fired the **dragstart** event, saved this code in the variable **code** and then sent the variable as data through the **setData()** method. Because we are sending text, we declared the **Text** type for this data.

> **IMPORTANT:** We could have used a more appropriate type in our example, such as **text/html** or even a customized type, but several browsers only admit a small set of types at this moment, so **Text** makes our application more compatible and our examples ready to be tested.

When we retrieved the data in the **dropped()** function using the **getData()** method, we had to specify the type of data to be read. This is because different kinds of data can be sent at the same time by the same element. For example, an image might send the image itself, the url, and text declaring what the image is about. All this information may be sent using several **setData()** with different type values and then retrieved by **getData()** specifying those same types.

> **IMPORTANT:** To get more information about data types for the drag and drop operation, go to our website and follow the links for this chapter.

The **dataTransfer** object has a few more methods and properties that sometimes might be useful for our applications:

> **setDragImage(element, x, y)**—Some browsers show a thumbnail of the element that is being dragged. This method is used to customize that image and select a position relative to the mouse pointer with the **x** and **y** attributes.

> **types**—This property returns an array containing the types that were set in the **dragstart** event (by the code or the browser). You can save this array in a variable (**list=dataTransfer.types**) and then read it with a **for** loop.

> **files**—This property returns an array containing information about the files that are being dragged.

> **dropEffect**—This property returns the type of operation currently selected. It can also be set to change the selected operation. The possible values are **none**, **copy**, **link** and **move**.

> **effectAllowed**—This property returns the types of operations that are allowed. It can be set to change the operations allowed. The possible values are **none**, **copy**, **copyLink**, **copyMove**, **link**, **linkMove**, **move**, **all** and **uninitialized**.

We will apply some of these properties and methods in the following examples.

dragenter, dragleave and dragend

Nothing has been done with the **dragenter** event so far. We just cancelled the event to prevent browsers' default behaviour. And we didn't take advantage of the **dragleave** and **dragend** events either. These are important events that let us provide feedback that will guide users while moving elements all over the screen.

```
function initiate(){
    source1=document.getElementById('image');
    source1.addEventListener('dragstart', dragged, false);
    source1.addEventListener('dragend', ending, false);

    drop=document.getElementById('dropbox');
    drop.addEventListener('dragenter', entering, false);
    drop.addEventListener('dragleave', leaving, false);
    drop.addEventListener('dragover', function(e){
e.preventDefault(); }, false);
    drop.addEventListener('drop', dropped, false);
}
function entering(e){
    e.preventDefault();
    drop.style.background='rgba(0,150,0,.2)';
}
function leaving(e){
    e.preventDefault();
    drop.style.background='#FFFFFF';
}
function ending(e){
    elem=e.target;
    elem.style.visibility='hidden';
}
function dragged(e){
    var code='<img src="'+source1.getAttribute('src')+'">';
    e.dataTransfer.setData('Text', code);
}
function dropped(e){
    e.preventDefault();
    drop.style.background='#FFFFFF';
    drop.innerHTML=e.dataTransfer.getData('Text');
}
window.addEventListener('load', initiate, false);
```

Listing 8-4: controlling the whole drag and drop process

The Javascript code in Listing 8-4 replaces the code in Listing 8-3. In this new code, we added two functions for the drop box and one for the source. The functions **entering()** and **leaving()** will change the background color of our drop box every time the mouse is dragging something and enters or leaves the area occupied by the element (These actions are firing the **dragenter** and **dragleave** events.). In addition, the **ending()** function will be called by the listener for the **dragend** event when the element is dropped. Notice that this event and function do not control whether the process was successful or not; you have to do it by yourself.

Thanks to these functions, every time the mouse drags something and enters the drop box area, the box will turn green, and when the element is dropped, the source image will be hidden. These visible changes are not affecting the drag or drop process, but rather providing feedback to guide users during the operation.

To prevent default actions, we have to use the **preventDefault()** method in every function, even when customized actions are declared.

> **Do It Yourself:** Copy the code in Listing 8-4 into your Javascript file, open the HTML document of Listing 8-1 in your browser, and drag the image into the drop box.

Selecting a Valid Source

There is no specific method to detect whether the source is valid or not. We can't rely on the information returned by the **getData()** method because even when we only get the data of the type specified in the attribute, other sources might originate the same type and provide data we didn't expect. There is a property of the **dataTransfer** object called **types** that returns an array with a list of the types set by the **dragstart** event, but it's also useless for validation purposes.

For this reason, the techniques for selecting and validating data transferred in a drag and drop operation are variable and can be as simple or complex as needed.

```
<!DOCTYPE html>
<html lang="en">
<head>
  <title>Drag and Drop</title>
  <link rel="stylesheet" href="dragdrop.css">
  <script src="dragdrop.js"></script>
</head>
<body>
  <section id="dropbox">
    Drag and drop images here
  </section>
  <section id="picturesbox">
    <img id="image1"
src="http://www.minkbooks.com/content/monster1.gif">
    <img id="image2"
src="http://www.minkbooks.com/content/monster2.gif">
    <img id="image3"
src="http://www.minkbooks.com/content/monster3.gif">
```

```
  <img id="image4"
src="http://www.minkbooks.com/content/monster4.gif">
  </section>
</body>
</html>
```

Listing 8-5: new template with more sources

Using the new HTML document in Listing 8-5, we are going to filter sources by checking the image's **id** attribute. The following Javascript code will indicate which image can be dropped and which not:

```
function initiate(){
  var images=document.querySelectorAll('#picturesbox > img');
  for(var i=0; i<images.length; i++){
    images[i].addEventListener('dragstart', dragged, false);
  }

  drop=document.getElementById('dropbox');
  drop.addEventListener('dragenter', function(e){
e.preventDefault(); }, false);
  drop.addEventListener('dragover', function(e){
e.preventDefault(); }, false);
  drop.addEventListener('drop', dropped, false);
}
function dragged(e){
  elem=e.target;
  e.dataTransfer.setData('Text', elem.getAttribute('id'));
}
function dropped(e){
  e.preventDefault();
  var id=e.dataTransfer.getData('Text');
  if(id!="image4"){
    var src=document.getElementById(id).src;
    drop.innerHTML='<img src="'+src+'">';
  }else{
    drop.innerHTML='not admitted';
  }
}
window.addEventListener('load', initiate, false);
```

Listing 8-6: sending the id attribute

Not many things changed in Listing 8-6 from previous codes. We are using the **querySelectorAll()** method to add a listener for the **dragstart** event to every image inside the **picturesbox** element, sending the **id** attribute with **setData()** every time an image is dragged and checking the value of this **id** in the **dropped()** function to prevent the user from dropping the image with the **id="image4"** (The "not admitted" message is shown in the drop box when the user tries to drop this particular image.).

This is a simple filter. You can use the `querySelectorAll()` method in the `dropped()` function to check that the image received is inside the `picturesbox` element, for example, or use properties from the `dataTransfer` object (like `types` or `files`), but it is always a customized process. In other words, you have to take care of it by yourself.

setDragImage()

Changing the image that is dragged along with the mouse's pointer in a drag and drop operation may sound useless, but sometimes it avoids headaches. The `setDragImage()` method not only lets us change the image, but also takes two attributes, **x** and **y**, to set the position of that image relative to the mouse's pointer. Usually the browser generates a thumbnail with the source, but the position in which this thumbnail is located relative to the mouse's pointer is set according to the position of the mouse when the drag started. The `setDragImage()` method lets us declare a specific position that will be the same in every drag and drop operation.

```
<!DOCTYPE html>
<html lang="en">
<head>
  <title>Drag and Drop</title>
  <link rel="stylesheet" href="dragdrop.css">
  <script src="dragdrop.js"></script>
</head>
<body>
  <section id="dropbox">
    <canvas id="canvas" width="500" height="300"></canvas>
  </section>
  <section id="picturesbox">
    <img id="image1"
src="http://www.minkbooks.com/content/monster1.gif">
    <img id="image2"
src="http://www.minkbooks.com/content/monster2.gif">
    <img id="image3"
src="http://www.minkbooks.com/content/monster3.gif">
    <img id="image4"
src="http://www.minkbooks.com/content/monster4.gif">
  </section>
</body>
</html>
```

Listing 8-7: <canvas> as a drop box

With the new HTML document of Listing 8-7, we are going to show you the importance of the **setDragImage()** method using a **<canvas>** element as the drop box.

```
function initiate(){
    var images=document.querySelectorAll('#picturesbox > img');
    for(var i=0; i<images.length; i++){
        images[i].addEventListener('dragstart', dragged, false);
        images[i].addEventListener('dragend', ending, false);
    }

    drop=document.getElementById('canvas');
    canvas=drop.getContext('2d');

    drop.addEventListener('dragenter', function(e){
e.preventDefault(); }, false);
    drop.addEventListener('dragover', function(e){
e.preventDefault(); }, false);
    drop.addEventListener('drop', dropped, false);
}
function ending(e){
    elem=e.target;
    elem.style.visibility='hidden';
}
function dragged(e){
    elem=e.target;
    e.dataTransfer.setData('Text', elem.getAttribute('id'));
    e.dataTransfer.setDragImage(e.target, 0, 0);
}
function dropped(e){
    e.preventDefault();
    var id=e.dataTransfer.getData('Text');
    var elem=document.getElementById(id);

    var posx=e.pageX-drop.offsetLeft;
    var posy=e.pageY-drop.offsetTop;

    canvas.drawImage(elem,posx,posy);
}
window.addEventListener('load', initiate, false);
```

Listing 8-8: a small drag and drop application

Probably, with this example, we are getting close to a real-life application. The code in Listing 8-8 will control three different aspects of the process. When the image is dragged, the **dragged()** function is called and sets a customized drag image with the **setDragImage()** method. The code also gets the context to work with canvas and draws the image dropped using the **drawImage()** method and the reference to the source. Finally, the source is hidden with the **ending()** function.

For the custom thumbnail, we used the same element that is being dragged. We didn't change anything about this aspect, but we set the position as 0,0, and this means that now we know exactly where the thumbnail is positioned relative to the mouse. We took advantage of this information in the **dropped()** function. Using the same technique introduced in previous chapters, we calculated where exactly the source was dropped on the canvas and drew the image in that precise place. If you test this example in browsers that already support the **setDragImage()** method (for example, Firefox 4), you will see that the image is drawn in the canvas exactly in the position of the thumbnail, making it easy for users to find the right place to drop the image.

> **IMPORTANT:** The code in Listing 8-8 uses the **dragend** event to hide the original image when the operation is over. This event is fired by the source when a drag operation is finished, either in success or failure. In our example, the image will be hidden in both cases. You will have to create the proper controls to proceed only in case of success.

Files

Possibly the most interesting characteristic of the Drag and Drop API is the ability to work with files. The API is not only available within the document, but also integrated with the system, allowing users to drag elements from the browser to other applications and vice versa. And usually the most required elements from external applications are files.

As we saw before, there is a special property for this purpose in the **dataTransfer** object that will return an array containing the list of files that have been dragged. We can use this information to build complex scripts to help users work with files or upload them to the server.

```
<!DOCTYPE html>
<html lang="en">
<head>
  <title>Drag and Drop</title>
  <link rel="stylesheet" href="dragdrop.css">
  <script src="dragdrop.js"></script>
</head>
<body>
  <section id="dropbox">
    Drag and drop FILES here
  </section>
</body>
</html>
```

Listing 8-9: simple template to drop files

The HTML document of Listing 8-9 is just providing a drop box. The files will be dragged into this box from an external application (for example, File Explorer). The data from the files is processed by the following code:

```
function initiate(){
   drop=document.getElementById('dropbox');
   drop.addEventListener('dragenter', function(e){
e.preventDefault(); }, false);
   drop.addEventListener('dragover', function(e){
e.preventDefault(); }, false);
   drop.addEventListener('drop', dropped, false);
}
function dropped(e){
   e.preventDefault();
   var files=e.dataTransfer.files;
   var list='';
   for(var f=0;f<files.length;f++){
     list+='File: '+files[f].name+' '+files[f].size+'<br>';
   }
   drop.innerHTML=list;
}
window.addEventListener('load', initiate, false);
```

Listing 8-10: processing the data in `files`

The information returned by the **files** property can be saved in a variable and then read by a **for** loop. In the code in Listing 8-10, we are just showing the name and size of every file in the drop box. To use this information to build more complex applications, we need to resort to other APIs and programming techniques, as we will see later in this book.

> **Do It Yourself:** Create new files with the codes in Listings 8-9 and 8-10, and open the template in your browser. Drag files from the File Explorer or any other similar program to the drop box of the template. You should see a list with the name and size of every file dropped inside this box.

The Drag and Drop API introduces specific events, methods and properties to help us build applications that take advantage of this feature.

Events

There are seven new events for this API:

dragstart—This event is fired by the source when a drag operation starts.

drag—This event is fired by the source during the time a drag operation is performing.

dragend—This event is fired by the source when a drag operation is finished, either because the drop action was successful or the drag was cancelled.

dragenter—This event is fired by the target when the mouse enters the area occupied by the element. This event always has to be cancelled using the `preventDefault()` method.

dragover—This event is fired by the target while the mouse is over it. This event always has to be cancelled using the `preventDefault()` method.

drop—This event is fired by the target when the source is dropped over it. This event always has to be cancelled using the `preventDefault()` method.

dragleave—This event is fired by the target when the mouse leaves the area occupied by the element.

Methods

The following is a list of the most important methods introduced by this API:

setData(type, data)—This method is used to prepare the data to be sent when a `dragstart` event is fired. The `type` attribute can be any regular data type (like `text/plain` or `text/html`) or a customized type.

getData(type)—This method returns the data of the type specified. It's used when a drop event is fired.

clearData(type)—This method removes the data for the type specified.

setDragImage(element, x, y)—This method replaces the default thumbnail created by the browser with a customized image and sets its position relative to the mouse's pointer.

Properties

The `dataTransfer` object that holds the data transferred in a drag and drop operation also introduces a few useful properties:

> **types**—This property returns an array with all the types set in the `dragstart` event.
>
> **files**—This property returns an array with information about the files that have been dragged.
>
> **dropEffect**—This property returns the type of operation currently selected. It can also be set to change the selected operation. The possible values are **none**, `copy`, `link` and `move`.
>
> **effectAllowed**—This property returns the types of operations that are allowed. It can be set to change the operations allowed. The possible values are **none**, `copy`, `copyLink`, `copyMove`, `link`, `linkMove`, `move`, `all` and `uninitialized`.

Chapter 9
Geolocation API

Finding Your Place

The Geolocation API was designed for browsers to provide a detection mechanism by default that will let developers determine the user's physical location. Previously, we only had the option of building a big database with IP addresses and programming resource-consuming scripts into the server that would give us just an approximate idea of the user's location (usually as vague as by country).

This API takes advantage of new systems, such as network triangulation or GPS, to return an accurate location of the device running the application. The valuable information returned will let us create applications that adapt themselves according to the user's particular needs or provide localized information automatically.

Three specific methods are provided to use the API:

getCurrentPosition(location, error, configuration)—This is the method used for single requests. It can take three attributes: a function to process the location returned, a function to process the errors returned and an object to configure how the information will be acquired. Only the first attribute is required for the method to work properly.

watchPosition(location, error, configuration)—This is similar to the previous method, except that it will start a watch process for the detection of new locations. It works in a way similar to the `setInterval()` Javascript method, repeating the process automatically throughout a period of time according to the configuration by default or the value of its attributes.

clearWatch(id)—The `watchPosition()` method returns a value that can be saved in a variable and then used as an id by the `clearWatch()` method to stop the watch. This is similar to the `clearInterval()` method used to stop the process started by `setInterval()`.

getCurrentPosition(location)

As we said, only the first attribute is required for the `getCurrentPosition()` method to work properly. This attribute is a callback function that will receive an object called `Position` that holds all the information retrieved by the geolocation systems.

The `Position` object has two attributes:

> **coords**—This attribute contains a set of values that establish the position of the device and other important information. The values are accessible through seven internal attributes: `latitude, longitude, altitude` (in meters), `accuracy` (in meters), `altitudeAccuracy` (in meters), `heading` (in degrees) and `speed` (in meters per second).
>
> **timestamp**—This indicates the time when the information was acquired.

This object is passed to the callback function and then the values are accessible inside this function. Let's see a practical example of using this method:

```
<!DOCTYPE html>
<html lang="en">
<head>
  <title>Geolocation</title>
  <script src="geolocation.js"></script>
</head>
<body>
  <section id="location">
    <button id="getlocation">Get my location</button>
  </section>
</body>
</html>
```

Listing 9-1: HTML document for geolocation

Listing 9-1 will be our template for the rest of this chapter. It's as simple as can be, with just a **<button>** element inside a **<section>** element that we are going to use to show the information retrieved by the geolocation system.

```
function initiate(){
  var get=document.getElementById('getlocation');
  get.addEventListener('click', getlocation, false);
}
function getlocation(){
  navigator.geolocation.getCurrentPosition(showinfo);
}
```

```
function showinfo(position){
  var location=document.getElementById('location');
  var data='';
  data+='Latitude: '+position.coords.latitude+'<br>';
  data+='Longitude: '+position.coords.longitude+'<br>';
  data+='Accuracy: '+position.coords.accuracy+'mts.<br>';
  location.innerHTML=data;
}
window.addEventListener('load', initiate, false);
```

Listing 9-2: getting location information

An implementation of the Geolocation API is simple: we use the **getCurrentPosition()** method and create a function that will show the values returned. The **getCurrentPosition()** method is a method of the **geolocation** object. This is a new object that is part of the **navigator** object, a Javascript object that was previously implemented to return information about the browser and the system. So to access the **getCurrentPosition()** method, the syntax is the following: **navigator.geolocation.getCurrentPosition(function)** where **function** is a custom function that will receive the **Position** object returned and process the information.

In the code in Listing 9-2, we called this function **showinfo**. When the **getCurrentPosition()** method is called, a new **Position** object is created with the information and sent to the **showinfo()** function. We referenced that object inside the function with the variable **position**, and then used this variable to show the data.

The **Position** object has two important attributes: **coords** and **timestamp**. In our example, we are just using **coords** to access the information we want (latitude, longitude and accuracy). These values are saved in the variable **data** and then shown on the screen as the new content of the element **location**.

> **Do It Yourself:** Create files with the codes in Listings 9-1 and 9-2 and then open the HTML document in your browser. When you click the button, the browser will ask you whether or not to activate the geolocation system for this application. If you allow the application to access this information, then your latitude, longitude and the accuracy of this information will be shown on the screen.

getCurrentPosition(location, error)

However, what happen if you don't allow the browser to access the information about your location? By adding a second attribute (another function), we are able to capture errors produced in the process, and one of those errors occurs when the user denies access.

Along with the **Position** object, the **getCurrentPosition()** method returns the **PositionError** object if an error is detected. The object is sent to the second attribute of **getCurrentPosition()**, and has two attributes, **error** and **message**, to provide the value and description of the error. The four possible errors are represented by constants:

> **UNKNOWN_ERROR**—value 0. When this is returned by `PositionError` it means than an error not covered by the definition occurs.
> **PERMISSION_DENIED**—value 1. This error occurs when the user denies access for the Geolocation API to his or her location information.
> **POSITION_UNAVAILABLE**—value 2. This error occurs when the position of the device couldn't be determined.
> **TIMEOUT**—value 3. This error occurs when the position couldn't be determined in the period of time declared in the configuration.

```
function initiate(){
    var get=document.getElementById('getlocation');
    get.addEventListener('click', getlocation, false);
}
function getlocation(){
    navigator.geolocation.getCurrentPosition(showinfo, showerror);
}
function showinfo(position){
    var location=document.getElementById('location');
    var data='';
    data+='Latitude: '+position.coords.latitude+'<br>';
    data+='Longitude: '+position.coords.longitude+'<br>';
    data+='Accuracy: '+position.coords.accuracy+'mts.<br>';
    location.innerHTML=data;
}
function showerror(error){
    alert('Error: '+error.code+' '+error.message);
}
window.addEventListener('load', initiate, false);
```

Listing 9-3: showing error messages

The error messages are intended for internal use. The purpose is to provide a mechanism for the application to acknowledge the situation and proceed accordingly. In the code in Listing 9-3, we added the second parameter to the `getCurrentPosition()` method (another callback function) and created the `showerror()` function to show the information of the **code** and **message** attributes. The value of **code** will be a number between 0 and 3 according to the number of the error (listed above).

For learning purposes, we used an `alert()` method to show the data, but you should process the response in a silent way, without alerting the user of anything, if possible.

The `PositionError` object is sent to the `showerror()` function and represented by the variable **error**. We could also check for the errors individually (error.PERMISSION_DENIED, for example) and show an alert only if that particular condition is true.

getCurrentPosition(location, error, configuration)

The third possible value of the getCurrentPosition() method is an object containing up to three possible attributes:

enableHighAccuracy—This is a boolean attribute to inform the system that the most accurate possible location is required. The browser will try to get information through systems like GPS, for example, to provide the exact location of the device. These are high resource-consuming systems and their use should be limited to specific circumstances. For this reason the default value of this attribute is false.

timeout—This indicates the maximum time for the operation to take place. If the information is not acquired in the time limit, the TIMEOUT error is returned. Its value is in milliseconds.

maximumAge—The previous positions are cached in the system. If we consider it appropriate to get the last information saved instead of retrieving a new location (to avoid resource consumption or for a quick response), this attribute can be set with a specific time limit. If the last cached location is older than the value of this attribute, then a new location will be retrieved from the system. Its value is in milliseconds.

```
function initiate(){
  var get=document.getElementById('getlocation');
  get.addEventListener('click', getlocation, false);
}
function getlocation(){
  var geoconfig={
    enableHighAccuracy: true,
    timeout: 10000,
    maximumAge: 60000
  };
  navigator.geolocation.getCurrentPosition(showinfo, showerror,
geoconfig);
}
function showinfo(position){
  var location=document.getElementById('location');
  var data='';
  data+='Latitude: '+position.coords.latitude+'<br>';
  data+='Longitude: '+position.coords.longitude+'<br>';
  data+='Accuracy: '+position.coords.accuracy+'mts.<br>';
  location.innerHTML=data;
}
```

```
function showerror(error){
    alert('Error: '+error.code+' '+error.message);
}
window.addEventListener('load', initiate, false);
```

Listing 9-4: system configuration

The code in Listing 9-4 will try to get the most accurate location for the device in no more than 10 seconds, but only if there is no previous location in the cache captured less than 60 seconds ago (If there is, this will be the `Position` object returned.).

The object containing the configuration values was created first and then referenced from the `getCurrentPosition()` method. Nothing changed in the rest of the code. The `showinfo()` function will show the information on the screen independently of its origin (if it's cached or brand new).

> **Review the Basics:** Javascript provides different ways to build an object. For clarity's sake, we chose to create the object first, save it in the variable `geoconfig` and then use this reference in the `getCurrentPosition()` method. However, you could have inserted the object directly into the method as an attribute. In small applications, objects can usually be avoided, but it's not the case for more complex codes. To learn more about objects, go to our website and visit the links for this chapter.

With the last code, we start to see the real purpose of the Geolocation API and what the API was intended for. The most effective and useful features are oriented toward mobile devices. The value `true` for the `enableHighAccuracy` attribute, for example, will suggest the browser use systems like GPS to get the most accurate location. The methods `watchPosition()` and `clearWatch()`, which we will see next, work over location updates, and this is only possible, of course, when the device accessing the application is mobile (and moving). This brings up two important subjects. First, most of our codes will have to be tested in a mobile device to know exactly how they will perform in a real situation. And second, we have to be responsible with the use of this API. GPS and other location systems consume a lot of resources and in most cases devices will run out of battery if we are not careful enough. Regarding the first point, we have an alternative; just go to dev.w3.org/geo/api/test-suite/ and check the test suite for the Geolocation API. Regarding the second point, here is a little advice: set the `enableHighAccuracy` attribute to `true` only when it is strictly necessary, and don't abuse this possibility.

watchPosition(location, error, configuration)

Similar to `getCurrentPosition()`, the `watchPosition()` method takes three attributes and performs the same task: namely, the method gets the location of the device that is accessing to the application. The only difference is that the first one is a one-time operation while `watchPosition()` offers new data automatically every time the location changes. The method will be watching all the time and sending information to the callback function when there is a new location to show, unless we cancel the process with the `clearWatch()` method.

Here is an example of how to implement the `watchPosition()` method based on previous codes:

```
function initiate(){
  var get=document.getElementById('getlocation');
  get.addEventListener('click', getlocation, false);
}
function getlocation(){
  var geoconfig={
    enableHighAccuracy: true,
    maximumAge: 60000
  };
  control=navigator.geolocation.watchPosition(showinfo,
showerror, geoconfig);
}
function showinfo(position){
  var location=document.getElementById('location');
  var data='';
  data+='Latitude: '+position.coords.latitude+'<br>';
  data+='Longitude: '+position.coords.longitude+'<br>';
  data+='Accuracy: '+position.coords.accuracy+'mts.<br>';
  location.innerHTML=data;
}
function showerror(error){
  alert('Error: '+error.code+' '+error.message);
}
window.addEventListener('load', initiate, false);
```

Listing 9-5: *testing the* `watchPosition()` *method*

You won't notice anything in a static PC using this code, but on a mobile device, new information will be shown every time there is a modification in the device's location. The `maximumAge` attribute determines how often this information will be sent to `showinfo()`. If the new location is retrieved after 60 seconds (60000 milliseconds) from the previous one, then it's shown; otherwise the `showinfo()` function won't be called.

Notice that the value returned by the `watchPosition()` method was saved in the `control` variable. This variable is like the id for this operation. If later we want to cancel the processing of this method, we just have to execute the line `clearWatch(control)` and `watchPosition()` will stop updating information.

If you run this code on a desktop computer, the `watchPosition()` method will work like `getCurrentPosition()`; no information will be updated. The callback function is called only when the location changes.

Practical Uses with Google Maps

So far we have shown the location data on the screen exactly the way we receive it. However, these are values that usually mean nothing to regular people. I cannot immediately say my current location's latitude and longitude, let alone identify a different location in the world with these values. We have two alternatives: use this information internally to calculate position, distance and other variables that will let us offer specific results to users (such as products or restaurants in the area) or we can actually show directly the information retrieved by the Geolocation API in a more comprehensible way. And what can be better at representing a geographic location than a map?

Earlier in this book, we talked about the Google Maps API. This is an external Javascript API provided by Google that has nothing to do with HTML5 but is widely used in modern websites and applications these days. It offers a variety of alternatives to work with interactive maps and even real views of very specific locations through the StreetView technology.

We are going to show you a simple example using one part of the API called Static Maps API. With this specific API, we only have to build a URL with the information of the location, and an image of the selected area in a map will be returned.

```
function initiate(){
  var get=document.getElementById('getlocation');
  get.addEventListener('click', getlocation, false);
}
function getlocation(){
  navigator.geolocation.getCurrentPosition(showinfo, showerror);
}
function showinfo(position){
  var location=document.getElementById('location');
  var
mapurl='http://maps.google.com/maps/api/staticmap?center='+positi
on.coords.latitude+','+position.coords.longitude+'&zoom=12&size=4
00x400&sensor=false&markers='+position.coords.latitude+','+positi
on.coords.longitude;
  location.innerHTML='<img src="'+mapurl+'">';
}
function showerror(error){
  alert('Error: '+error.code+' '+error.message);
}
window.addEventListener('load', initiate, false);
```

***Listing 9-6**: representing the location on a map*

The code is simple. We used the **getCurrentPosition()** method and send the information to **showinfo()** as always, but now in this function the values of the **Position** object are added to a Google URL and then the address is inserted as the source of an **<img>** element to show the map on the screen.

Do It Yourself: Test the code in Listing 9-6 on your browser using the template in Listing 9-1. Go to the Google Maps API web page to check other alternatives: code.google.com/apis/maps/. Change the values of the attributes `zoom` and `size` in the URL to modify the map returned by the API.

Determining the user's location has become more critical in modern web applications. The success of mobile devices provides the possibility of creating applications that take advantage of this information.

Methods

The Geolocation API provides three methods to get location information from devices:

getCurrentPosition(location, error, configuration)—This method returns the location information every time it is invoked. The first attribute is a callback function to receive the information; the second attribute is another callback function to process errors; and the third attribute is an object to provide values for configuration (See Configuration Object below.).

watchPosition(location, error, configuration)—This method returns the location information automatically every time the location changes. The first attribute is a callback function to receive the information; the second attribute is another callback function to process errors; and the third attribute is an object to provide values for configuration (See Configuration Object below.).

clearWatch(id)—This method cancels the process started by the `watchPosition()` method. The attribute `id` is the identification returned by `watchPosition()` when it was called.

Objects

Two objects are generated by the `getCurrentPosition()` and `watchPosition()` methods to communicate the information retrieved from the geolocation system and the status of the operation.

Position object—This object is generated to hold the information about the location detected. It has two attributes: `coords` and `timestamp`.

coords—This is an attribute of the `Position` object. It has seven internal attributes to return the location information: `latitude, longitude, altitude` (in meters), `accuracy` (in meters), `altitudeAccuracy` (in meters), `heading` (in degrees) and `speed` (in meters per second).

timestamp—This is an attribute of the `Position` object. It returns the time in which the location was detected.

PositionError object—This object is generated when an error occurs. It provides two general attributes with the error value and message, and four specific values for individual error identification.

message—This is an attribute of the `PositionError` object. It returns a message describing the error detected.

error—This is an attribute of the `PositionError` object. It holds the value of the error detected. The possible values are listed in the individual errors below:

UNKNOWN_ERROR—value 0 in the `error` attribute. This constant will be `true` when an error not covered by the definition occurs.

PERMISSION_DENIED—value 1 in the `error` attribute. This constant will be `true` when the user doesn't allow the Geolocation API to have access to his or her location.

POSITION_UNAVAILABLE—value 2 in the `error` attribute. This constant will be `true` when the location of the device couldn't be determined.

TIMEOUT—value 3 in the `error` attribute. This constant will be `true` when the location couldn't be determined before the period of time declared by configuration.

The following object is required by the `getCurrentPosition()` and `watchPosition()` methods for configuration purposes.

Configuration Object—This object provides configuration values for the `getCurrentPosition()` and `watchPosition()` methods.

enableHighAccuracy—This is one of the possible attributes for the Configuration Object. If set to `true`, it will ask the browser to get the most accurate location possible.

timeout—This is one of the possible attributes for the Configuration Object. It indicates the maximum time for the operation to take place.

maximumAge—This is one of the possible attributes for the Configuration Object. It indicates for how long the last cached location will be valid.

Chapter 10
Web Storage API

Two Storage Systems

The World Wide Web was first thought of as a way to show information—just to *show* it. The information processing started later, first with applications in servers and then inefficiently with short scripts and plugins on the client side. However, the essence of the web was still basically the same: the information was cooked on the server and then shown to users. The hard work was almost always on the server side because the system wasn't taking advantage of the resources in user's computer.

HTML5 put this situation into balance. Motivated by the particular characteristics of mobile devices, the emergence of cloud computing and the need to standardize technologies and innovations incorporated by plugins throughout all these years, the HTML5 specification included features that make it possible to run full and completely functional applications in a user's computers, even when no network connection is available.

One of the most necessary features for any application is the possibility of storing data and making this data available when it's needed, but there was no effective mechanism that allowed data storage. Cookies were used to store small pieces of information on the client side, but due to their nature, they were limited to short strings and only useful in specific circumstances.

The Web Storage API is basically an improvement on cookies. The API lets us save data in the user's hard drive and use it later as a desktop application would do. The storage process provided by this API may be used in two particular situations: when the information has to be available only during a session and when it has to be preserved as long as is determined by the user. To make this clear for developers, the API was divided into two parts called `sessionStorage` and `localStorage`.

> **sessionStorage**—This is a storage mechanism that will keep data available only for the duration of a page session. Actually, unlike real sessions, the information stored through this mechanism is only accessible from a single window or tab and it lasts until the window is closed. The specification is still talking about "sessions" because the information is preserved even when the window is refreshed or a new page from the same website is loaded.

localStorage—This mechanism works similar to a storage system for a desktop application. The data saved is permanently preserved and always available from the application that created it.

Both mechanisms work through a similar interface, sharing the same methods and properties. And both are origin dependent, which means the information is available only through the website that created it. Every website will have its own storage space that will last until the window is closed or will be permanent, according to the mechanism used.

The API clearly differentiates temporary data from permanent data, making easy the construction of small applications that need to preserve just a few strings as temporary reference (for example, shopping carts) or big and more complex ones that have to save entire documents for as much time as needed.

IMPORTANT: Most browsers only work properly with this API when the source is a real server. To test the following codes, we recommend that you first upload the files to your server.

sessionStorage

This part of the API, **sessionStorage**, is like a replacement for session cookies. Cookies, as well as **sessionStorage**, keep the data available during a specific period of time, but while cookies use the browser as reference, **sessionStorage** uses a single window or tab. This means that cookies created for a session are available as long as any browser's window is still open, but the data created by **sessionStorage** is only available until the window is closed (and only for that particular window or tab).

Data Storage Implementation

Because both systems, **sessionStorage** and **localStorage**, work with the same interface, we are going to need only one HTML document and a simple form to test the codes and experiment with this API:

```
<!DOCTYPE html>
<html lang="en">
<head>
  <title>Web Storage API</title>
  <link rel="stylesheet" href="storage.css">
  <script src="storage.js"></script>
</head>
<body>
  <section id="formbox">
    <form name="form">
      <p>Keyword:<br><input type="text" name="keyword"
id="keyword"></p>
      <p>Value:<br><textarea name="text"
id="text"></textarea></p>
      <p><input type="button" name="save" id="save"
value="Save"></p>
    </form>
  </section>
  <section id="databox">
    No Information available
  </section>
</body>
</html>
```

***Listing 10-1:** template for the Storage API*

We also created a simple set of styles to shape the page and differentiate the form area from the box where the data will be shown and listed:

```
#formbox{
   float: left;
   padding: 20px;
   border: 1px solid #999999;
}
#databox{
   float: left;
   width: 400px;
   margin-left: 20px;
   padding: 20px;
   border: 1px solid #999999;
}
#keyword, #text{
   width: 200px;
}
#databox > div{
   padding: 5px;
   border-bottom: 1px solid #999999;
}
```

Listing 10-2: *styles for our template*

> **Do It Yourself:** Create an HTML file with the code in Listing 10-1 and a CSS file called **storage.css** with the styles in Listing 10-2. You will also need a file named **storage.js** to save and test the Javascript codes presented next.

Creating Data

Either **sessionStorage** or **localStorage** store data as items. The items are formed by a keyword/value pair, and every value will be converted to a string before being stored. Think of items as variables each with a name and a value that can be created, modified or deleted.

There are two new API specific methods to create and get an item from the storage space:

> **setItem(key, value)**—This is the method we have to call to create an item. The item will be created with a keyword and a value according to the specified attributes. If there is already an item with the same keyword, it will be updated with the new value, so this method may be also used to modify data.
>
> **getItem(key)**—To retrieve the value of an item, we must call this method by specifying the keyword of the item we want. The keyword in this case is the same as the keyword declared when the item was created by **setItem()**.

```
function initiate(){
  var button=document.getElementById('save');
  button.addEventListener('click', newitem, false);
}
function newitem(){
  var keyword=document.getElementById('keyword').value;
  var value=document.getElementById('text').value;
  sessionStorage.setItem(keyword,value);

  show(keyword);
}
function show(keyword){
  var databox=document.getElementById('databox');
  var value=sessionStorage.getItem(keyword);
  databox.innerHTML='<div>'+keyword+' - '+value+'</div>';
}
window.addEventListener('load', initiate, false);
```

Listing 10-3: *storing and retrieving data*

The process is extremely simple. The methods are part of **sessionStorage** and called with the syntax **sessionStorage.setItem()**. In the code in Listing 10-3, the **newitem()** function is executed every time the user clicks the button in the form. This function creates an item with the information inserted in the form and then calls the **show()** function. This function gets the item according to the keyword received using the **getItem()** method, and then it shows the content of this item on the screen.

Besides these methods, the API also provides a shortcut to create and get an item from the storage space. We can use the keyword of the item as a property and access the item this way. This method uses two syntaxes according to the type of information we are using to create the item. We can enclose a variable for the keyword in square brackets (for example, **sessionStorage[keyword]=value**) or we can use the string as a property name (for example, **sessionStorage.myitem=value**).

```
function initiate(){
  var button=document.getElementById('save');
  button.addEventListener('click', newitem, false);
}
function newitem(){
  var keyword=document.getElementById('keyword').value;
  var value=document.getElementById('text').value;
  sessionStorage[keyword]=value;

  show(keyword);
}
```

```
function show(keyword){
  var databox=document.getElementById('databox');
  var value=sessionStorage[keyword];
  databox.innerHTML='<div>'+keyword+' - '+value+'</div>';
}
window.addEventListener('load', initiate, false);
```

Listing 10-4: *using a shortcut to work with items*

Reading Data

The previous example only retrieves the last item saved. We are going to improve the code to make it more useful by taking advantage of more methods and properties provided by the API to manipulate items:

> **length**—This property returns the number of items accumulated in the storage space for this application. It works exactly like the **length** property used regularly in Javascript for arrays, and it is useful for sequential readings.
>
> **key(index)**—The items are stored sequentially, enumerated with an automatic index that starts from 0. With this method, we can retrieve a specific item or create a loop to retrieve all the information stored.

```
function initiate(){
  var button=document.getElementById('save');
  button.addEventListener('click', newitem, false);
  show();
}
function newitem(){
  var keyword=document.getElementById('keyword').value;
  var value=document.getElementById('text').value;

  sessionStorage.setItem(keyword,value);
  show();
  document.getElementById('keyword').value='';
  document.getElementById('text').value='';
}
function show(){
  var databox=document.getElementById('databox');
  databox.innerHTML='';
  for(var f=0;f<sessionStorage.length;f++){
    var keyword=sessionStorage.key(f);
    var value=sessionStorage.getItem(keyword);
    databox.innerHTML+='<div>'+keyword+' - '+value+'</div>';
  }
}
window.addEventListener('load', initiate, false);
```

Listing 10-5: *listing items*

The purpose of the code in Listing 10-5 is to get a complete list of items in the right box on the screen. The **show()** function was improved using the **length** property and the method **key()**. We created a **for** loop that goes from 0 to the number of items that exist in the storage space. Inside the loop, the **key()** method will return the corresponding keyword for the element in every position. For example, if the item in the position 0 of the storage space was created with the keyword "myitem", the code **sessionStorage.key(0)** will return "myitem". Calling this method from a loop allows us to list all the items on the screen each with their corresponding keyword and value.

The **show()** function is called from the **initiate()** function to show the items already saved in the storage space as soon as the application starts running.

> **Do It Yourself:** You can take advantage of the Forms API studied in Chapter 6 to check the validity of the input fields and not allow the insertion of invalid or empty items.

Deleting Data

The items can be created, read, and of course, deleted. There are two methods incorporated for this purpose:

> **removeItem(key)**—This method will delete one single item. The keyword to identify the item must be the same declared when it was created with the **setItem()** method.
>
> **clear()**—This method will simply empty the storage space. Every item will be erased.

```
function initiate(){
  var button=document.getElementById('save');
  button.addEventListener('click', newitem, false);
  show();
}
function newitem(){
  var keyword=document.getElementById('keyword').value;
  var value=document.getElementById('text').value;

  sessionStorage.setItem(keyword,value);
  show();
  document.getElementById('keyword').value='';
  document.getElementById('text').value='';
}
```

```
function show(){
    var databox=document.getElementById('databox');
    databox.innerHTML='<div><button onclick="removeAll()">erase
everything</button></div>';
    for(var f=0;f<sessionStorage.length;f++){
        var keyword=sessionStorage.key(f);
        var value=sessionStorage.getItem(keyword);
        databox.innerHTML+='<div>'+keyword+' - '+value+'<br><button
onclick="remove(\''+keyword+'\')">remove</button></div>';
    }
}
function remove(keyword){
    if(confirm('Are you sure?')){
        sessionStorage.removeItem(keyword);
        show();
    }
}
function removeAll(){
    if(confirm('Are you sure?')){
        sessionStorage.clear();
        show();
    }
}
window.addEventListener('load', initiate, false);
```

Listing 10-6: deleting items

The `initiate()` and `newitem()` functions in Listing 10-6 are the same from the previous code. Only the `show()` function changes to incorporate the event handler `onclick` to call the functions that will delete an individual item or all of them. The list of items is built the same way than before, but this time a "remove" button is added for every item to be able to remove it. Also another button is added at the top of the list to erase everything.

The `remove()` and `removeAll()` functions are in charge of deleting the selected item or clearing the storage space, respectively. Each function calls the `show()` function at the end to update the list of items on the screen.

> **Do It Yourself:** With the code in Listing 10-6, you will be able to test how the information is processed by `sessionStorage`. Open the template of Listing 10-1 in your browser, create new items and then open the template in a new window. The information on every window is different; the old window will keep its data available and the storage space for the new window will be empty. Unlike other systems (like cookies), for `sessionStorage`, every window is considered an independent instance of the application and the information of the session is not spread between them.

The system `sessionStorage` preserves the data created in a window only until the window is closed. It is useful for controlling shopping carts or any other application that requires short-term data access.

localStorage

Having a reliable system to store data during a window session may be extremely useful in some circumstances, but when you try to emulate powerful desktop applications on the web, a temporary data storage system is not enough.

To cover this aspect, the Storage API provides a second system that will reserve a storage space for every origin and keep the information permanently available. With **localStorage**, we can finally save large amounts of data and let the user decide whether the information is still useful and must be preserved or not.

This system uses the same interface as **sessionStorage**, therefore every method and property studied so far in this chapter is available for **localStorage** as well. Only the substitution of the prefix **session** by **local** is required to prepare the codes.

```
function initiate(){
  var button=document.getElementById('save');
  button.addEventListener('click', newitem, false);
  show();
}
function newitem(){
  var keyword=document.getElementById('keyword').value;
  var value=document.getElementById('text').value;

  localStorage.setItem(keyword,value);
  show();
  document.getElementById('keyword').value='';
  document.getElementById('text').value='';
}
function show(){
  var databox=document.getElementById('databox');
  databox.innerHTML='';
  for(var f=0;f<localStorage.length;f++){
    var keyword=localStorage.key(f);
    var value=localStorage.getItem(keyword);
    databox.innerHTML+='<div>'+keyword+' - '+value+'</div>';
  }
}
window.addEventListener('load', initiate, false);
```

Listing 10-7: *using* `localStorage`

In Listing 10-7, we just took a previous code and replaced **sessionStorage** with **localStorage**. Now every item created will be preserved through different windows or even after the browser is completely closed.

Do It Yourself: Using the template in Listing 10-1, test the code in Listing 10-7. This code will create a new item with the information from the form and automatically list every item available in the storage space reserved for this application. Close the browser and open the HTML file again. You will still be able to see all the items on the list.

storage Event

Because `localStorage` makes the information available in every window where the same application is loaded, at least two problems arise: how these windows will communicate and how we will update the information in a window that is not active or focused. To solve both problems the `storage` event was included in the specification.

> **storage**—This event will be fired by the window every time a change occurs in the storage space. It can be used to inform every window opened with the same application that something has changed in the storage space and that something needs to be done about it.

```
function initiate(){
   var button=document.getElementById('save');
   button.addEventListener('click', newitem, false);
   window.addEventListener("storage", show, false);

   show();
}
function newitem(){
   var keyword=document.getElementById('keyword').value;
   var value=document.getElementById('text').value;

   localStorage.setItem(keyword,value);
   show();
   document.getElementById('keyword').value='';
   document.getElementById('text').value='';
}
function show(){
   var databox=document.getElementById('databox');
   databox.innerHTML='';
   for(var f=0;f<localStorage.length;f++){
      var keyword=localStorage.key(f);
      var value=localStorage.getItem(keyword);
      databox.innerHTML+='<div>'+keyword+' - '+value+'</div>';
   }
}
window.addEventListener('load', initiate, false);
```

Listing 10-8: listening to the `storage` event to keep the item list updated

We just had to start listening to the `storage` event in the `initiate()` function with the code in Listing 10-8 to execute the `show()` function every time an item is created, modified or eliminated. Now, if something is changed in one window, it will be automatically shown in the rest of the windows that are running the same application.

Storage Space

The information stored by `localStorage` will be permanent unless the user decides that is no longer necessary. This means that the physical space in the hard drive occupied by this information will probably grow every time the application is used. Up to this point, the HTML5 specification recommends to browser vendors to reserve a minimum of 5 megabytes for every origin (website or application). This is just a recommendation and will probably change dramatically in the coming years. Some browsers are consulting the user about whether or not to expand this space when the application needs it, but you should be aware of this limitation and keep it in mind while developing your own applications.

Quick Reference
Web Storage API

With the help of the Storage API, now web applications can offer local storage. Using a keyword/value pair, information is stored in the user's computer for fast access or offline work.

Storage Type

Two different mechanisms are provided to store data:

sessionStorage—This mechanism keeps the information stored only available for a single window and until the window is closed.

localStorage—This mechanism stores permanent data that is shared by every window running the same application and will be always available unless the user decides it is no longer necessary.

Methods

This API includes a common interface with new methods, properties and events:

setItem(key, value)—This method creates a new item that is stored in the storage space reserved for the application. The item is composed of a keyword/value pair created from the attributes `key` and `value`.

getItem(key)—This method retrieves the content of the item identified with the keyword specified by the attribute `key`. The value of this keyword must be the same used when the item was created by the `setItem()` method.

key(index)—This method returns the keyword of the item found in the storage space at the position specified by the attribute `index`.

removeItem(key)—This method deletes an item with the keyword specified by the attribute `key`. The value of this keyword must be the same used when the item was created by the `setItem()` method.

clear()—This method deletes every item from the storage space reserved for the application.

Properties

length—This property returns the number of items available in the storage space reserved for the application.

Events

storage—This event is fired every time a change occurs in the storage space reserved for the application.

Chapter 11
IndexedDB API

A Low-Level API

The Storage API studied in the previous chapter is useful for storing small amounts of data, but when it comes to large amounts of structured data, we must resort to a database system. The IndexedDB API is the solution provided by HTML5 for this matter.

IndexedDB is a database system to store indexed information in the user's computer. It was developed as a low-level API with the intention of allowing a wide range of uses. This turns it into the most powerful API of all, but also the most complex. The goal was to provide the most basic infrastructure possible to allow developers build things on top of it and create high-level interfaces for very specific needs. In a low-level API like this, we have to take care of everything and control the condition of every process in every operation performed. The result is an API that most developers will take time to get used to and probably apply indirectly through popular libraries such as jQuery or others that will come out in the near future.

The structure proposed by IndexedDB is also different from SQL or other popular database systems that developers are used to. The information is stored in the database as objects (records) inside what is called Object Stores (tables). The Object Stores have no specific structure, just a name and indexes to be able to find the objects inside. These objects don't have a predefined structure either; they can be different from one to another and as complex as we want. The only condition for objects is that they have at least one property declared as the index in order for the Object Store to be able to find them.

Database

The database itself is simple. Because every database is associated with one computer and one website or application, there are no users to associate or any other access restrictions to take care of. We just need to specify the name and the version, and the database will be ready.

The interface declared by the API provides the attribute `indexedDB` and the method `open()` to create a database. This method returns an object over which two events will be fired to indicate an error or a success in creating the database.

The second aspect we have to consider in order to create or open a database is the version. The API requires a version to be assigned to the database. This is to make the system ready for future migrations. When you have to update the structure of a database on the server side to add more tables or indexes, you usually turn off the server, migrate the information to the new structure and then turn the server back on. However, you can't turn off the user's computer to do this process in a browser. As a result, the version of the database has to be changed and then the information migrated from the old version to the new one.

To work with database versions, the API provides the **version** property and the **setVersion()** method. The property returns the current version value and the method assigns a new version value to the database in use. This value can be a number or any string you want.

Objects and Object Stores

What we used to call records are called objects in IndexedDB. These objects include properties to store and identify values. The number of properties and how the objects are structured is irrelevant. They just must include at least one property declared as index for the Object Store to be able to find them.

The Object Stores (tables) don't have a specific structure either. Only the name and one or more indexes must be declared at the time they are created in order to be able to find objects inside.

Object Store

Object 1	Object 2
Id Name DVD Video	Id Name DVD

Object 3	Object 4
Id Name DVD Book	Id Name Book

Figure 11-1: objects with different properties stored in an Object Store

As you can see in Figure 11-1, an Object Store contains diverse objects with different properties. Some objects have the **DVD** property, others have the **Book** property, etc. Each one has its own structure, but they must have at least one property selected as index to be found. In Figure 11-1's example, it could be the **Id** property).

To work with objects and Object Stores, we just need to create the Object Store, declare the properties that will be used as indexes and then start storing objects in it. We don't have to think about the structure and content of the objects at this moment, but only consider the indexes we are going to need to be able to find them later.

The API provides several methods to manipulate Object Stores:

createObjectStore(name, keyPath, autoIncrement)—This method creates a new Object Store with the name and configuration sets by its attributes. The attribute `name` is mandatory. The `keyPath` will declare a common index for every object. And `autoIncrement` is a boolean value that determines if the Object Store will have a key generator.

objectStore(name)—To access the objects in an Object Store, a transaction must be started and the Object Store opened for that transaction. This method will open the Object Store with the name declared by the `name` attribute.

deleteObjectStore(name)—This will destroy the Object Store with the name declared by the `name` attribute.

The `createObjectStore()` and `deleteObjectStore()` methods, as well as other methods responsible for the configuration of the database, can only be applied when the database is created or upgraded to a new version.

Indexes

To find objects in an Object Store, we need to set some properties of these objects as indexes. An easy way to do it is to declare the `keyPath` attribute in the `createObjectStore()` method. The property declared as `keyPath` will be a common index for every object stored in that particular Object Store. When we set a `keyPath`, this property must be present in every object.

Besides the `keyPath`, we can set all the indexes we want for an Object Store using special methods provided for this purpose:

createIndex(name, property, unique)—This method creates an index for a specific object. The `name` attribute is a name to identify the index, the `property` attribute is the object's property used for the index and `unique` is a boolean value to indicate the possibility of two or more objects sharing the same index's value.

index(name)—To use an index we have to create a reference to the index first and then assign this reference to the transaction. The `index()` method creates a reference to the index declared by the `name` attribute.

deleteIndex(name)—If we don't need an index anymore, we can delete it using this method.

Transactions

A database system working on a browser must contemplate some unique circumstances that are not present in other platforms. The browser could fail, it could be closed abruptly, the process could be stopped by the user, or just another website could be loaded in the same window, for example. There are many situations in which working directly with the database can cause a malfunction or even data corruption. To prevent this from happening, every action is performed through transactions.

The method for generating a transaction is called `transaction()`, and several attributes set the type of the transaction.

> **READ_ONLY**—This attribute sets a read-only transaction. Modifications are not allowed.
>
> **READ_WRITE**—Using this type of transaction, we can read and write. Modifications are allowed.
>
> **VERSION_CHANGE**—This type of transaction is only used for updating the version of the database.

The most common are read-and-write transactions. However, to prevent misuse, the read-only type is set by default, so when we just need to get some information from the database, the only thing we need to do is to specify the scope of the transaction (usually the name of the Object Store we are going to get the information from).

Object Stores Methods

To interact with Object Stores, read and store information, the API provides several methods:

> **add(object)**—This method receives a keyword/value pair or an object containing several keyword/value pairs, and it adds an object to the selected Object Store with this information. If an object with the same index already exist, the `add()` method returns an error.
>
> **put(object)**—This method is similar to the previous one, except it overwrites an existing object with the same index. This method is useful to modify an object already stored in the selected Object Store.
>
> **get(key)**—We can retrieve a specific object from an Object Store using this method. The `key` attribute is the value of the index of the object we want to read.
>
> **delete(key)**—To delete an object from the selected Object Store, we just have to call this method with the value of the index as attribute.

Implementing IndexedDB

Enough with theory! Let's create our first database and apply some of the methods mentioned already in this chapter. We are going to simulate an application to store information about movies. You can add your own information, but for reference, we are going to mention the following:

> **id:** tt0068646 **name:** The Godfather **date:** 1972
> **id:** tt0086567 **name:** WarGames **date:** 1983
> **id:** tt0111161 **name:** The Shawshank Redemption **date:** 1994
> **id:** tt1285016 **name:** The Social Network **date:** 2010

> **IMPORTANT:** The names of the properties (**id, name** and **date**) are the ones we are going to use for our examples in the rest of the chapter. The information was collected from the www.imdb.com website, but you can make your own list or use random information to test the codes.

Template

As always, we need an HTML document and some CSS styles to get the boxes for a form and to show the information retrieved. The form will let us insert new movies into the database by asking for a keyword, the title of the movie and the year when it was made.

```
<!DOCTYPE html>
<html lang="en">
<head>
  <title>IndexedDB API</title>
  <link rel="stylesheet" href="indexed.css">
  <script src="indexed.js"></script>
</head>
<body>
  <section id="formbox">
    <form name="form">
      <p>Keyword:<br><input type="text" name="keyword"
id="keyword"></p>
      <p>Title:<br><input type="text" name="text" id="text"></p>
      <p>Year:<br><input type="text" name="year" id="year"></p>
      <p><input type="button" name="save" id="save"
value="Save"></p>
    </form>
  </section>
```

```
  <section id="databox">
    No Information available
  </section>
</body>
</html>
```

Listing 11-1: template for the IndexedDB API

The CSS styles define the boxes for the form and how to render the information on the screen:

```
#formbox{
  float: left;
  padding: 20px;
  border: 1px solid #999999;
}
#databox{
  float: left;
  width: 400px;
  margin-left: 20px;
  padding: 20px;
  border: 1px solid #999999;
}
#keyword, #text{
  width: 200px;
}
#databox > div{
  padding: 5px;
  border-bottom: 1px solid #999999;
}
```

Listing 11-2: styles for boxes

> **Do It Yourself:** You will need an HTML file for the template in Listing 11-1, a CSS file called **indexed.css** for the styles in Listing 11-2 and a Javascript file called **indexed.js** for all the codes studied next.

Opening the Database

The first thing to do in the Javascript code is to open the database. The **indexedDB** attribute and the **open()** method open the database with the given name or create a new one if it doesn't exist:

```
function initiate(){
  databox=document.getElementById('databox');
  var button=document.getElementById('save');
  button.addEventListener('click', addobject, false);
```

```
if('webkitIndexedDB' in window){
  window.indexedDB=window.webkitIndexedDB;
  window.IDBTransaction=window.webkitIDBTransaction;
  window.IDBKeyRange=window.webkitIDBKeyRange;
  window.IDBCursor=window.webkitIDBCursor;
}else if('mozIndexedDB' in window){
  window.indexedDB=window.mozIndexedDB;
}

var request=indexedDB.open('mydatabase');
request.addEventListener('error', showerror, false);
request.addEventListener('success', start, false);
}
```

Listing 11-3: opening the database

The **initiate()** function in Listing 11-3 prepares the elements of the template and opens the database. The **indexedDB.open()** instruction tries to open a database with the name **mydatabase** and returns the request object with the result of the operation. The **error** or **success** events are fired over this object according to the result of the operation.

> **IMPORTANT:** At the moment of this writing, the API is experimental. Some attributes, including **indexedDB**, needs a prefix for some browsers in order to work properly. Before opening the database in the **initiate()** function, we detected the existence of **webkitIndexedDB** or **mozIndexedDB**, and we prepared the attributes for the specific browser's engine. After this experimental period is over, you will be able to erase the conditional **if** at the beginning of the code in Listing 11-3.

Events are an important part of this API. IndexedDB is both a synchronous and asynchronous API. The synchronous part is been developed at this moment and it's intended to work with the Web Workers API. In contrast, the asynchronous part is intended for normal web use and is already available. An asynchronous system performs tasks in the background and returns the results later. For this purpose, this API fires different events for every operation. Any action over the database and its content is processed in the background (while the system is executing other codes) and events are fired later to inform the results.

After the API processes the request for the database, an **error** or **success** event is fired, and the **showerror()** or the **start()** function in our code is executed to control the errors or continue with the definition of the database.

Database Version

There are a few things we must do to complete the database definition. As we said before, IndexedDB databases are versioned. When the database is created, a **null** value is assigned to its version. So, by checking this value, we are able to know whether the database is new or not:

```
function showerror(e){
  alert('Error: '+e.code+' '+e.message);
}
function start(e){
  db=e.result || e.target.result;
  if(db.version==''){
    var request=db.setVersion('1.0');
    request.addEventListener('error', showerror, false);
    request.addEventListener('success', createdb, false);
  }
}
```

Listing 11-4: setting the version and *responding to events*

Our **showerror()** function is simple (we don't need to process errors for this small application). Here we just used the **code** and **message** attributes of the IDBErrorEvent interface to generate an alert message. The **start()** function, on the other hand, follows the right steps to detect the version of the database and provide one in case it is the first time the user runs our application. The function assigns the **result** object created by the event to the **db** variable and uses this variable to represent the database later.

> **IMPORTANT:** At the moment, some browsers are sending the result object through the event and others through the element that fired the event. To select the right reference automatically, we used the logic **e.result ||**
> **e.target.result**. Probably you will have to use only one of the references when the final specification is ready.

The IDBDatabase interface provides the **version** property to inform the value of the current version and also provides the **setVersion()** method to set a new version. What we do on the **start()** function in Listing 11-4 is detect the value of the current version of the database and then set a new version or not according to this value. If the database already exists, the value of the **version** property will be different than **null** and we won't have to configure anything, but if this is the first time the user runs our application, the **version** property will be **null** and we will have to set a new version and configure the database.

The **setVersion()** method receives a string that can be a number or any string you want to declare the version. You only have to be sure to always use the same string in every code to open the version of the database you want to use. This method is, as well as any other procedure in this part of the API, asynchronous. The version will be set in the background and the result will be informed through events. If an error occurs, we call the **showerror()** function again, but if the version was set correctly, then the `createdb()` function is called to declare the Object Stores and indexes for this new version.

Object Stores and Indexes

At this moment you have to think about what kind of objects you need to store in the database and how you are going to get this information from the Object Stores later. If something is wrong or you want to add something to the configuration of your database in the future, you will have to set a new version and migrate the data from the previous one. This is because the creation of Object Stores and indexes can only be made during a **setVersion** transaction.

```
function createdb(){
  var objectstore=db.createObjectStore('movies',{keyPath:'id'});
  objectstore.createIndex('SearchYear', 'date',{unique: false});
}
```

Listing 11-5: declaring Object Stores and indexes

For our example, we only need one Object Store (to store the movies) and two indexes. The first index, **id**, is set as the **keyPath** attribute for the **createObjectStore()** method when the Object Store is created. The second index is assigned to the Object Store using the **createIndex()** method. This index was identified with the name **SearchYear** and declared for the **date** property. We are going to use this index to order the movies by year.

Adding Objects

So far, we have a database name **mydatabase** that will have the version **1.0** and one Object Store named **movies** with two indexes: **id** and **date**. Now it's time to start adding objects to this Object Store.

```
function addobject(){
  var keyword=document.getElementById('keyword').value;
  var title=document.getElementById('text').value;
  var year=document.getElementById('year').value;

  var transaction=db.transaction(['movies'],
IDBTransaction.READ_WRITE);
  var objectstore=transaction.objectStore('movies');
  var request=objectstore.add({id: keyword, name: title, date:
year});
  request.addEventListener('success', function(){ show(keyword)
}, false);
```

```
    document.getElementById('keyword').value='';
    document.getElementById('text').value='';
    document.getElementById('year').value='';
}
```

Listing 11-6: adding objects

At the beginning of the **initiate()** function, we added a listener for the **click** event to the button in the form. This listener executes the **addobject()** function when the event is fired. This function takes the values from the form (**keyword**, **text** and **year**) and then generates a transaction to store a new object using this information.

To start a transaction, we must use the **transaction()** method and specify the Object Stores involved in the transaction and the type of transaction. In this case, the Object Store is only **movies** and the type is set as **READ_WRITE**.

The next step is to select the Object Store we are going to use. Because the transaction can be originated for several Object Stores, we have to declare which one corresponds to the following operation. Using the **objectStore()** method we open the Object Store and assign it to the transaction with the following line: **transaction.objectStore('movies')**.

Now it's time to add the object to the Object Store. In this example, we use the **add()** method because we want to create new objects, but we could have used the **put()** method instead if we wanted to modify or replace old objects. The **add()** method takes the properties **id**, **name** and **date** and the variables **keyword**, **title** and **year** and creates the object using these values as keyword/value pairs.

Finally, we listen to the event fired by this request and execute the **show()** function in case of success. There is also an **error** event, of course, but since the answer depends on your application, we are not considering that possibility in this example.

Getting Objects

If the object is correctly stored, the **success** event is fired and the **show()** function is executed. In the code in Listing 11-6, this function was declared inside an anonymous function to be able to pass the variable **keyword**. Now we are going to take this value to read the object previously stored:

```
function show(keyword){
    var transaction=db.transaction(['movies']);
    var objectstore=transaction.objectStore('movies');
    var request=objectstore.get(keyword);
    request.addEventListener('success', showlist, false);
}
```

```
function showlist(e){
  var result=e.result || e.target.result;
  databox.innerHTML='<div>'+result.id+' - '+result.name+' -
'+result.date+'</div>';
}
```

Listing 11-7: showing the new object

The code in Listing 11-7 generates a **READ_ONLY** transaction and uses the **get()** method to retrieve the object with the keyword received. We don't have to declare the transaction type because **READ_ONLY** is set by default.

The **get()** method returns the object stored with the property **id=keyword**. If we, for example, inserted the movie *The Godfather* from our list, the variable **keyword** will have the value "tt0068646". This value is received by the **show()** function and used by the **get()** method to retrieve the movie *The Godfather*. As you can see, this code is just for illustration purposes because it only returns the same movie we just added.

Because every operation is asynchronous, we need two functions to show this information. The **show()** function generates the transaction and the **showlist()** function shows the value of the properties on the screen in case of success. Again, we are only listening to the **success** event but an **error** event is also fired from this operation in case of failure.

The **showlist()** function receives an object, and so to access its properties we just have to write the variable representing the object and the name of the property (for example, **result.id**). The variable **result** represents the object and **id** is one of its properties.

Finishing the Code and Testing

As with any previous codes, to end this example, we must add a listener for the **load** event to execute the **initiate()** function as soon as the application is loaded in the browser:

```
window.addEventListener('load', initiate, false);
```

Listing 11-8: initiating the application

> **Do It Yourself:** Copy all the Javascript codes in Listings 11-3 to 11-8 in the file **indexed.js** and open the HTML document of Listing 11-1 in your browser. Using the form on the screen, insert the information about the movies listed at the beginning of this chapter. Every time a new movie is inserted, the same information will be shown in the box at the right of the form.

Listing Data

The `get()` method implemented in the code in Listing 11-7 only returns one object at a time (the last movie inserted). In this example, we are going to use a cursor to generate a list including all the movies stored in the **movies** Object Store.

Cursors

Cursors are the alternative provided by the API to retrieve and navigate through a group of objects returned by the database in a transaction. A cursor gets a specific list of objects from the Object Store and starts a pointer that points to one object of the list at a time

The API provides the `openCursor()` method to generate a cursor. This method extracts information from the selected Object Store and returns an IDBCursor object that has its own attributes and methods to manipulate the cursor:

> **continue()**—This method moves the pointer of the cursor one position and the **success** event of the cursor is fired again. When the pointer reaches the end of the list, the **success** event is also fired but the object returned is empty. The pointer can be moved to a specific position by providing an index value within the parentheses.
>
> **delete()**—This method deletes the object in the current cursor position.
>
> **update(value)**—This method is similar to `put()` but updates the value of the object in the current cursor position.

The `openCursor()` method also has attributes to specify the kind of objects returned and the order. The values by default return all the objects available in the selected Object Store in ascending order. We will see more of this later.

```
function initiate(){
  databox=document.getElementById('databox');
  var button=document.getElementById('save');
  button.addEventListener('click', addobject, false);
  if('webkitIndexedDB' in window){
    window.indexedDB=window.webkitIndexedDB;
    window.IDBTransaction=window.webkitIDBTransaction;
    window.IDBKeyRange=window.webkitIDBKeyRange;
    window.IDBCursor=window.webkitIDBCursor;
  }else if('mozIndexedDB' in window){
    window.indexedDB=window.mozIndexedDB;
  }
```

```
  var request=indexedDB.open('mydatabase');
  request.addEventListener('error', showerror, false);
  request.addEventListener('success', start, false);
}
function showerror(e){
  alert('Error: '+e.code+' '+e.message);
}
function start(e){
  db=e.result || e.target.result;
  if(db.version==''){
    var request=db.setVersion('1.0');
    request.addEventListener('error', showerror, false);
    request.addEventListener('success', createdb, false);
  }else{
    show();
  }
}
function createdb(){
  var objectstore=db.createObjectStore('movies',{keyPath: 'id'});
  objectstore.createIndex('SearchYear', 'date',{unique: false});
}
function addobject(){
  var keyword=document.getElementById('keyword').value;
  var title=document.getElementById('text').value;
  var year=document.getElementById('year').value;
  var transaction=db.transaction(['movies'],
IDBTransaction.READ_WRITE);
  var objectstore=transaction.objectStore('movies');
  var request=objectstore.add({id: keyword, name: title, date:
year});
  request.addEventListener('success', show, false);
  document.getElementById('keyword').value='';
  document.getElementById('text').value='';
  document.getElementById('year').value='';
}
function show(){
  databox.innerHTML='';
  var transaction=db.transaction(['movies']);
  var objectstore=transaction.objectStore('movies');
  var newcursor=objectstore.openCursor();
  newcursor.addEventListener('success', showlist, false);
}
function showlist(e){
  var cursor=e.result || e.target.result;
  if(cursor){
    databox.innerHTML+='<div>'+cursor.value.id+' -
'+cursor.value.name+' - '+cursor.value.date+'</div>';
    cursor.continue();
  }
}
window.addEventListener('load', initiate, false);
```

Listing 11-9: list of objects

Listing 11-9 shows the full Javascript code necessary for this example. Of all the functions used to configure the database, only **start()** presents a small change. Now when the version of the database is different from **null** (which means that the database has been already created) the **show()** function is executed. This function is now in charge of showing the list of objects stored in the Object Store, so if the database already exists you will see a list of objects in the box at the right of the screen as soon as the web page is loaded.

The big innovations of this code are in the **show()** and **showlist()** functions. Here, we are working with cursors for the first time.

Reading information from the database with a cursor is also an operation that has to be made through a transaction. So the first thing we do in the **show()** function is to generate a **READ_ONLY** transaction over the **movies** Object Store. This Object Store is selected as the one to be involved in the transaction and then the cursor is open over this Object Store with the **openCursor()** method.

If the operation is successful, an object is returned with all the information gotten from the Object Store, a **success** event is fired over this object and the **showlist()** function is executed.

To read the information, the object returned by the operation provides several attributes:

> **key**—This attribute returns the value of the key for the object in the current cursor position.
>
> **value**—This attribute returns the value of any property of the object in the current cursor position. The name of the property must be specified as a property of the attribute—for example, **value.year**.
>
> **direction**—The objects can be read in ascending or descending order; this attribute returns the current condition.
>
> **count**—This returns the approximate number of objects in the cursor.

In the **showlist()** function of Listing 11-9, we used the conditional **if** to test the content of the cursor. If no objects are returned or the pointer reaches the end of the list, then the object will be empty and the loop is over. However, when the pointer is pointing to a valid object, the information is shown on the screen and the pointer is moved to the next position with **continue()**.

It's important to mention that we don't have to use a **while** loop here because the **continue()** method fires the **success** event again, and the whole function is executed one more time until the cursor returns **null** and **continue()** is not called anymore.

> **Do It Yourself:** The code in Listing 11-9 replaces all the previous Javascript codes. Empty the file **indexed.js** and copy this new code. Open the template in Listing 11-1 and, if you didn't do it already, insert all the movies listed at the beginning of this chapter. You will see the complete list of the movies in the right box in ascending order according to the value of the **id** property.

Changing Order

There are two things we probably need to modify to finally get the list we want. All the movies in our example are listed in ascending order and the property used to organize the objects is **id**. This property is the **keyPath** for the **movies** Object Store, but it is not usually the value that our users will be interested in.

Considering this situation, we created another index in the **createdb()** function. The name of this additional index is **SearchYear** and the property assigned to the index is **date**. This index will let us order the movies according to the value of the year in which they were made.

```
function show(){
  databox.innerHTML='';
  var transaction=db.transaction(['movies']);
  var objectstore=transaction.objectStore('movies');
  var index=objectstore.index('SearchYear');

  var newcursor=index.openCursor(null, IDBCursor.PREV);
  newcursor.addEventListener('success', showlist, false);
}
```

Listing 11-10: descending order by year

The function in Listing 11-10 replaces the **show()** function of the code in Listing 11-9. This new function generates a transaction, then assigns the index **SearchYear** to the Object Store used in the transaction, and finally uses **openCursor()** to get the objects that have the property corresponding to that index (in this case, **date**).

There are two attributes we can provide to select and order the information returned by the cursor. The first attribute specifies the range to select the objects, and the second is one of the following constants:

> **NEXT**—The order of the objects returned will be ascendant (which is the value by default).
> **NEXT_NO_DUPLICATE**—The order of the objects returned will be ascendant and the duplicated objects will be ignored (Only the first object is returned if a duplicated keyword is found.).
> **PREV**—The order of the objects returned will be descendent.
> **PREV_NO_DUPLICATE**—The order of the objects returned will be descendent and the duplicated objects will be ignored (Only the first object is returned if a duplicated keyword is found.).

With the **openCursor()** method used in the **show()** function in Listing 11-10, we retrieved the objects in descending order and declared the range attribute as **null**. We are going to see how to build a range at the end of this chapter.

Do It Yourself: Take the previous code in Listing 11-9 and replace the `show()` function with the new function in Listing 11-10. This new function lists the movies on the screen by year in descending order (the newest first). The result should be the following:

id: tt1285016 **name:** The Social Network **date:** 2010
id: tt0111161 **name:** The Shawshank Redemption **date:** 1994
id: tt0086567 **name:** WarGames **date:** 1983
id: tt0068646 **name:** The Godfather **date:** 1972

Deleting Data

We have learned how to add, get and list data. It's time to provide the possibility to delete objects from the Object Store. As we mentioned previously, the method `delete()` provided by the API receives a value and deletes the object with the keyword corresponding to that value.

The code is simple; it only needs to create a button for every object listed on the screen and generate a **READ_WRITE** transaction to be able to perform the delete operation:

```
function showlist(e){
  var cursor=e.result || e.target.result;
  if(cursor){
    databox.innerHTML+='<div>'+cursor.value.id+' -
'+cursor.value.name+' - '+cursor.value.date+' <button
onclick="remove(\''+cursor.value.id+'\')">remove</button></div>';
    cursor.continue();
  }
}
function remove(keyword){
  if(confirm('Are you sure?')){
    var transaction=db.transaction(['movies'],
IDBTransaction.READ_WRITE);
    var objectstore=transaction.objectStore('movies');
    var request=objectstore.delete(keyword);
    request.addEventListener('success', show, false);
  }
}
```

Listing 11-11: deleting objects

The button added for every object in the `showlist()` function in Listing 11-11 has an inline event handler. Every time the user clicks on one of these buttons, the `remove()` function is executed with the value of the `id` property as the attribute. This function generates the **READ_WRITE** transaction first, and then using the received keyword, proceeds to delete the corresponding object from the `movies` Object Store.

At the end, if the operation is successful, the `success` event is fired and the `show()` function is executed to update the list of movies on the screen.

> **Do It Yourself:** Take the previous code in Listing 11-9, replace the `showlist()` function and add the `remove()` function from the code in Listing 11-11. Finally, open the HTML document of Listing 11-1 to test the application.

You will see the list of movies but now every line includes a button to delete the movie from the Object Store.

Searching Data

Probably the most important operation performed in a database system is search. The entire purpose of this kind of system is to index stored information to make it easier to find. As we studied earlier in this chapter, the `get()` method is useful to return one object at a time when we know the value of its keyword, but a search operation is usually more complex than that.

In order to get a specific list of objects from an Object Store, we have to pass a range as the first argument for the `openCursor()` method. The API provides the IDBKeyRange interface with several methods and properties to declare a range and limit the objects returned:

only(value)—Only the objects with the keyword corresponding to `value` are returned. For example, if we search movies by year using `only("1972")`, only the movie *The Godfather* will be returned from our list.

bound(lower, upper, lowerOpen, upperOpen)—To really create a range, we must have starting and ending values and must specify whether those values will be included or not in the list. The value of the attribute `lower` for this method specifies the starting point of the list. The `upper` attribute is for the ending point. And `lowerOpen` and `upperOpen` are boolean values to declared if the objects that matches exactly the values of the `lower` and `upper` attributes will be ignored. For example, `bound("1972", "2010", false, true)` will return the list of movies made from the year 1972 to the year 2010, but not including those made in 2010 (because the boolean value is `true` for the ending point and the movies made that year are not included).

lowerBound(value, open)—This method creates an open range that will start from `value` and go up to the end of the list. For example, `lowerBound("1983", true)` will return all the movies made after 1983 not including the ones made that year.

upperBound(value, open)—This is the opposite of the previous method. It will create an open range, but the objects returned will be from the beginning of the list to `value`. For example, `upperBound("1983", false)` will return the movies made before 1983 including those made that year.

Let's first prepare a new template to provide a form for searching movies:

```html
<!DOCTYPE html>
<html lang="en">
<head>
  <title>IndexedDB API</title>
  <link rel="stylesheet" href="indexed.css">
  <script src="indexed.js"></script>
</head>
<body>
  <section id="formbox">
    <form name="form">
      <p>Find Movie by Year:<br><input type="text" name="year"
id="year"></p>
      <p><input type="button" name="find" id="find"
value="Find"></p>
    </form>
  </section>
  <section id="databox">
    No Information available
  </section>
</body>
</html>
```

Listing 11-12: *search form*

This new HTML document provides a button and a text field to let us type the year and find movies according to the range specified in the code bellow:

```javascript
function initiate(){
  databox=document.getElementById('databox');
  var button=document.getElementById('find');
  button.addEventListener('click', findobjects, false);

  if('webkitIndexedDB' in window){
    window.indexedDB=window.webkitIndexedDB;
    window.IDBTransaction=window.webkitIDBTransaction;
    window.IDBKeyRange=window.webkitIDBKeyRange;
    window.IDBCursor=window.webkitIDBCursor;
  }else if('mozIndexedDB' in window){
    window.indexedDB=window.mozIndexedDB;
  }

  var request=indexedDB.open('mydatabase');
  request.addEventListener('error', showerror, false);
  request.addEventListener('success', start, false);
}
function showerror(e){
  alert('Error: '+e.code+' '+e.message);
}
```

```
function start(e){
  db=e.result || e.target.result;
  if(db.version==''){
    var request=db.setVersion('1.0');
    request.addEventListener('error', showerror, false);
    request.addEventListener('success', createdb, false);
  }
}
function createdb(){
  var objectstore=db.createObjectStore('movies', {keyPath:
'id'});
  objectstore.createIndex('SearchYear', 'date', { unique: false
});
}
function findobjects(){
  databox.innerHTML='';
  var find=document.getElementById('year').value;

  var transaction=db.transaction(['movies']);
  var objectstore=transaction.objectStore('movies');
  var index=objectstore.index('SearchYear');
  var range=IDBKeyRange.only(find);

  var newcursor=index.openCursor(range);
  newcursor.addEventListener('success', showlist, false);
}
function showlist(e){
  var cursor=e.result || e.target.result;
  if(cursor){
    databox.innerHTML+='<div>'+cursor.value.id+' -
'+cursor.value.name+' - '+cursor.value.date+'</div>';
    cursor.continue();
  }
}
window.addEventListener('load', initiate, false);
```

Listing 11-13: searching for movies

The **findobjects()** function is the most important in Listing 11-13. In this function, we generated a **READ_ONLY** transaction for the **movies** Object Store, opened the index **SearchYear** to use the **date** property as index, and created a range from the value of the variable **find** (the year inserted in the form). The method used for the range is **only()**, but you can test any other mentioned before. This range is passed as an argument to the **openCursor()** method. After a successful operation, the **showlist()** function will print on the screen the list of the movies that match the selected year.

The **only()** method returns only movies that match exactly the value of the variable **find**. To test other methods, you can provide your own values for the attributes—for example, **bound(find, "2011", false, true)**.

The **openCursor()** method can take the two possible attributes at the same time. Therefore, an instruction like **openCursor(range, IDBCursor.PREV)** is valid and will get the objects inside the range in descending order (using the same index as a reference).

> **IMPORTANT:** A full-text search feature is under consideration at this moment but it hasn't been developed or even included in the official specification yet. To get updated codes for this API, visit our website and follow the links for this chapter.

Quick Reference
IndexedDB API

The IndexedDB API has a low-level infrastructure. The methods and properties studied in this chapter are only part of what this API has to offer. With the purpose of simplifying the examples, we didn't follow any specific structure. However, this API, as well as others, is organized in interfaces. For example, there is a specific interface to deal with the database organization, another for the creation and manipulation of Object Stores, etc. Every interface includes its own methods and properties, and now we are going to present the information shared in this chapter following this official classification.

> **IMPORTANT:** The descriptions presented in this quick reference only describe the most relevant aspects of each interface. For the full specification, visit our website and follow the links for this chapter.

Environment Interface (IDBEnvironment and IDBFactory)

The Environment Interface, or IDBEnvironment, includes an IDBFactory attribute. Together these interfaces provide the elements necessary to operate databases:

indexedDB—This attribute provides a mechanism for accessing the indexed database system.

open(name)—This method opens a database with the name specified in its attributes. If no previous database exists, a new one is created using the name provided.

deleteDatabase(name)—This method deletes the database with the name specified in its attributes.

Database Interface (IDBDatabase)

The object returned after the opening or creation of the database is processed by this interface. For this purpose, the interface provides several methods and properties:

version—This property returns the value of the current version of the open database.

name—This property returns the name of the open database.

objectStoreNames—This property returns a list of the names of the Object Stores in the opened database.

setVersion(value)—This method sets a new version for the opened database. The `value` attribute can be any string we want.

createObjectStore(name, keyPath, autoIncrement)—This method creates a new Object Store for the opened database. The `name` attribute represents the name of the Object Store, `keyPath` is a common index for the objects stored in this Object Store and `autoIncrement` is a boolean value to activate a key generator.

deleteObjectStore(name)—This method deletes an Object Store with the name specified in its attribute.

transaction(stores, type, timeout)—This method initiates a transaction. The transaction can be specific for one or more Object Stores declared in the `stores` attribute, and it can be created for different access modes according to the `type` attribute. It can also receive a `timeout` attribute in milliseconds to specify the time the operation is allowed to take. For information on how to configure a transaction, see Transaction Interface in this Quick Reference.

Object Store Interface (IDBObjectStore)

This interface provides all the methods and properties necessary to manipulate objects in an Object Store.

name—This property provides the name of the Object Store currently in use.

keyPath—This property returns the `keyPath`, if any, for the Object Store currently in use.

IndexNames—This property returns a list of the names of the indexes created for the Object Store currently in use.

add(object)—This method adds an object to the selected Object Store with the information provided in its attributes. If an object with the same index already exists, an error is returned. The method can receive a keyword/value pair or an object containing several keyword/value pairs as attribute.

put(object)—This method adds an object to the selected Object Store with the information provided in its attributes. If an object with the same index already exists, the object is overwritten with the new information. The method can receive a keyword/value pair or an object containing several keyword/value pairs as attribute.

get(key)—This method returns the object with the index corresponding to `key`.

delete(key)—This method deletes the object with the index corresponding to `key`.

createIndex(name, property, unique)—This method creates a new index for the selected Object Store. The `name` attribute specifies the name of the index, the `property` attribute declares the property of the objects that will be associated with this index and the `unique` attribute indicates whether objects with the same index value are allowed or not.

index(name)—This method opens the index with the name specified in its attribute.

deleteIndex(name)—This method deletes an index with the name specified in its attribute.

openCursor(range, direction)—This method creates a cursor over the object of the selected Object Store. The `range` attribute takes a range object to determine which objects are selected. The `direction` attribute set the order of these objects. For more information about how to configure and manipulate a cursor, see the Cursor Interface in this Quick Reference. For more information about how to build a range, see the Range Interface in this Quick Reference.

Cursors Interface (IDBCursor)

This interface provides configuration values to specify the order of the objects selected from the Object Store. These values must be declared as the second attribute of the `openCursor()` method, as in `openCursor(null, IDBCursor.PREV)`.

NEXT—This constant determines an ascending order for the objects pointed to by the cursor (This is the value by default.).

NEXT_NO_DUPLICATE—This constant determines an ascending order for the objects pointed to by the cursor and ignores the duplicates.

PREV—This constant determines a descending order for the objects pointed to by the cursor.

PREV_NO_DUPLICATE—This constant determines a descending order for the objects pointed to by the cursor and ignores the duplicates.

The interface also provides several methods and properties to manipulate the objects pointed to by the cursor.

continue(key)—This method moves the pointer of the cursor to the next object on the list or to the object referenced by the `key` attribute, if it's present.

delete()—This method deletes the object currently pointed to by the cursor.

update(value)—This method updates the object currently pointed to by the cursor with the value provided in its attribute.

key—This property returns the value of the index for the object currently pointed to by the cursor.

value—This property returns the value of any property of the object currently pointed to by the cursor.

direction—This property returns the order for the objects read by the cursor (ascending or descending).

Transactions Interface (IDBTransaction)

This interface provides configuration values to specify the type of transaction that is going to take place. These values must be declared as the second attribute of the `transaction()` method, as in `transaction(stores, IDBTransaction.READ_WRITE)`.

READ_ONLY—This constant configures the transaction as a read_only transaction (This is the value by default.).
READ_WRITE—This constant configures the transaction as a read_write transaction.
VERSION_CHANGE—This type of transaction is used solely for updating the version number.

Range Interface (IDBKeyRangeConstructors)

This interface provides several methods to construct a range to use with cursors:

only(value)—This method returns a range with both the ending and starting point set to `value`.
bound(lower, upper, lowerOpen, upperOpen)—This method returns a range with the starting point set by `lower`, the ending point set by `upper` and whether this values will be excluded from the list of objects or not.
lowerBound(value, open)—This method returns a range starting from `value` and ending at the end of the object list. The `open` attribute determines whether the objects that match `value` will be excluded or not.
upperBound(value, open)—This method returns a range starting from the beginning of the object list and ending at `value`. The `open` attribute determines whether the objects that match `value` will be excluded or not.

Error Interface (IDBDatabaseException)

The errors returned by the database operations are informed through this interface.

code—This property represents the number of the error.
message—This property returns a message describing the error.

The value returned can also be compared with the following list to find the corresponding error.

UNKNOWN_ERR—value 0
NON_TRANSIENT_ERR—value 1
NOT_FOUND_ERR—value 2
CONSTRAINT_ERR—value 3

DATA_ERR—value 4
NOT_ALLOWED_ERR—value 5
TRANSACTION_INACTIVE_ERR—value 6
ABORT_ERR—value 7
READ_ONLY_ERR—value 11
RECOVERABLE_ERR—value 21
TRANSIENT_ERR—value 31
TIMEOUT_ERR—value 32
DEADLOCK_ERR—value 33

Chapter 12
File API

File Storage

Files are units of information that users can easily share with others. Users can't share the value of a variable, but they can surely make copies of their files and send them on a DVD, on portable memories or hard drives, through the Internet, etc. Files can store a large amount of data and be moved, duplicated or transmitted independently of the nature of their content.

Files were always an essential part of every application, but up to now there was no possible way to work with them on the web. The options were limited to downloading or uploading pre-existing files in servers' or users' computers. There was no file creation, copying nor processing on the web until HTML5 arrived.

The HTML5 specification was developed considering every aspect of the construction and operability of web applications. From design to elemental data structure, everything has been covered. And files couldn't be ignored. For this reason, the specification incorporates the File API.

The File API shares some characteristics with the storage APIs studied in previous chapters. The File API has a low-level infrastructure, although not as complex as IndexedDB, and it can work synchronously or asynchronously. The synchronous part was developed to be used on the Web Workers API, like IndexedDB and other APIs, and the asynchronous part is for normal web applications. These characteristics mean that we will have to take care of each aspect of the process, check for success or failure and probably adopt (or develop ourselves) simpler APIs built over it in the future.

The File API is an old API that has been improved and expanded. At this point, it is composed of at least three specifications—File API, File API: Directories & System, and File API: Writer—but this situation might change in the following months with the incorporation of new specifications or even the unification of some of them. Basically, the File API lets us interact with local files and process their content in our application, the File API: Directories & System extension provides the tools to work with a small file system created specifically for each application, and the File API: Writer extension is for writing content within files that were created or downloaded by the application.

Processing User's Files

Working with local files from a web application is dangerous. Browsers have to consider safety measures before even contemplating the possibility of letting applications have access to the user's files. In this respect, the File API provides only two loading methods: the **<input>** tag and the drag and drop operation.

In Chapter 8, we learned how to use the Drag and Drop API to drag files from desktop applications to a drop space in our web page. The **<input>** tag with the **file** type shares similar characteristics. Both this tag and the Drag and Drop API transmit files through the **files** property. Just as we did before, we just have to explore the value of this property to get every file that was selected or dropped.

> **IMPORTANT:** This API and its extensions are not working at this moment from a local host, and only Chrome and Firefox have implementations available. At the time of this writing, some of these implementations are so new that they only work in experimental browsers such as Chromium (www.chromium.org) or Firefox Beta. To run the codes of this chapter, you will have to upload every file to a server and test them in new browser versions.

Template

In this part of the chapter, we are going to use the **<input>** tag to select files, but you can always take advantage of the information in Chapter 8 to integrate these codes with the Drag and Drop API.

```
<!DOCTYPE html>
<html lang="en">
<head>
  <title>File API</title>
  <link rel="stylesheet" href="file.css">
  <script src="file.js"></script>
</head>
<body>
  <section id="formbox">
    <form name="form">
      <p>File:<br><input type="file" name="myfiles"
id="myfiles"></p>
    </form>
  </section>
```

```
<section id="databox">
   No File Selected
</section>
</body>
</html>
```

Listing 12-1: template to work with user's files

The CSS file includes styles for this template and others we are going to use later:

```
#formbox{
   float: left;
   padding: 20px;
   border: 1px solid #999999;
}
#databox{
   float: left;
   width: 500px;
   margin-left: 20px;
   padding: 20px;
   border: 1px solid #999999;
}
.directory{
   color: #0000FF;
   font-weight: bold;
   cursor: pointer;
}
```

Listing 12-2: styles for the form and the databox

Reading Files

To read users' files from their computer, we have to use the **FileReader** interface. This interface returns an object with several methods to get each file's content:

> **readAsText(file, encoding)**—To process the content as text, you can use this method. A **load** event is fired over the **FileReader** object when the file is loaded. The content is returned decoded as UTF-8 text unless the **encoding** attribute is specified. This method will try to interpret every byte or multi-byte sequences as text characters.
>
> **readAsBinaryString(file)**—The information is read by this method as a succession of integers in the range of 0 to 255. This method assures that each byte is read as it is, without any attempt to interpret it. It's useful to process binary content like images or videos.

readAsDataURL(file)—This method generates a base64 encoded data:url representing the file's data.

readAsArrayBuffer(file)—This method generates data as an ArrayBuffer from the file's data.

```
function initiate(){
   databox=document.getElementById('databox');
   var myfiles=document.getElementById('myfiles');
   myfiles.addEventListener('change', process, false);
}
function process(e){
   var files=e.target.files;
   var file=files[0];
   var reader=new FileReader();
   reader.onload=show;
   reader.readAsText(file);
}
function show(e){
   var result=e.target.result;
   databox.innerHTML=result;
}
window.addEventListener('load', initiate, false);
```

Listing 12-3: *reading a text file*

The input field of the HTML document in Listing 12-1 lets the user select the file to be processed. To detect the selection, in the `initiate()` function in Listing 12-3 a listener for the `change` event was added to the `<input>` element, and the `process()` function was set to handle the event.

The `files` property sent by the `<input>` element (and the Drag and Drop API, as well) is an array containing all the files selected. When the `multiple` attribute is not present in the `<input>` element, it is not possible to select multiple files, so the first element of the array will be the only one available. At the beginning of the `process()` function, we took the content of the `files` property, put it into the `files` variable and then select the first element of this array with the line `var file=files[0]`.

> **IMPORTANT:** To learn more about the `multiple` attribute, go to Chapter 6, Listing 6-17. You can also find an example of how to work with multiple files in the code from Chapter 8, Listing 8-10.

The first thing we have to do to process the file is to use the `FileReader()` constructor to get a `FileReader` object. In the `process()` function in Listing 12-3, we called this object `reader`. Next, we must register the `onload` event handler for `reader` to detect when the file to be read is loaded and is ready to be processed. Finally, the `readAsText()` method reads the file and gets its content as text.

When the `readAsText()` method finishes reading the file, the `load` event is fired and the `show()` function is called. This function takes the content of the file from the `result` property of the `reader` object and shows it on the screen.

This code, of course, is expecting text files, but the `readAsText()` method takes everything and interprets it as text, including files with binary content (for example, images). You will see a lot of crazy characters on the screen when a non-text file is selected.

> **Do It Yourself:** Create files with the codes in Listings 12-1, 12-2 and 12-3. The names for the CSS and Javascript files were declared in the HTML document as `file.css` and `file.js` respectively. Open the template in your browser and use the form to select a file from your computer. Try with text files as well as images to see how the content of these files is rendered on the screen.

> **IMPORTANT:** At this moment, the File API and every one of its specifications are being implemented by browser vendors. The codes in this chapter were tested on Chrome and Firefox 4, but the last release of Chrome had not yet implemented the `addEventListener()` method for `FileReader` and other objects. For this reason, we used event handlers in our examples, such as `onload`, every time it was necessary for the code to work properly. For example, `reader.onload=show` was used instead of `reader.addEventListener('load', show, false)`. As always, you will have to try the codes in every browser to find what implementations are ready to work with this API.

File Properties

In a real application, information such as the name of the file, its size or its type are necessary to inform the user about the files being processed or even to control the user's input. The file object sent by the `<input>` tag provides several properties for this purpose:

> **name**—This property returns the full name of the file (name and extension).
> **size**—This property returns the size of the file in bytes.
> **type**—This property returns the type of the file as a MIME type.

```
function initiate(){
  databox=document.getElementById('databox');
  var myfiles=document.getElementById('myfiles');
  myfiles.addEventListener('change', process, false);
}
```

```
function process(e){
  var files=e.target.files;
  databox.innerHTML='';
  var file=files[0];
  if(!file.type.match(/image.*/i)){
    alert('insert an image');
  }else{
    databox.innerHTML+='Name: '+file.name+'<br>';
    databox.innerHTML+='Size: '+file.size+' bytes<br>';

    var reader=new FileReader();
    reader.onload=show;
    reader.readAsDataURL(file);
  }
}
function show(e){
  var result=e.target.result;
  databox.innerHTML+='<img src="'+result+'">';
}
window.addEventListener('load', initiate, false);
```

Listing 12-4: *loading images*

The example in Listing 12-4 is similar to the previous one except this time we used the **readAsDataURL()** method to read the file. This method returns the file's content in data:url format that can later be used as the source for an **<img>** tag to show the selected image on the screen.

When we want to process a particular type of file, the first thing to do is to check the file's **type** property. In the **process()** function in Listing 12-4, we do the checking by taking advantage of the old **match()** method. If the file is not an image, the **alert()** method shows an error message. If the file is an image, the name and size of the file are shown on the screen and the file is opened.

Despite the use of **readAsDataURL()**, the opening process is exactly the same. The **FileReader** object is created, the **onload** event handler is registered and the file is loaded. Once the process is over, the **show()** function uses the content of the **result** property as source for an **<img>** tag and the image is shown on the screen.

> **Review the Basics:** To build the filter, we took advantage of Regular Expressions and the old Javascript method **match()**. This method searches for a match between the regular expression and the string, returning an array of matches or null. The MIME type for images is something like **image/jpeg** for JPG images, or **image/gif** for GIF images, so the expression **/image.*/i** allows only images to be read. For more information on Regular Expressions or MIME types, visit our website and follow the links for this chapter.

Blobs

In addition to files, the API works with other types of source called blobs. A blob is an object representing raw data. It was created with the purpose of overcoming Javascript limitations to work with binary data. A blob is usually generated from a file, but not necessarily. It's a good alternative to work with data without loading the entire file into memory, and it provides the possibility of processing binary information in small pieces.

A blob has multiple purposes, but it's focused on providing better ways to process big pieces of raw data or large files. To generate blobs from a previous blob or file, the API offers the `slice()` method:

> **slice(start, length, type)**—This method returns a new blob generated from another blob or a file. The first attribute indicates the start point, the second is the length of the new blob and the last one is an optional parameter to specify the type of data.

```
function initiate(){
  databox=document.getElementById('databox');
  var myfiles=document.getElementById('myfiles');
  myfiles.addEventListener('change', process, false);
}
function process(e){
  var files=e.target.files;
  databox.innerHTML='';
  var file=files[0];
  var reader=new FileReader();
  reader.onload=function(e){ show(e, file); };
  var blob=file.slice(0,1000);
  reader.readAsBinaryString(blob);
}
function show(e, file){
  var result=e.target.result;
  databox.innerHTML='Name: '+file.name+'<br>';
  databox.innerHTML+='Type: '+file.type+'<br>';
  databox.innerHTML+='Size: '+file.size+' bytes<br>';
  databox.innerHTML+='Blob size: '+result.length+' bytes<br>';
  databox.innerHTML+='Blob: '+result;
}
window.addEventListener('load', initiate, false);
```

Listing 12-5: *working with blobs*

> **IMPORTANT:** Due to inconsistencies with previous methods, a replacement of `slice` is being developed at this moment. Until the new method is available, to test the code of Listing 12-5 in latest versions of Firefox and Google Chrome you will have to replace `slice` by `mozSlice` and `webkitSlice` respectively. For more information, go to our website and follow the links for this chapter.

In the code in Listing 12-5, we did exactly the same we have done before, but this time (instead of reading the entire file) we created a blob with the `slice()` method. The blob is 1000 bytes long and starts from the byte 0 of the file. If the file loaded is smaller than 1000 bytes, the blob will be as long as the file (from the starting point to the EOF, or End of File).

To show the information retrieved by this process, we registered the `onload` event handler with an anonymous function to send a reference to the `file` object. This reference is received by the `show()` function, and the values of its properties are shown on the screen.

The advantages offered by blobs are countless. You can create a loop to generate several blobs from a file, for example, and then process this information part by part, creating asynchronous uploaders or image-processing applications, among others. Blobs provide new possibilities to Javascript code.

Events

The time it takes for a file to be loaded into memory depends on its size. For small files, the process looks like an instant operation, but large files can take several minutes to load. Besides the `load` event already studied, the API provides special events to inform every instance of the process.

> **loadstart**—This event is fired from the `FileReader` object when the reading starts.
> **progress**—This event is fired periodically while the file or blob is being read.
> **abort**—This event is fired in case the process is aborted.
> **error**—This event is fired when the reading has failed.
> **loadend**—This event is similar to `load`, but is fired either in success or failure.

```
function initiate(){
  databox=document.getElementById('databox');
  var myfiles=document.getElementById('myfiles');
  myfiles.addEventListener('change', process, false);
}
function process(e){
  var files=e.target.files;
  databox.innerHTML='';
  var file=files[0];
  var reader=new FileReader();
  reader.onloadstart=start;
  reader.onprogress=status;
  reader.onloadend=function(){ show(file); };
  reader.readAsBinaryString(file);
}
```

```
function start(e){
   databox.innerHTML='<progress value="0"
max="100">0%</progress>';
}
function status(e){
   var per=parseInt(e.loaded/e.total*100);
   databox.innerHTML='<progress value="'+per+'"
max="100">'+per+'%</progress>';
}
function show(file){
   databox.innerHTML='Name: '+file.name+'<br>';
   databox.innerHTML+='Type: '+file.type+'<br>';
   databox.innerHTML+='Size: '+file.size+' bytes<br>';
}
window.addEventListener('load', initiate, false);
```

Listing 12-6: using events to control the process

In the code in Listing 12-6, we created an application that loads a file and shows the progress of the operation through a progress bar. Three event handlers were registered for the **FileReader** object to control the reading process and two new functions were created to respond to these events: **start()** and **status()**. The **start()** function will initiate the progress bar to 0% and show it on the screen. This progress bar can use any value or range, but we decided to use percentages to make it easier to understand for the user. In the **status()** function, this percentage was calculated from the properties **loaded** and **total** returned by the **progress** event. The progress bar is recreated on the screen every time the **progress** event is fired.

> **Do It Yourself:** Using the template in Listing 12-1 and the Javascript code in Listing 12-6, try to load a large file, a video or a big data file to test the progress bar. If the browser doesn't recognize the **<progress>** element, the content of this element will be shown instead.

> **IMPORTANT:** We used **innerHTML** to add a new **<progress>** element to the document. This is not the recommended practice but it's useful and convenient for our example. Usually elements are added to the DOM using the Javascript method **createElement()** along with **appendChild()**.

Creating Files

The main File API is useful for loading and processing files from the user's computer, but it takes files that already exist in the hard drive. It doesn't contemplate the possibility of creating new files or directories. An expansion of this API called File API: Directories and System takes care of this issue. The API reserves a specific space in the hard drive, a special storage space, in which the web application can create and process files and directories just as a desktop application would do. The space is unique and only accessible with the application that created it.

> **IMPORTANT:** At the time of this writing, Chrome is the only browser that has implemented this expansion of the File API, but the browser is not reserving storage space. If you try to execute the following codes, a QUOTA_EXCEEDED error will be shown. To be able to use the File API: Directories and System, Chrome must be opened with the flag as follows: **--unlimited-quota-for-files**. To incorporate this flag in Windows, go to your desktop, click the mouse's right button over Chrome's icon, and select the Properties option. Within the opened window, you will see a Target field with the path and name of the Chrome file. At the end of this line add the flag **--unlimited-quota-for-files**. The path will end up something like this:
> C:\Users\...\Chrome\Application\chrome.exe --unlimited-quota-for-files

Template

To test this part of the API, we are going to need a new form with an input field and a button to create and process files and directories:

```
<!DOCTYPE html>
<html lang="en">
<head>
  <title>File API</title>
  <link rel="stylesheet" href="file.css">
  <script src="file.js"></script>
</head>
```

```
<body>
  <section id="formbox">
    <form name="form">
      <p>Name:<br><input type="text" name="myentry" id="myentry"
required></p>
      <p><input type="button" name="fbutton" id="fbutton"
value="Do It"></p>
    </form>
  </section>
  <section id="databox">
    No entries available
  </section>
</body>
</html>
```

Listing 12-7: new template for the File API: Directories and System

Do It Yourself: The new HTML document provides a new form but preserves the same structure and CSS styles. You just need to replace the previous HTML code for this one and copy the Javascript codes into the file `file.js` to test the following examples.

IMPORTANT: The `request` attribute was included in the `<input>` element, but it won't be considered in the codes of this chapter. To make the validation process effective, the Forms API has to be applied. Check the code in Chapter 10, Listing 10-5 to find an example of how to do it.

The Hard Drive

The space reserved for the application is like a sandbox, a small hard drive unit with its own root directory and configuration. To start working with it, first we have to request a `FileSystem` to be initialized for our application.

requestFileSystem(type, size, success function, error function)—This method creates the File System of the size and type specified in its attributes. The value of the `type` attribute can be either **TEMPORARY** or **PERSISTENT** according to how long the data should be preserved. The `size` attribute determines the space reserved in the hard drive for this File System in bytes. In case of error or success, this method will call the corresponding callback functions.

The `requestFileSystem()` method returns a File System object with two properties:

root—The value of this property is a reference to the root directory of the File System. This is also a `DirectoryEntry` object and has the methods assigned to this kind of object, as we will see later. By using this property, we are able to reference the storage space and work with files and directories.

name—This property returns information about the File System, such as the name assigned by the browser and its condition.

```
function initiate(){
   databox=document.getElementById('databox');
   var button=document.getElementById('fbutton');
   button.addEventListener('click', create, false);

   window.webkitRequestFileSystem(window.PERSISTENT, 5*1024*1024,
createhd, showerror);
}
function createhd(fs) {
   hd=fs.root;
}
function create(){
   var name=document.getElementById('myentry').value;
   if(name!=''){
      hd.getFile(name, {create: true, exclusive: false}, show,
showerror);
   }
}
function show(entry){
   document.getElementById('myentry').value='';

   databox.innerHTML='Entry created!<br>';
   databox.innerHTML+='Name: '+entry.name+'<br>';
   databox.innerHTML+='Path: '+entry.fullPath+'<br>';
   databox.innerHTML+='FileSystem: '+entry.filesystem.name;
}
function showerror(e){
   alert('Error: '+e.code);
}
window.addEventListener('load', initiate, false);
```

Listing 12-8: setting our own File System

IMPORTANT: Google Chrome is the only browser at this moment with a working implementation of this part of the API. Because the implementation is experimental, we had to replace the `requestFileSystem()` method by the Chrome specific method `webkitRequestFileSystem()`. Using this method you will be able to test the codes for this and the following examples in your browser.

By using the HTML document in Listing 12-7 and the code in Listing 12-8, we have our first application to work with new files in the user's computer. The code calls the `requestFileSystem()` method to create or get a reference to our File System. If this is the first visit, the File System will be created as permanent with a size of 5 megabytes (5*1024*1024). If that is successful, the `createhd()` function is executed, continuing with the initialization process. For errors, we use the simple `showerror()` function, as we did before for other APIs.

When the File System is created or opened, the `createhd()` function receives a `FileSystem` object and saves a reference in the `hd` variable with the value of the `root` property.

Creating Files

The starting process for the File System is over. The rest of the functions in the code in Listing 12-8 will create a new file and show the entry's data on the screen. When the "Do It" button is pressed in the form, the `create()` function is called. This function assigns the text inserted in the `<input>` element to the variable `name` and creates a file with that name using the `getFile()` method.

This method is part of the `DirectoryEntry` interface included in the API. The interface provides a total of four methods to create and handle files and directories:

> **getFile(path, options, success function, error function)**—This method creates or opens a file. The `path` attribute must include the name of the file and the path in which the file is located (from the root of the File System). There are two flags we can use to set the options for this method: `create` and `exclusive`. Both receive boolean values. The flag `create` indicates whether the file will be created or not, and the `exclusive` flag, when it is set to `true`, forces the `getFile()` method to return an error if we are trying to create a file that already exists. This method also receives two callback functions—for success or failure.
>
> **getDirectory(path, options, success function, error function)**—This method has exactly the same characteristics as the previous method but exclusive for directories.
>
> **createReader()**—This method returns a `DirectoryReader` object to read entries from a specified directory.
>
> **removeRecursively()**—This is a specific method to delete a directory and all of its content.

In the code in Listing 12-8, the `getFile()` method uses the value of the `name` variable to create or get the file. The file will be created if it doesn't already exist (`create: true`) or will be fetched otherwise (`exclusive: false`). The `create()` function also checks the value of the `name` variable before to execute `getFile()`.

The `getFile()` method uses two functions, `show()` and `showerror()`, to respond to success or failure. The `show()` function receives an `Entry` object and shows the value of its properties on the screen. This type of objects has several methods and properties associated that we will study later. For now, we are just using the `name`, `fullPath` and `filesystem` properties.

Creating Directories

The **getFile()** method (specific for files) and the **getDirectory()** method (specific for directories) are exactly the same. To create a directory from our template in Listing 12-7, we just have to replace the name of **getFile()** with **getDirectory()**, as shown in the following code:

```
function create(){
   var name=document.getElementById('myentry').value;
   if(name!=''){
     hd.getDirectory(name, {create: true, exclusive: false}, show,
showerror);
   }
}
```

Listing 12-9: using `getDirectory()` *to create a directory*

Notice that both methods are part of the **DirectoryEntry** object called **root**, that we are representing with the **hd** variable, so we always have to use this variable to call the methods and create files and directories in the File System of our application.

> **Do It Yourself:** Use the function in Listing 12-9 to replace the **create()** function in Listing 12-8 in order to create directories instead of files. Upload the files to your server, open the HTML document of Listing 12-7 in your browser and create a directory using the form on the screen.

Listing Files

As we mentioned before, the **createReader()** method allows us to get a list of entries (files and directories) from a specific path. This method returns a **DirectoryReader** object that contains the **readEntries()** method to read entries from a specific directory:

> **readEntries(success function, error function)**—This method reads the next block of entries from the selected directory. Every time the method is called, the success function returns an object with the list of entries or null when no entries were found.

The **readEntries()** method reads the list of entries by blocks. As a consequence, there is no guarantee that all the entries will be returned in one call. We will have to call this method until the object returned is empty.

There is another consideration we have to make before writing our next code. The **createReader()** method returns a **DirectoryReader** object for a specific directory.

To get the files we want, we have to get first the **Entry** object for the directory we want to read.

```
function initiate(){
  databox=document.getElementById('databox');
  var button=document.getElementById('fbutton');
  button.addEventListener('click', create, false);

  window.webkitRequestFileSystem(window.PERSISTENT, 5*1024*1024,
createhd, showerror);
}
function createhd(fs) {
  hd=fs.root;
  path='';
  show();
}
function showerror(e){
  alert('Error: '+e.code);
}
function create(){
  var name=document.getElementById('myentry').value;
  if(name!=''){
    name=path+name;
    hd.getFile(name, {create: true, exclusive: false}, show,
showerror);
  }
}
function show(){
  document.getElementById('myentry').value='';

  databox.innerHTML='';
  hd.getDirectory(path,null,readdir,showerror);
}
function readdir(dir){
  var reader=dir.createReader();
  var read=function(){
      reader.readEntries(function(files){
          if(files.length){
            list(files);
            read();
          }
      }, showerror);
  }
  read();
}
```

```
function list(files){
   for(var i=0; i<files.length; i++) {
     if(files[i].isFile) {
        databox.innerHTML+=files[i].name+'<br>';
     }else if(files[i].isDirectory){
        databox.innerHTML+='<span
onclick="changedir(\''+files[i].name+'\')"
class="directory">+'+files[i].name+'</span><br>';
     }
   }
}
function changedir(newpath){
  path=path+newpath+'/';
  show();
}
window.addEventListener('load', initiate, false);
```

Listing 12-10: File System application

This code will not replace Windows File Explorer, but at least provides all the information you need to understand how to build a useful File System in your browser. Let's analyze it part by part:

The **initiate()** function does the same as previous codes: it starts or creates the File System and calls the **createhd()** function if it's successful. Along with declaring the **hd** variable to reference the File System, the **createhd()** function also initializes the **path** variable with an empty string (representing the root) and calls the **show()** function to show the list of files on the screen as soon as the application is loaded.

The **path** variable will be used in the rest of the application to save the current path in which the user is working. For instance, you can see how the **create()** function was modified in the code in Listing 12-10 to use this value. Now, every time a new name is sent from the form, the path is added to that name and the file is created in the current directory.

As we said before, to show the list of entries we have to open the directory to be read first. Using the **getDirectory()** method in the **show()** function, the current directory is opened according to the value of **path**, and a reference to that directory is sent to the **readdir()** function if it's successful. This function keeps this reference in the **dir** variable, creates a new **DirectoryReader** object for the current directory and retrieves the list of entries with the **readEntries()** method.

In **readdir()**, anonymous functions are used to keep everything organized and within the same scope. First, **createReader()** creates a **DirectoryReader** object for the directory represented by **dir**. Next, a new function called **read()** is created dynamically to read the entries using the **readEntries()** method. The **readEntries()** method reads entries by blocks, which means that the method has to be called several times to be sure every entry available in the directory is retrieved. The **read()** function helps us accomplish this purpose. The process is as follows: at the end of the **readdir()** function, the **read()** function is called for the first time. Inside the **read()** function, we call the **readEntries()** method. This method uses another anonymous function as the success callback function to receive the **files** object and check its content. If this object is not empty, the `list()` function is called to show on the screen the entries already read, and the `read()` function is executed again to check for the next block of entries (The function calls itself until no more entries are returned.).

The `list()` function is in charge of rendering the list of entries (files and directories) on the screen. It takes the `files` object and checks for the characteristic of each entry using two other important properties of the `Entry` interface: `isFile` and `isDirectory`. As their names indicate, these properties contain boolean values to inform whether the entry is a file or a directory. After the condition of the entry is checked, the `name` property is used to show information on the screen.

There is a difference in how a file or a directory is shown on the screen. When an entry is detected to be a directory, it is shown through a `<span>` element with an `onclick` event handler that will call the `changedir()` function when the element is clicked. The purpose of this function is to set the new current path. It receives the name of the directory, adds the directory to the path and calls the `show()` function to update the list of entries on the screen. This feature lets us open directories and see the content with just a click of the mouse, exactly as a normal file explorer would.

This example doesn't contemplate the possibility of going backwards. To do that, we have to use another method provided by the `Entry` interface:

> **getParent(success function, error function)**—This method returns an `Entry` object of the directory containing the selected entry. Once you get the `Entry` object you can read its properties to obtain all the information needed about the parent of that particular entry.

How the `getParent()` method works is simple: let's suppose a directory tree such as **pictures/myvacations** was created and the user is listing the content of `myvacations` at this moment. To go back to `pictures`, you could provide a link in the HTML document with an `onclick` event handler registered to call a function that moves the current path to the new position. The function called by this event handler might be something like this:

```
function goback(){
    hd.getDirectory(path,null,function(dir){
        dir.getParent(function(parent){
            path=parent.fullPath;
            show();
        }, showerror);
    },showerror);
}
```

Listing 12-11: moving back to the parent

The `goback()` function in Listing 12-11 is changing the value of the `path` variable to point to the parent of the current directory. The first thing we do is to get a reference to the current directory using the `getDirectory()` method. If that is successful, an anonymous function is executed by this method. In the function, the `getParent()` method is used to find the parent of the directory referenced by `dir` (the current directory). If that is successful, this method executes another anonymous function to take the parent object and set the value of the current path to the value of its `fullPath` property. The `show()` function is also called at the end to update the information on the screen (show the entries in the new path).

Of course, this application can be extremely improved, but that's your homework.

> **Do It Yourself:** Append the function in Listing 12-11 to the code in Listing 12-10 and create a link in the HTML document to call this function (e.g., `<span onclick="goback()">go back</span>`).

Handling Files

We already mentioned that the `Entry` interface provides a set of properties and methods to get information and operate with files. You will find most of the properties available applied in previous examples. We already took advantage of the `isFile` and `isDirectory` properties to check the condition of an entry and we used the values of `name`, `fullPath` and `filesystem` to show information on the screen. The `getParent()` method studied in the previous code is also part of this interface. However, there are still a few more methods that are useful to perform regular operations for files and directories. Using these methods, we will be able to move, copy and delete entries just as in any desktop application:

> **moveTo(parent, new name, success function, error function)**—This method moves an entry to a different location in the File System. If the **new name** attribute is provided, the name of the entry will change to this value.
> **copyTo(parent, new name, success function, error function)**—This method makes a copy of an entry in another location of the File System. If the **new name** attribute is provided, the name of the new entry will change to this value.
> **remove**—This deletes a file or an empty directory (To delete a directory with content, we have to use the `removeRecursively()` method mentioned before.).

A new template will be necessary to test these methods. To simplify the codes, we are just going to provide two input fields for the origin and destination of every operation:

```
<!DOCTYPE html>
<html lang="en">
<head>
  <title>File API</title>
  <link rel="stylesheet" href="file.css">
  <script src="file.js"></script>
</head>
<body>
  <section id="formbox">
    <form name="form">
      <p>Origin:<br><input type="text" name="origin" id="origin"
required></p>
      <p>Destination:<br><input type="text" name="destination"
id="destination" required></p>
      <p><input type="button" name="fbutton" id="fbutton"
value="Do It"></p>
    </form>
  </section>
  <section id="databox"></section>
</body>
</html>
```

Listing 12-12: *new template to handle files*

Moving

The **moveTo()** method requires an **Entry** object for the file and another for the directory in which the file will be moved. So first we have to create a reference to the file using **getFile()**, then get the reference to the directory of destination using **getDirectory()** and finally apply **moveTo()** with this information:

```
function initiate(){
  databox=document.getElementById('databox');
  var button=document.getElementById('fbutton');
  button.addEventListener('click', modify, false);

  window.webkitRequestFileSystem(window.PERSISTENT, 5*1024*1024,
createhd, showerror);
}
function createhd(fs){
  hd=fs.root;
  path='';
  show();
}
function showerror(e){
  alert('Error: '+e.code);
}
```

```
function modify(){
   var origin=document.getElementById('origin').value;
   var destination=document.getElementById('destination').value;

   hd.getFile(origin,null,function(file){
      hd.getDirectory(destination,null,function(dir){
         file.moveTo(dir,null,success,showerror);
       },showerror);
     },showerror);
}
function success(){
   document.getElementById('origin').value='';
   document.getElementById('destination').value='';
   show();
}
function show(){
   databox.innerHTML='';
   hd.getDirectory(path,null,readdir,showerror);
}
function readdir(dir){
   var reader=dir.createReader();
   var read=function(){
      reader.readEntries(function(files){
          if(files.length){
             list(files);
             read();
          }
        }, showerror);
     }
   read();
}
function list(files){
   for(var i=0; i<files.length; i++) {
      if(files[i].isFile) {
         databox.innerHTML+=files[i].name+'<br>';
      }else if(files[i].isDirectory){
         databox.innerHTML+='<span
onclick="changedir(\''+files[i].name+'\')"
class="directory">+'+files[i].name+'</span><br>';
      }
   }
}
function changedir(newpath){
   path=path+newpath+'/';
   show();
}
window.addEventListener('load', initiate, false);
```

Listing 12-13: moving files

We used functions from previous examples to create or open our file system and show the list of entries on the screen. The only new function in the code in Listing 12-13 is **modify()**. This function takes the values of the origin and destination fields from the form and uses them to open the file from the origin first, and if that is successful, the directory of destination later. If both operations are successful, the **moveTo ()** method is applied over the **file** object and this file is moved to the directory represented by **dir**. If that's successful, the **success ()** function is called to clear the form fields and run the **show ()** function again to update the list of entries on the screen.

> **Do It Yourself:** To test this example, you need an HTML file with the template in Listing 12-12, the CSS file used since the beginning of this chapter, and a file called **file.js** with the code in Listing 12-13 (Remember to upload the files to your server before testing.). Create files and directories in your File System to have something to work with. You can use previous codes for this purpose. Use the form from the last HTML document to insert the values of the file to be moved (with the entire path from the root) and the directory to which the file will be moved (If the directory is in the root of the File System, you don't need slashes, only its name.).

Copying

Of course, the only difference between the **moveTo ()** method and the **copyTo ()** method is that the latter preserves the original file. To use the **copyTo ()** method, you just have to change the name of the method in the code in Listing 12-13. The **modify ()** function will end up like this:

```
function modify(){
   var origin=document.getElementById('origin').value;
   var destination=document.getElementById('destination').value;

   hd.getFile(origin,null,function(file){
     hd.getDirectory(destination,null,function(dir){
         file.copyTo(dir,null,success,showerror);
      },showerror);
    },showerror);
}
```

Listing 12-14: copying files

> **Do It Yourself:** Replace the **modify ()** function in Listing 12-13 with this one and open the template in Listing 12-12 to test the code. You must repeat the same procedure used for moving a file in order to copy it. Insert the path of the file to be copied in the **origin** field and the path of the directory you want to copy the file to in the **destination** field.

Deleting

Deleting files and directories is even simpler than moving and copying. All we have to do is get the **Entry** object for the file or directory we want to delete and apply the **remove()** method over that reference:

```
function modify(){
   var origin=document.getElementById('origin').value;
   var origin=path+origin;
   hd.getFile(origin,null,function(entry){
        entry.remove(success,showerror);
      },showerror);
}
```

Listing 12-15: deleting files and directories

The code in Listing 12-15 is only taking the value of the **origin** field from the form. This value, along with the value of the **path** variable, represents the path of the file we want to delete. So, using the **getFile()** method, we create the **Entry** object for that file and then apply **remove()** over it.

> **Do It Yourself:** Replace the **modify()** function in the code in Listing 12-13 with the new one in Listing 12-15. This time you only have to provide the value of the **origin** field to specify the file to be deleted.

To delete a directory instead of a file, the **Entry** object must be created for the directory using **getDirectory()**, but the **remove()** method works exactly the same. There is one situation we have to consider for directories though: if the directory is not empty, the **remove()** method will return an error. To delete a directory and its content altogether we have to use another method (mentioned previously in this chapter) called **removeRecursively()**:

```
function modify(){
   var destination=document.getElementById('destination').value;
   hd.getDirectory(destination,null,function(entry){
        entry.removeRecursively(success,showerror);
      },showerror);
}
```

Listing 12-16: deleting non-empty directories

In the function in Listing 12-16, we used the value of the **destination** field to indicate the directory to be deleted. The **removeRecursively()** method will erase the directory and its content in just one execution and call the **success ()** function if it is successful.

> **Do It Yourself:** The **modify ()** functions presented in Listings 12-14, 12-15 and 12-16 were made to replace the same function in Listing 12-13. To test these examples, take the code in Listing 12-13, replace the **modify ()** function for the one you want to try and open the template of Listing 12-12 in your browser. According to the method you are testing, you will have to provide one or two values from the form.

> **IMPORTANT:** If you have problems running these examples in your browser, we recommend that you use Chromium instead (www.chromium.org). The codes for this part of the API were tested in the last version available of Google Chrome.

File Content

In addition to the main File API and the File API's expansion we just studied, there is another important expansion called File API: Writer. This specification declares new interfaces for writing and adding content to files. It works along with the rest of the API by combining methods and sharing objects to achieve its goal.

> **IMPORTANT:** The integration between all the specifications involved in the File API caused debate about whether some interfaces proposed had to be moved from one API to another or not. For updates about this, you can find the links for every API reviewed in this book on our website or visit the W3C website at www.w3.org.

Writing Content

To write content into a file, we have to create a `FileWriter` object. These objects are returned by the `createWriter()` method of the `FileEntry` interface. This interface is an addition to the `Entry` interface and provides a total of two methods to work with files:

> **createWriter(success function, error function)**—This method returns a `FileWriter` object associated with the entry selected.
>
> **file(success function, error function)**—This is a method we are going to use later to read the file's content. It creates a `File` object (like the one returned by the `<input>` element or a drag and drop operation) associated with the entry selected.

The `FileWriter` object returned by the `createWriter()` method has its own methods, properties and events to facilitate the process of adding content to a file:

> **write(data)**—This is the method that actually writes content into the file. The content is provided by the `data` attribute as a blob.
>
> **seek(offset)**—This method sets the file position in which the content will be added. The value of the `offset` attribute must be declared in bytes.
>
> **truncate(size)**—This changes the length of the file according to the value of the `size` attribute (in bytes).
>
> **position**—This property returns the actual position in which the next writing will occur. The position will be 0 for a new file or different from 0 if some content was written into the file or the `seek()` method was applied previously.

length—This returns the length of the file.

writestart—This event is fired when the process starts.

progress—This event is fired periodically to report progress.

write—This event is fired when the data has been fully written.

abort—This event is fired if the process is aborted.

error—This event is fired if an error occurs.

writeend—This event is fired when the process is over.

There is another object we need to create in order to prepare the content to be added to a file. The **BolbBuilder()** constructor returns a **BlobBuilder** object with the following methods:

getBlob(type)—This returns the content of the **BlobBuilder** object as a blob. This is useful to create the blob we need for the **write()** method.

append(data)—This appends the value of **data** to the **BlobBuilder** object. The **data** attribute can be a blob, an ArrayBuffer or just text.

The HTML document in Listing 12-17 incorporates a second field to insert a text that will represent the content of the file. We are going to use this template for the following examples:

```
<!DOCTYPE html>
<html lang="en">
<head>
  <title>File API</title>
  <link rel="stylesheet" href="file.css">
  <script src="file.js"></script>
</head>
<body>
  <section id="formbox">
    <form name="form">
      <p>File:<br><input type="text" name="myentry" id="myentry"
required></p>
      <p>Text:<br><textarea name="mytext" id="mytext"
required></textarea></p>
      <p><input type="button" name="fbutton" id="fbutton"
value="Do It"></p>
    </form>
  </section>
  <section id="databox">
    No information available
  </section>
</body>
</html>
```

Listing 12-17: template to insert the file name and content

For the writing, we are going to open the File System, get or create the file with `getFile()` and insert content into the opened file with the values provided by the user using two different functions: `writefile()` and `writecontent()`.

> **IMPORTANT:** We tried to keep every code as simple as we can for learning purposes. However, you can always take advantage of anonymous functions to keep everything within the same scope (inside the same function), or use Object Oriented Programming for a more advanced and scalable implementation.

```
function initiate(){
   databox=document.getElementById('databox');
   var button=document.getElementById('fbutton');
   button.addEventListener('click', writefile, false);
   window.webkitRequestFileSystem(window.PERSISTENT, 5*1024*1024,
createhd, showerror);
}
function createhd(fs){
   hd=fs.root;
}
function showerror(e){
   alert('Error: '+e.code);
}
function writefile(){
   var name=document.getElementById('myentry').value;
   hd.getFile(name, {create: true, exclusive:
false},function(entry){
        entry.createWriter(writecontent, showerror);
     }, showerror);
}
function writecontent(fileWriter) {
   var text=document.getElementById('mytext').value;
   fileWriter.onwriteend=success;
   var blob=new WebKitBlobBuilder();
   blob.append(text);
   fileWriter.write(blob.getBlob());
}
function success(){
   document.getElementById('myentry').value='';
   document.getElementById('mytext').value='';
   databox.innerHTML='Done!';
}
window.addEventListener('load', initiate, false);
```

Listing 12-18: writing content

> **IMPORTANT:** As well as the `requestFileSystem()` method, Google Chrome has prefixed the `BlobBuilder()` constructor in the current implementation. You will have to use `WebKitBlobBuilder()` in this and following examples to test the codes in your browser.

When the "Do It" button is clicked, the information in the fields is processed by the functions `writefile()` and `writecontent()`. The `writefile()` function takes the value of `myentry` and uses `getFile()` to open or create the file. The `Entry` object returned is used by `createWriter()` to create a `FileWriter` object. If the operation is successful, the `writecontent()` function is called.

The `writecontent()` function receives the `FileWriter` object, and using the value of the `mytext` field, writes content into the file. The text must be first turned into a blob to be ready to use. For this purpose, the `BlobBuilder()` constructor is used to create a `BlobBuilder` object, the text is added to this object by the `append()` method and the content is retrieved as a blob with `getBlob()`. Now the information is in the appropriate format to be written into the file using `write()`.

All the process is asynchronous, which means the status of the operation is constantly informed by events. In the `writecontent()` function, we only listen to the **writeend** event (using the event handler **onwriteend**) to call the **success()** function and write the string "Done!" on the screen when the operation is successful. However, you can control the progress or check for errors by watching the rest of the events fired by the `FileWriter` object.

> **Do It Yourself:** Copy the template in Listing 12-17 into a new HTML file (This template uses the same CSS styles as in Listing 12-2.). Create a Javascript file called `file.js` with the code in Listing 12-18. Open the HTML document in your browser and insert the name and the text of the file you want to create. If the string "Done!" appears on your screen, the process was successful.

Adding Content

Because we didn't specify the position in which the content had to be written, the previous code will simply write the blob from the beginning of the file. To select a specific position or to append content at the end of an existing file, we have to use the **seek()** method.

```
function writecontent(fileWriter) {
  var text=document.getElementById('mytext').value;
  fileWriter.seek(fileWriter.length);
  fileWriter.onwriteend=success;
  var blob=new WebKitBlobBuilder();
  blob.append(text);
  fileWriter.write(blob.getBlob());
}
```

Listing 12-19: adding more content

The function in Listing 12-19 improves the previous `writecontent()` function by incorporating a **seek()** method to move the writing position to the end of the file. In this way, the content written by the **write()** method won't overwrite the existing content of the file.

To calculate the position at the end of the file in bytes, we used the **length** property. The rest of the code is exactly the same as in Listing 12-18.

> **Do It Yourself:** Replace the **writecontent()** function in Listing 12-18 with the function in Listing 12-19 and open the HTML file in your browser. Insert in the form the same name of the file you created using the previous code and the text you want to add at the end of this file.

Reading Content

It's time to read what we just wrote. The reading process uses techniques of the main File API specification, which we studied at the beginning of this chapter. We are going to use the **FileReader()** constructor and reading methods such as **readAsText()** to read and get the content of the file.

```
function initiate(){
   databox=document.getElementById('databox');
   var button=document.getElementById('fbutton');
   button.addEventListener('click', readfile, false);

   window.webkitRequestFileSystem(window.PERSISTENT, 5*1024*1024,
createhd, showerror);
}
function createhd(fs){
   hd=fs.root;
}
function showerror(e){
   alert('Error: '+e.code);
}
function readfile(){
   var name=document.getElementById('myentry').value;
   hd.getFile(name, {create: false}, function(entry) {
     entry.file(readcontent, showerror);
   }, showerror);
}
function readcontent(file){
   databox.innerHTML='Name: '+file.name+'<br>';
   databox.innerHTML+='Type: '+file.type+'<br>';
   databox.innerHTML+='Size: '+file.size+' bytes<br>';

   var reader=new FileReader();
   reader.onload=success;
   reader.readAsText(file);
}
```

```
function success(e){
   var result=e.target.result;
   document.getElementById('myentry').value='';
   databox.innerHTML+='Content: '+result;
}
window.addEventListener('load', initiate, false);
```

Listing 12-20: *reading a file from the File System*

The methods provided by the **FileReader** interface to read the content of a file, such as **readAsText()**, take a blob or take a **File** object as attribute. The **File** object represents the file to be read and is generated by the **<input>** element or a drag and drop operation. As we said before, the **FileEntry** interface provides the option to create this kind of object using a method called **file()**.

When the "Do It" button is clicked, the **readfile()** function takes the value of the **myentry** field and opens the file with that name using **getFile()**. The **Entry** object returned by this method if it's successful is represented by the **entry** variable and used to generate the **File** object with the **file()** method.

Because the **File** object is exactly the same object generated by the **<input>** element or a drag and drop operation, all the same properties used before are available and we are able to show basic information about the file even before the reading process is started. In the **readcontent()** function, the values of these properties are shown on the screen and the content of the file is read.

The reading process is an exact copy of the code in Listing 12-3. The **FileReader** object is created with the **FileReader()** constructor, the **onload** event handler is registered to call the **success()** function when the process is over and the file's content is read by the **readAsText()** method.

In the **success()** function, instead of printing a string as we did before, the file's content is shown on the screen. To do this, we take the **result** property's value of the **FileReader** object and print it in the **databox**.

> **Do It Yourself:** The code in Listing 12-20 takes only the value of the **myentry** field. Open the HTML file with the last template in your browser and insert the name of the file you want to read. It has to be a file you have already created or the system will return an error message (**create: false**). If the file's name is correct, the information and content of the file will be shown on the screen.

File System in Real Life

It's always good to see a real-life example that allows us to understand the potential of the concepts already studied. To end this chapter, we are going to create an application that combines several techniques of the File API with the possibilities of image manipulation provided by Canvas.

This example takes multiple image files and draws the images onto the canvas in a random position. Every change in the canvas element is saved in a file for further reading, so every time you access the application, the last work is shown on the screen.

The HTML document for this example is similar to the first template of this chapter. However, this time it includes a canvas element inside the **databox**:

```html
<!DOCTYPE html>
<html lang="en">
<head>
  <title>File API</title>
  <link rel="stylesheet" href="file.css">
  <script src="file.js"></script>
</head>
<body>
  <section id="formbox">
    <form name="form">
      <p>Images:<br><input type="file" name="myfiles"
id="myfiles" multiple></p>
    </form>
  </section>
  <section id="databox">
    <canvas id="canvas" width="500" height="350"></canvas>
  </section>
</body>
</html>
```

Listing 12-21: *new template with a* <canvas> *element*

The code for our example includes methods and programming techniques you are already familiar with, but the combination of specifications may be confusing at first. Let's list the code and analyze everything later step by step.

```
function initiate(){
  var elem=document.getElementById('canvas');
  canvas=elem.getContext('2d');
  var myfiles=document.getElementById('myfiles');
  myfiles.addEventListener('change', process, false);
  window.webkitRequestFileSystem(window.PERSISTENT, 5*1024*1024,
createhd, showerror);
}
function createhd(fs){
  hd=fs.root;
  loadcanvas();
}
function showerror(e){
  alert('Error: '+e.code);
}
function process(e){
  var files=e.target.files;
  for(var f=0;f<files.length;f++){
    var file=files[f];
    if(file.type.match(/image.*/i)){
      var reader=new FileReader();
      reader.onload=show;
      reader.readAsDataURL(file);
    }
  }
}
function show(e){
  var result=e.target.result;
  var image=new Image();
  image.src=result;
  image.addEventListener("load", function(){
    var x=Math.floor(Math.random()*451);
    var y=Math.floor(Math.random()*301);
    canvas.drawImage(image,x,y,100,100);
    savecanvas();
  }, false);
}
function loadcanvas(){
  hd.getFile('canvas.dat', {create: false}, function(entry) {
    entry.file(function(file){
        var reader=new FileReader();
        reader.onload=function(e){
            var image=new Image();
            image.src=e.target.result;
            image.addEventListener("load", function(){
                canvas.drawImage(image,0,0);
              }, false);
          };
        reader.readAsBinaryString(file);
      }, showerror);
  }, showerror);
}
```

```
function savecanvas(){
  var elem=document.getElementById('canvas');
  var info=elem.toDataURL();
  hd.getFile('canvas.dat', {create: true, exclusive: false},
function(entry) {
      entry.createWriter(function(fileWriter){
          var blob=new WebKitBlobBuilder();
          blob.append(info);
          fileWriter.write(blob.getBlob());
        }, showerror);
    }, showerror);
}
window.addEventListener('load', initiate, false);
```

Listing 12-22: canvas application using the File API

In this example, we are working with two APIs: the File API (with its extensions) and the Canvas API. In the `initiate()` function, both APIs are initialized. The drawing context for the canvas is generated first using `getContext()`, and the File System is requested later by `requestFileSystem()`.

As always, once the File System is ready, the `createhd()` function is called and the **hd** variable is initialized in this function with a reference to the root of the File System. This time, a call to a new function was added at the end of `createhd()` with the purpose of loading the file containing the image generated by the application the last time it was executed.

However, let's see first how this image is generated. When the user selects new image files from the form provided by the HTML document, the **change** event is fired by the <input> element and the `process()` function is called. This function takes the files sent by the input, extracts every **File** object from this array, checks whether the file is an image or not, and reads the content of every entry with the `readAsDataURL()` method, returning a value in data:url format.

As you can see, every file is read by the `process()` function, one at a time. If it's successful, the **load** event is fired and the **show()** function is called for each one of them. As a result, this function will process every image the user has selected.

The **show()** function takes the data from the **reader** object, creates a new image object with the **Image()** constructor and assigns the data as the source of that image with the line `image.src=result`.

When working with images, you always have to consider the time the image takes to be loaded. For this reason, after declaring the new source for the image object, we added a listener for the **load** event to be sure the image is fully loaded before processing its data. Once the **load** event is fired (the image was loaded), the anonymous function declared in the **addEventListener()** method is executed. This function calculates a random position for the image and draws it onto the canvas using **drawImage()** and a fixed size of 100x100 (Check the **show()** function in Listing 12-22 to follow the process.).

After the image is drawn, the **savecanvas()** function is called. This function will take care of saving the canvas' status every time it is modified, allowing the application to recover the last work the next time it is opened. A method from the Canvas API called **toDataURL()** is used to return the canvas content as data:url. A series of operations are performed in the **savecanvas()** to process this data. First, the data:url generated from the canvas is saved into the **info** variable. Then, the **canvas.dat** file is created (in case it doesn't exist) and opened with **getFile()**. If **getFile()** is successful, the entry is taken by an anonymous function and the **FileWriter** object is created by the **createWriter()** method. If it's successful, this method also calls an anonymous function where the value of the **info** variable is appended to a **BlobBuilder** object and the blob is written into the file with **write()**.

> **IMPORTANT:** This time we didn't listen to any event of the **FileWriter** object because there is nothing we want to do in case of success or failure. However, you can always take advantage of events to report status on the screen or to have absolute control of every part of the process.

OK, it's time to go back to **loadcanvas()**. We already mentioned that this function is called in the **createhd()** function as soon as the application is started. It has the purpose of loading the file with previous work and drawing it onto the canvas. At this point, you already know which file we are talking about and how it was generated, so now let's see the work performed by this function.

The **loadcanvas()** function is called from **createhd()** as soon as the File System is ready. Its work (as its name indicates) is to load the **canvas.dat** file to get the data:url generated the last time a modification occurred in the canvas element, and to draw its content. If the file doesn't exist, the **getFile()** method will return an error, but when the file is found, the method calls an anonymous function that will take the entry and use the **file()** method to generate a **File** object from it. This method, if successful, also calls an anonymous function to read the file and get its content as a binary string using **readAsBinaryString()**. The content we get from this file is a data:url string that has to be assigned as the source of an image before it can be drawn on the canvas. So, what we do inside the anonymous function called by the **load** event is to create the image object, declare the data:url from the file as the source of the image and (when the image is already loaded) draw it on the canvas with **drawImage()**.

The final effect is simple: the images selected from the **<input>** element are drawn on the canvas in a random position, and this work is preserved in a file. If the browser is closed, the file is loaded, the canvas is restored and our work is still there. It's not a really useful example, but you can see the potential, right?

> **Do It Yourself:** Using the Drag and Drop API you can drag and drop image files onto the canvas instead of loading the images from an **<input>** element. Try combining the code in Listing 12-22 with some codes from Chapter 8 to practice integrating these APIs.

Quick Reference
File API

Just as with the IndexedDB API, the features provided by the File API and its extensions are organized in interfaces. Every interface provides methods, properties and events that work combined with the rest to offer different alternatives to create, read and process files. In the following, we are going to present all the features already studied in this chapter in an order according to the official organization.

> **IMPORTANT:** The descriptions presented in this quick reference only describe the most relevant aspects of each interface. For a full specification, visit our website and follow the links for this chapter.

Blob Interface (File API)

This interface provides properties and methods to operate with blobs. This interface is inherited by the File Interface.

> **size**—This property represents the size of the blob or file in bytes.
> **type**—This property represents the media type of the blob or file.
> **slice(start, length, type)**—This method returns the part of the blob or file indicated by the values in bytes of the `start` and `length` attributes.

File Interface (File API)

This interface is an extension of the Blob Interface to process files.

> **name**—This property represents the name of the file.

FileReader Interface (File API)

This interface provides specific methods, properties and events for reading files and blobs into memory.

> **readAsArrayBuffer(file)**—This method returns a file or blob's content as an ArrayBuffer.
> **readAsBinaryString(file)**—This method returns a file or blob's content as a binary string.
> **readAsText(file)**—This method interprets a file or blob's content and returns it as a text.

readAsDataURL(file)—This method returns a file or blob's content as a data:url.

abort()—This method aborts the reading process.

result—This property represents the data returned by the reading methods.

loadstart—This event is fired when the read starts.

progress—This event is fired periodically to report reading status.

load—This event is fired when the reading is complete.

abort—This event is fired when the reading process is aborted.

error—This event is fired in case of failure.

loadend—This event is fired when the request is completed, either in success or failure.

LocalFileSystem Interface (File API: Directories and System)

This interface is provided to initiate a File System for the application.

requestFileSystem(type, size, success function, error function)—This method requests the initialization of a File System configured according to the value of its attributes. The `type` attribute can take two values: `TEMPORARY` or `PERSISTENT`. The size must be specified in bytes.

FileSystem Interface (File API: Directories and System)

This interface provides information about the File System.

name—This property represents the name of the File System.

root—This property references the root directory of the File System.

Entry Interface (File API: Directories and System)

This interface provides methods and properties to process entries (files and directories) in the File System.

isFile—This property is a boolean value indicating whether the entry is a file or not.

isDirectory—This property is a boolean value indicating whether the entry is a directory or not.

name—This property represents the name of the entry.

fullPath—This property represents the full path from the root of the File System to the entry.

filesystem—This property contains a reference to the File System.

moveTo(parent, new name, success function, error function)—This method moves an entry to a different location. The **parent** attribute represents the directory in which the entry will be moved. The **new name** attribute, if specified, changes the name of the entry in the new location.

copyTo(parent, new name, success function, error function)—This method makes a copy of the entry. The **parent** attribute represents the directory in which the copy of the entry will be created. The **new name** attribute, if specified, changes the name of the copy.

remove(success function, error function)—This method deletes a file or an empty directory.

getParent(success function, error function)—This method returns the parent **DirectoryEntry** of the selected entry.

DirectoryEntry Interface (File API: Directories and System)

This interface provides methods to create and read files and directories.

createReader()—This method creates a DirectoryReader object to read entries.

getFile(path, options, success function, error function)—This method creates or reads the file indicated by the **path** attribute. The **options** attribute is set by two flags: **create** and **exclusive**. The first one indicates whether the file will be created or not, and **exclusive**, when it is set to **true**, forces this method to return an error if the file already exists.

getDirectory(path, options, success function, error function)—This method creates or reads the directory indicated by the **path** attribute. The **options** attribute is set by two flags: **create** and **exclusive**. The first one indicates whether the directory will be created or not, and **exclusive**, when it is set to **true**, forces this method to return an error if the directory already exists.

removeRecursively(success function, error function)—This method deletes a directory and all its content.

DirectoryReader Interface (File API: Directories and System)

This interface provides the alternative to get a list of entries in a specific directory.

readEntries(success function, error function)—This method reads a block of entries from the selected directory. It returns **null** if no more entries are found.

FileEntry Interface (File API: Directories and System)

This interface provides methods to get a File object from a specific file and a FileWriter object in order to add content to the file.

> **createWriter(success function, error function)**—This method creates a FileReader object to write content into a file.
>
> **file(success function, error function)**—This method returns a File object that represents the selected file.

BlobBuilder Interface (File API: Writer)

This interface provides methods to work with blob objects.

> **getBlob(type)**—This method returns the content of a blob object as a blob.
>
> **append(data)** —This method appends data to a blob object. The interface provides three `append()` methods to append data as text, as a blob or as ArrayBuffer.

FileWriter Interface (File API: Writer)

The FileWriter interface is an expansion of the FileSaver interface. The latter is not described here, but the events listed below are part of it.

> **position**—This property represents the current position in which the next writing will occur.
>
> **length**—This property represents the length of the file in bytes.
>
> **write(blob)**—This method writes content in a file.
>
> **seek(offset)**—This method sets a new position in which the next writing will occur.
>
> **truncate(size)**—This method changes the length of the file to the value of the `size` attribute (in bytes).
>
> **writestart**—This event is fired when the write starts.
>
> **progress**—This event is fired periodically to report writing status.
>
> **write**—This event is fired when the writing is complete.
>
> **abort** – this event is fired when the writing process is aborted.
>
> **error**—This event is fired in case of failure.
>
> **writeend**—This event is fired when the request is completed, either in success or failure.

FileError Interface (File API and extensions)

Several methods in this API return a value through a callback function when the process fails. This value can be compared with the following list to find the corresponding error:

NOT_FOUND_ERR—value 1
SECURITY_ERR—value 2
ABORT_ERR—value 3
NOT_READABLE_ERR—value 4
ENCODING_ERR—value 5
NO_MODIFICATION_ALLOWED_ERR—value 6
INVALID_STATE_ERR—value 7
SYNTAX_ERR—value 8
INVALID_MODIFICATION_ERR—value 9
QUOTA_EXCEEDED_ERR—value 10
TYPE_MISMATCH_ERR—value 11
PATH_EXISTS_ERR—value 12

Chapter 13
Communication API

Ajax Level 2

This is the first part of what we call the Communication API. What is unofficially considered the Communication API is composed of the XMLHttpRequest Level 2, the Cross Document Messaging (Web Messaging API), and Web Sockets (WebSocket API). The first of these three communication technologies is an enhancement of the old XMLHttpRequest object used extensively up to now to communicate with servers and build Ajax applications.

The Level 2 of XMLHttpRequest incorporates new features such as cross-origin communication and events to control the evolution of the request. These improvements simplify scripts and provide new options, such as interacting with several servers from the same application or working with small pieces of data instead of entire files, to name a few.

The most important element of this API is, of course, the XMLHttpRequest object. A constructor was specified to create this object:

> **XMLHttpRequest()**—This returns an XMLHttpRequest object from which we can start a request and listen to the events to control the communication process.

The object created by the **XMLHttpRequest()** constructor has important methods to initiate and control the request:

> **open(method, url, async)**—This method configures a pending request. The **method** attribute specifies the HTTP method used to open the connection, such as **GET** or **POST**. The **url** attribute declares the location of the script that is going to process the request. And **async** is a boolean value to make the communication synchronous (**false**) or asynchronous (**true**). The method can also include values for the user and password when it's necessary.

send(data)—This is the method that actually initiates the request. There are several versions of this method in an XMLHttpRequest object to process different kinds of data. The **data** attribute may be omitted, declared as an ArrayBuffer, a blob, a document, a string, or a FormData.

abort()—This is a simple method to cancel the request.

Retrieving Data

Let's begin building an example to take information from a text file in the server using the **GET** method. We are going to need a new HTML document with a button to start the request:

```
<!DOCTYPE html>
<html lang="en">
<head>
  <title>Ajax Level 2</title>
  <link rel="stylesheet" href="ajax.css">
  <script src="ajax.js"></script>
</head>
<body>
  <section id="formbox">
    <form name="form">
      <p><input type="button" name="button" id="button" value="Do
It"></p>
    </form>
  </section>
  <section id="databox"></section>
</body>
</html>
```

Listing 13-1: *template for Ajax requests*

To make the codes as simple as possible, we are keeping the same HTML structure as always and applying some essential styles for visual purposes:

```
#formbox{
  float: left;
  padding: 20px;
  border: 1px solid #999999;
}
```

```css
#databox{
   float: left;
   width: 500px;
   margin-left: 20px;
   padding: 20px;
   border: 1px solid #999999;
}
```

Listing 13-2: *styles to shape boxes on the screen*

Do It Yourself: You need to create an HTML file with the template in Listing 13-1 and a CSS file called **ajax.css** with the rules in Listing 13-2. To be able to test the following examples, you will have to upload all the files, including the Javascript file and the file to which the request is made, to your server. We are going to provide more instructions in each example.

The code for this example will read a file in the server and show its content on the screen. No data is sent to the server; we just have to make a **GET** request and show the information retrieved.

```javascript
function initiate(){
   databox=document.getElementById('databox');

   var button=document.getElementById('button');
   button.addEventListener('click', read, false);
}
function read(){
   var url="textfile.txt";
   var request=new XMLHttpRequest();
   request.addEventListener('load',show,false);
   request.open("GET", url, true);
   request.send(null);
}
function show(e){
   databox.innerHTML=e.target.responseText;
}
window.addEventListener('load', initiate, false);
```

Listing 13-3: *reading a file*

In the code in Listing 13-3, we have our typical **initiate()** function. This function is called when the document is loaded. It creates a reference to the **databox** and adds a listener to the button for the **click** event.

When the "Do It" button is pressed, the **read()** function is executed. Here we can see in action all the methods studied before. First, the URL of the file to be read is declared. We didn't explain how to make cross-origin requests yet, so this file will have to be in the same domain (and in this example, also the same directory) as the Javascript code. In the next step, the object was created with the **XMLHttpRequest()**

constructor and assigned to the **request** variable. This variable is used next to add an event listener for the **load** event and use the **open()** and **send()** methods to start the request. Since no data will be sent in this request, the **send()** method is empty (**null**), but the **open()** method needs its attributes to configure the request. Using this method, we declared the request as **GET**, the URL of the file to be read and the type of operation (**true** for asynchronous).

An asynchronous operation means that the browser will continue processing the code while the file is being read. The end of the operation will be informed through the **load** event. When the file is finally loaded, this event is fired and the **show()** function is called. This function replaces the content of the **databox** by the value of the **responseText** property, and the process is over.

> **Do It Yourself:** To test this example, create a text file called **textfile.txt** and add some content to it. Upload this file and the rest of the files created with the codes of Listing 13-1, 13-2 and 13-3 to your server and open the HTML document in your browser. After clicking the "Do It" button, the content of the text file is shown on the screen.

> **IMPORTANT:** When the response is processed using **innerHTML**, the HTML and Javascript code are interpreted. For security reasons it is always better to use **innerText** instead. You will have to make that decision according to the demands of your application.

Response Properties

There are three different types of response properties we can use to process information returned by a request:

> **response**—This is a general purpose property. It returns the response to the request according to the value of the **responseType** attribute.
> **responseText**—This returns the response to the request as text.
> **responseXML**—This returns the response to the request as if it were an XML document.

Events

In addition to **load**, the specification includes other events for the XMLHttpRequest object:

> **loadstart**—This event is fired when the request starts.
> **progress**—This event is fired periodically while sending or loading data.
> **abort**—This event is fired when the request is aborted.
> **error**—This event is fired when an error occurs during the request.
> **load**—This event is fired when the request has been completed.

timeout—If a `timeout` value has been specified, this event will be fired when the request couldn't be completed in that specified period of time.

loadend—This event is fired when the request has been completed (either in success or failure).

Maybe the most attractive event of all is **progress**. This event is fired approximately every 50 milliseconds to inform about the state of the request. By taking advantage of **progress**, we can notify the user about every step of the process and create professional communication applications.

```
function initiate(){
  databox=document.getElementById('databox');

  var button=document.getElementById('button');
  button.addEventListener('click', read, false);
}
function read(){
  var url="trailer.ogg";
  var request=new XMLHttpRequest();
  request.addEventListener('loadstart',start,false);
  request.addEventListener('progress',status,false);
  request.addEventListener('load',show,false);
  request.open("GET", url, true);
  request.send(null);
}
function start(){
  databox.innerHTML='<progress value="0"
max="100">0%</progress>';
}
function status(e){
  if(e.lengthComputable){
    var per=parseInt(e.loaded/e.total*100);
    var progressbar=databox.querySelector("progress");
    progressbar.value=per;
    progressbar.innerHTML=per+'%';
  }
}
function show(e){
  databox.innerHTML='Done';
}
window.addEventListener('load', initiate, false);
```

Listing 13-4: informing the progress of the request

In Listing 13-4, the code uses three events, **loadstart, progress** and **load,** to control the request. The **loadstart** event calls the **start()** function to show the progress bar on the screen for the first time. While the file is being downloaded, the **progress** event will execute the **status()** function several times. This function informs about the progress through the `<progress>` element and the value of `ProgressEvent`'s properties.

Finally, when the file is fully downloaded, the `load` event is fired and the `show()` function shows the string "Done" on the screen.

> **IMPORTANT:** We used `innerHTML` to add a new `<progress>` element to the document. While it's useful and convenient for our example, this is not recommended practice. Usually elements are added to the DOM using the Javascript method `createElement()` along with `appendChild()`.

The `progress` event is declared by the specification in the `ProgressEvent` interface. This interface is common for every API and includes three valuable properties to return information about the process that is being monitoring by the event:

> **lengthComputable**—This is just a boolean value that returns `true` when the length of the progress is computable or `false` otherwise. We use it in our examples to be sure the values in the rest of the properties are valid.
>
> **loaded**—This property returns the total amount of bytes already downloaded or uploaded.
>
> **total**—This property returns the total size in bytes of the data to be downloaded or uploaded.

> **IMPORTANT:** Depending on your Internet connection, to see the progress bar working, you might have to use large files. In the code in Listing 13-4, we declared the URL as the name of the video used in Chapter 5 to work with the media API. You can use your own or download this file here:
>
> www.minkbooks.com/content/trailer.ogg

Sending Data

So far, we have been taking information from the server, but we haven't sent any data or even used another HTTP method than `GET`. In the following example, we are going to work with the `POST` method and a new object that allows us to send information using virtual form elements.

We didn't mention before how to send data through a `GET` method because, as usual, it's as simple as adding the values in the URL. You have to create a path for the `url` variable such as `textfile.txt?val1=1&val2=2` and the values are sent along with the request. The `val1` and `val2` attributes of this example will be read as `GET` variables at the server. Of course, a text file can't process that information, so usually you will have a PHP file or any other server-side script to receive these values. However, for `POST` requests, it is not that simple.

As you probably know, a `POST` request includes all the information sent by a `GET` method but also a message body. The message body allows us to send any type of information of any length we need. An HTML form is normally the best way to provide this information, but for dynamic applications this probably is not the best option or the most appropriate. To solve this issue, the API includes the `FormData` interface. This simple interface has just a constructor and a method to get and work with `FormData` objects.

> **FormData()**—This constructor returns a `FormData` object used by the `send()` method later to send the information.
>
> **append(name, value)**—This method adds data to the `FormData` object. It takes a keyword/value pair as attributes. The `value` attribute can be either a string or a blob. The data returned represents a form field.

```
function initiate(){
  databox=document.getElementById('databox');

  var button=document.getElementById('button');
  button.addEventListener('click', send, false);
}
function send(){
  var data=new FormData();
  data.append('name','John');
  data.append('lastname','Doe');

  var url="process.php";
  var request=new XMLHttpRequest();
  request.addEventListener('load',show,false);
  request.open("POST", url, true);
  request.send(data);
}
function show(e){
  databox.innerHTML=e.target.responseText;
}
window.addEventListener('load', initiate, false);
```

Listing 13-5: sending a virtual form

When information is sent to a server, it is with the purpose of processing it and producing a result. Usually this result is saved in the server and some information is returned to provide feedback. In our example in Listing 13-5, we are sending data to the `process.php` file and showing the information returned by that script on the screen.

To test this example, you can just print the values received by `process.php` with a code like the following:

```
<?PHP
  print('Your name is: '.$_POST['name'].'<br>');
  print('Your last name is: '.$_POST['lastname']);
?>
```

Listing 13-6: simple response for a POST request (`process.php`)

Let's see first how the information has been prepared for sending. In the **send()** function in Listing 13-5, the **FormData()** constructor was invoked and the **FormData** object returned was saved in the **data** variable. Two keyword/value pairs were added to this object with the names **name** and **lastname** using the **append()** method. These values represent form input fields.

The initialization of the request is exactly the same as in previous codes, except this time the first attribute for the **open()** method is **POST** instead of **GET**, and the attribute of the **send()** method is the **data** object rather than **null**.

When the "Do It" button is clicked, the **send()** function is called and the form created in the **FormData** object is sent to the server. The **process.php** file receives this data (**name** and **lastname**) and returns a text to the browser including this information. The **show()** function is executed when the process is over and the information received is shown on the screen through the **responseText** property.

> **Do It Yourself:** This example requires several files to be uploaded to a server. We are going to use the same HTML document and CSS styles in Listing 13-1 and 13-2. The Javascript code in Listing 13-5 replaces the previous one, and you also have to create a new file called **process.php** with the code from Listing 13-6. Upload all these files to a server and open the HTML document in your browser. By clicking the "Do It" button, you should be able to see on the screen the text returned by the **process.php** file.

Cross-Origin Requests

We have been working with scripts and data files in the same directory and the same domain, but XMLHttpRequest Level 2 lets us generate cross-origin requests, which means we are now able to interact with different servers from the same application.

The access from one origin to another must be authorized at the server. The authorization is made by declaring the origins allowed to access the application. This is done in the header sent by the server that allocates the file processing the request.

For example, if our application is located at www.domain1.com and we are accessing the **process.php** file of our example located at www.domain2.com, the second server must be configured to declare the origin www.domain1.com as a valid origin for an XMLHttpRequest call.

We can specify this configuration in our server's configuration files, or declare the header in the script. In the second case, the solution for our example is as simple as adding the header **Access-Control-Allow-Origin** to the **process.php** script:

```
<?PHP
  header('Access-Control-Allow-Origin: *');

  print('Your name is: '.$_POST['name'].'<br>');
  print('Your last name is: '.$_POST['lastname']);
?>
```

Listing 13-7: allowing multiple origin requests

The value * for the `Access-Control-Allow-Origin` header represents multiple origins. The code in Listing 13-7 may be accessed by any origin unless the value * is replaced by a specific origin—for example, `http://www.domain1.com` (This will only allow applications from www.domain1.com to access the script.).

> **IMPORTANT:** The PHP code in Listing 13-7 only adds the value at the header returned by the `process.php` script. To include this parameter in every header returned by the server, you have to modify the configuration files of your HTTP server. To find more information about it, check the links for this chapter in our website or follow the instructions for your HTTP server.

Uploading Files

Uploading files to a server is one of the major concerns for web developers. It's a feature required by almost every application online nowadays, but not contemplated by browsers. This API takes care of the situation by incorporating a new attribute to return an XMLHttpRequestUpload object to access all the methods, properties and events of an XMLHttpRequest objects but also to control the upload processes.

> **upload**—This attribute returns an XMLHttpRequestUpload object. The attribute must be called from an existent XMLHttpRequest object.

To work with this, we are going to need a new template with an `<input>` field to select the file to be uploaded:

```
<!DOCTYPE html>
<html lang="en">
<head>
  <title>Ajax Level 2</title>
  <link rel="stylesheet" href="ajax.css">
  <script src="ajax.js"></script>
</head>
```

```
<body>
  <section id="formbox">
    <form name="form">
      <p>File to Upload:<br><input type="file" name="myfiles"
id="myfiles"></p>
    </form>
  </section>
  <section id="databox"></section>
</body>
</html>
```

Listing 13-8: template to upload files

To upload a file, you have to use a file's reference and send it as a form field. The **FormData** object studied in the previous example is capable of handling this type of data. The system detects automatically the sort of information added to the **FormData** object and creates the proper headers for the request. The rest of the process is exactly the same as studied before in this chapter.

```
function initiate(){
   databox=document.getElementById('databox');

   var myfiles=document.getElementById('myfiles');
   myfiles.addEventListener('change', upload, false);
}
function upload(e){
   var files=e.target.files;
   var file=files[0];

   var data=new FormData();
   data.append('file',file);

   var url="process.php";
   var request=new XMLHttpRequest();
   var xmlupload=request.upload;
   xmlupload.addEventListener('loadstart',start,false);
   xmlupload.addEventListener('progress',status,false);
   xmlupload.addEventListener('load',show,false);
   request.open("POST", url, true);
   request.send(data);
}
function start(){
   databox.innerHTML='<progress value="0"
max="100">0%</progress>';
}
```

```
function status(e){
   if(e.lengthComputable){
      var per=parseInt(e.loaded/e.total*100);
      var progressbar=databox.querySelector("progress");
      progressbar.value=per;
      progressbar.innerHTML=per+'%';
   }
}
function show(e){
   databox.innerHTML='Done';
}
window.addEventListener('load', initiate, false);
```

Listing 13-9: *uploading a file with* FormData

The main function in the code in Listing 13-9 is **upload()**. This function is called when the user selects a new file from the **<input>** element on the template (when the **change** event is fired). The file selected is received and saved in the **file** variable, exactly the way we did before for the File API in Chapter 12 and also for the Drag and Drop API in Chapter 8. Every one of these methods returns the same File object.

Once we have a reference to the file, the **FormData** object is created and this file is added to the object by **append()**. To send this form, we started a **POST** request. First, a common XMLHttpRequest object is assigned to the request variable. Using the **upload** attribute, an XMLHttpRequestUpload object is created later and represented by the **xmlupload** variable. Using this new variable, we added event listeners for all the events fired by the upload process and finally the request is sent.

The rest of the code does the same than the example in Listing 13-4; in other words, a progress bar is shown on the screen when the upload process starts and then updated according to the progress of this process.

Real-Life Application

Uploading one file at a time probably is not what most web developers have in mind. Nor is using the **<input>** field to select the files for uploading. Usually every programmer wants their applications to be as intuitive as possible, and what a better way to do it than by combining techniques and methods that users are already familiar with. By taking advantage of the Drag and Drop API, we are going to create a real-life application to upload several files to the server at the same time just by dropping them into an area on the screen.

Let's create an HTML document with the drop box first:

```
<!DOCTYPE html>
<html lang="en">
```

```
<head>
  <title>Ajax Level 2</title>
  <link rel="stylesheet" href="ajax.css">
  <script src="ajax.js"></script>
</head>
<body>
  <section id="databox">
    <p>Drop Files Here</p>
  </section>
</body>
</html>
```

Listing 13-10: *dropping area to upload files*

The Javascript code for this example is probably the most complex we have seen so far. It not only combines two APIs but also works constantly with anonymous functions to keep everything organized and within the same scope (inside the same function). We have to take the files dropped into the **databox** element and list them on the screen, prepare the form with the file to be sent, make an upload request for every file and update each progress bar while the files are being uploaded.

```
function initiate(){
  databox=document.getElementById('databox');

  databox.addEventListener('dragenter', function(e){
e.preventDefault(); }, false);
  databox.addEventListener('dragover', function(e){
e.preventDefault(); }, false);
  databox.addEventListener('drop', dropped, false);
}
function dropped(e){
  e.preventDefault();
  var files=e.dataTransfer.files;
  if(files.length){
    var list='';
    for(var f=0;f<files.length;f++){
      var file=files[f];
      list+='<blockquote>File: '+file.name;
      list+='<br><span><progress value="0"
max="100">0%</progress></span>';
      list+='</blockquote>';
    }
    databox.innerHTML=list;

    var count=0;
```

```
    var upload=function(){
        var file=files[count];
        var data=new FormData();
        data.append('file',file);
        var url="process.php";
        var request=new XMLHttpRequest();
        var xmlupload=request.upload;

        xmlupload.addEventListener('progress',function(e){
            if(e.lengthComputable){
                var child=count+1;
                var per=parseInt(e.loaded/e.total*100);
                var
progressbar=databox.querySelector("blockquote:nth-
child("+child+") > span > progress");
                progressbar.value=per;
                progressbar.innerHTML=per+'%';
            }
        },false);
        xmlupload.addEventListener('load',function(){
            var child=count+1;
            var elem=databox.querySelector("blockquote:nth-
child("+child+") > span");
            elem.innerHTML='Done!';

            count++;
            if(count<files.length){
                upload();
            }
        },false);
        request.open("POST", url, true);
        request.send(data);
    }
    upload();
  }
}
window.addEventListener('load', initiate, false);
```

Listing 13-11: *uploading files one by one*

OK, it is not a nice code to follow, but it will be easier if we go step by step. As
always, everything starts from the **initiate()** function called as soon as the
document is loaded. This function creates a reference to the **databox** that will be our
drop box for this example and adds listeners for three events to control the drag and
drop operation. To know more about the Drag and Drop API, review Chapter 8.
Basically, the **dragenter** event is fired when the files that are being dragged enter the
area of the drop box, the **dragover** event is fired periodically while the files are over
the drop box, and the **drop** event is fired when the files are dropped into the drop box.
We don't have to do anything for **dragenter** and **dragover** in this example, so these
events are just canceled to prevent browser's default behavior. The only event we

respond to is **drop**. The listener for this event will call the **dropped()** function every time something is dropped into the **databox**.

The first line in the **dropped()** function also uses the **preventDefault()** method to do what we want to do with the files dropped and not what the browser would do by default. Now that we have absolute control over the situation, it is time to process the files dropped. First, we get the files from the **dataTransfer** object. The value returned is an array of files that we save in the **files** variable. To know for sure if files (and not another type of elements) were dropped in our drop box, we check the value of the **length** property with the conditional **if(files.length)**. If this value is different from 0 or **null**, it means that one or more files have been dropped and we can proceed.

Now it's time to work with the files received. With a **for** loop, we navigate through the **files** array and create a list of **<blockquote>** elements containing the file's name and a progress bar enclosed in **<span>** tags. Once the list is finished, the result is shown on the screen as the content of the **databox**.

It looks like the **dropped()** function does all the work, but inside this function, we created another one called **upload()** to take care of the uploading process for each file. So after being shown the files on the screen, the next action is to create this function and call it for every file in the list.

The **upload()** function was created using an anonymous function. Inside this function, we first select a file from the array using the **count** variable as an index. This variable was initialized to **0**, so the first time the **upload()** function is called the first file of the list is selected and uploaded.

To upload every file, we use the same method as in previous examples. A reference to the file is saved in the **file** variable, a **FormData** object is created using the **FormData()** constructor and the file is added to the object with the **append()** method.

This time, we only listen to two events to control the process: **progress** and **load**. Every time the **progress** event is fired, an anonymous function is called to update the status of the progress bar for the file that is being uploaded. To identify the **<progress>** element corresponding to that file, the **querySelector()** method with the **:nth-child()** pseudo-class was used. The index for the pseudo-class is calculated using the value of the **count** variable. This variable has the number of the index for the **files** array, but this index starts from **0** and the index used for the list of children accessed by **:nth-child()** starts from the value **1**. To get the corresponding index value to find the right **<progress>** element, we added **1** to the value of **count**, saved the result in the **child** variable and used this variable as index.

Every time the previous process is finished, we have to inform the situation and move to the next file in the **files** array. For this purpose, in the anonymous function executed when the **load** event is fired, we increased the value of **count** by **1** incrementally, replaced the **<progress>** element by the string "Done!" and called the **upload()** function again in case there are more files to be processed.

If you follow the code in Listing 13-11, you will see that, after declaring the **upload()** function, this function is called for the first time at the end of the **dropped()** function. Because the value of **count** was previously initialized to **0**, the first file of the **files** array will be processed first. Then, when the uploading of this file is over, the **load** event is fired and the anonymous function called to handle this event will increase the value of **count** incrementally by **1** and execute the **upload()** function again to process the next file in the array. At the end, every file dropped in the drop box will have been uploaded to the server, one by one.

Cross Document Messaging

This part of what we called Communication API is known officially as the Web Messaging API. Cross Document Messaging is a technique that allows applications from different origins to communicate with each other. Applications running in different frames, tabs or windows (or even other APIs) can communicate now by taking advantage of this technology. The procedure is simple: we post a message from one document and process this message at the target document.

Constructor

To post messages, the API provides the `postMessage()` method:

> **postMessage(message, target)**—This method is applied to the `contentWindow` of the Window object that receives the message. The `message` attribute is a string representing the message to be transmitted, and the `target` attribute is the domain of the target document (hostname or a port, as we will see later). The target can be declared as a specific domain, as any document with the * symbol or as the same as the origin using the / symbol. The method can also include an array of ports as a third attribute.

Message Event and Properties

The communication method is asynchronous. To listen to the messages posted for a particular document, the API provides the `message` event, which includes a few properties to return the information:

> **data**—This property returns the content of the message.
> **origin**—This returns the origin of the document that sent the message, usually the hostname. This value can be used to send a message back.
> **source**—This property returns an object to identify the source of the message. This value can be used to point to the sender and answer the message, as we will see later.

Posting a Message

For an example of this API, we have to consider the following: the communication process occurs between different windows (windows, frames, tabs, or other APIs), therefore we must provide documents and codes for each side. Our example includes a template with an iframe and the proper Javascript codes for each one. Let's start with the main HTML document:

```
<!DOCTYPE html>
<html lang="en">
<head>
  <title>Cross Document Messaging</title>
  <link rel="stylesheet" href="messaging.css">
  <script src="messaging.js"></script>
</head>
<body>
  <section id="formbox">
    <form name="form">
      <p>Your name: <input type="text" name="name" id="name"
required></p>
      <p><input type="button" name="button" id="button"
value="Send"></p>
    </form>
  </section>
  <section id="databox">
    <iframe id="iframe" src="iframe.html" width="500"
height="350"></iframe>
  </section>
</body>
</html>
```

Listing 13-12: main document with an iframe

As you can see, there are two **<section>** elements as in in previous templates, but **databox** this time includes an **<iframe>** that is loading the **iframe.html** file. We are going to get back to this later. Let's add a few styles to the structure:

```
#formbox{
  float: left;
  padding: 20px;
  border: 1px solid #999999;
}
#databox{
  float: left;
  width: 500px;
  margin-left: 20px;
  padding: 20px;
  border: 1px solid #999999;
}
```

Listing 13-13: styling the boxes (messaging.css)

The Javascript code for the main document has to take the value of the **name** input from the form and send it to the document inside the iframe using the **postMessage ()** method:

```
function initiate(){
   var button=document.getElementById('button');
   button.addEventListener('click', send, false);
}
function send(){
   var name=document.getElementById('name').value;
   var iframe=document.getElementById('iframe');

   iframe.contentWindow.postMessage(name, '*');
}
window.addEventListener('load', initiate, false);
```

Listing 13-14: *posting a message (messaging.js)*

In the code in Listing 13-14, the message was composed with the value of the **name** input. The * symbol was used as a target to send this message to every document running inside the iframe (no matter its origin).

Once the "Send" button is clicked, the **send()** function is called and the value of the input field is sent to the content of the iframe. Now it's time to take this message from the iframe and process it. We are going to create a small HTML document for the iframe to show this information on the screen:

```
<!DOCTYPE html>
<html lang="en">
<head>
   <title>iframe window</title>
   <script src="iframe.js"></script>
</head>
<body>
   <section>
      <div><b>Message from main window:</b></div>
      <div id="databox"></div>
   </section>
</body>
</html>
```

Listing 13-15: *template for the iframe (iframe.html)*

The template has its own **databox** that we can use to show the message on the screen and its own Javascript code to process this message:

```
function initiate(){
  window.addEventListener('message', receiver, false);
}
function receiver(e){
  var databox=document.getElementById('databox');
  databox.innerHTML='message from: '+e.origin+'<br>';
  databox.innerHTML+='message: '+e.data;
}
window.addEventListener('load', initiate, false);
```

Listing 13-16: processing messages in the target (`iframe.js`)

As we explained before, to listen to messages, the API provides the **message** event and some properties. In the code in Listing 13-16, a listener for this event was added and the **receiver()** function was set as the function to be called when the event is fired. This function shows the content of the message using the **data** property and information about the document that sent the message using the value of **origin**.

Remember that this code belongs to the HTML document for the iframe, and not the main document of Listing 13-12. These are two different documents with their own environment, scope and scripts: one is in the main browser window and the other one is inside the iframe.

> **Do It Yourself:** There are a total of five files that have to be created and uploaded to a server in order to test the example above. First, create a new HTML file with the code in Listing 13-12 for the main document. This document also requires the **messaging.css** file with the styles in Listing 13-13 and the **messaging.js** file with the Javascript code in Listing 13-14. The template from Listing 13-12 has an **<iframe>** element with the **iframe.html** file as its source. You will need to create this file with the code in Listing 13-15 and the corresponding **iframe.js** file with the code in Listing 13-16. Upload all the files to your server, open the first HTML document in your browser and send your name to the iframe using the form.

Filters and Cross-Origin

What we have done so far is not the best practice, especially considering security issues. The code in the main document is sending a message to a specific iframe, but not controlling which document is allowed to read it (Any document inside the iframe will be able to read the message.). As well, the code in the iframe is not controlling the origin and processing every message received. Both parts of the communication process must be improved to prevent abuse.

In the next example, we are going to correct this situation and show you how to answer a message from the target using another property of the message event called **source**.

```
<!DOCTYPE html>
<html lang="en">
<head>
  <title>Cross Document Messaging</title>
  <link rel="stylesheet" href="messaging.css">
  <script src="messaging.js"></script>
</head>
<body>
  <section id="formbox">
    <form name="form">
      <p>Your name: <input type="text" name="name" id="name"
required></p>
      <p><input type="button" name="button" id="button"
value="Send"></p>
    </form>
  </section>
  <section id="databox">
    <iframe id="iframe" src="http://www.domain2.com/iframe.html"
width="500" height="350"></iframe>
  </section>
</body>
</html>
```

Listing 13-17: communicating to specific origins/targets

Suppose that the new HTML document with the code in Listing 13-17 is located at www.domain1.com, but if you check the code you will see that the iframe is loading a file from a second location at www.domain2.com. To prevent abuse, you will have to declare these locations in your Javascript codes and be specific about who is able to read a message and from where.

In the code in Listing 13-17, we are not just providing the HTML file for the source of the iframe as we did before; we are now declaring the entire path to a different location (www.domain2.com). The main document will be at www.domain1.com and the iframe's content will be at www.domain2.com. The following codes consider this situation:

```
function initiate(){
  var button=document.getElementById('button');
  button.addEventListener('click', send, false);

  window.addEventListener('message', receiver, false);
}
function send(){
  var name=document.getElementById('name').value;
  var iframe=document.getElementById('iframe');
  iframe.contentWindow.postMessage(name,
'http://www.domain2.com');
}
```

```
function receiver(e){
   if(e.origin=='http://www.domain2.com'){
     document.getElementById('name').value=e.data;
   }
}
window.addEventListener('load', initiate, false);
```

Listing 13-18: communicating to specific origins

Pay attention to the **send()** function in the code in Listing 13-18. The **postMessage()** method is now declaring the specific target for the message (www.domain2.com). Only documents inside the iframe and from that specific origin will be able to read this message.

In the **initiate()** function on the code in Listing 13-18, we also added a listener for the **message** event. The purpose of this event listener and the **receiver()** function in this code is to listen to the answer sent by the document in the iframe. This will make sense later.

So let's look at the code for the iframe to see how a message from a specific origin is processed and how we answered this message (We are going to use exactly the same HTML document of Listing 13-15 for the iframe.).

```
function initiate(){
   window.addEventListener('message', receiver, false);
}
function receiver(e){
   var databox=document.getElementById('databox');
   if(e.origin=='http://www.domain1.com'){
     databox.innerHTML='valid message: '+e.data;
     e.source.postMessage('message received', e.origin);
   }else{
     databox.innerHTML='invalid origin';
   }
}
window.addEventListener('load', initiate, false);
```

Listing 13-19: responding to the main document (`iframe.js`)

The filter for the origin is as simple as comparing the value of the **origin** property with the domain we want to read messages from. Once the origin proves to be valid, the message is shown on the screen and then an answer is sent back using the value of the **source** property. The **origin** property is also used to declare this answer only available for the window that sent the message. Now, you can go back to Listing 13-18 and check how the **receiver()** function will process this answer.

> **Do It Yourself:** This example is a little bit tricky. We are using two different origins, so you need two different domains (or subdomains) to test the codes. Replace the domains in the codes for yours and then upload the codes for the

main document to one domain and the codes for the iframe to the other one. The main document will load in the iframe the code from the second domain and you will be able to see how the communication process works between these two different origins.

Web Sockets

In this part of the chapter, we are going to describe the last component of what we consider the Communication API. The WebSocket API provides connection support for faster and more effective two-way communication between browsers and servers. The connection is made through a TCP socket, without sending HTTP headers, thus reducing the size of data transmitted in every call. The connection is also persistent, thus allowing servers to keep clients updated without a previous request, which means we don't have to call the server for updates. Instead, the server itself automatically sends us information about the current condition.

WebSocket might be thought as an improved version of Ajax, but it is a totally different alternative for communication that allows the construction of real-time applications in a scalable platform—for example, multiplayer video games, chat rooms.

The Javascript API is simple; just a few methods and events are included to open and close the connection and send and listen for messages. However, no server supports this new protocol by default, so we have to install our own WS server (WebSocket server) to be able to establish communication between the browser and the server that allocates our application.

WS Server Configuration

If you are a savvy programmer probably you can figure out how to build your own WS server script, but for those who want to spend their time on something else, there are several scripts already available to configure a WS server and have your server ready to process WS connections. Depending on your own preferences, you can opt for scripts made on PHP, Java, Ruby, and others. For a complete list, visit our website and follow the links for this chapter.

> **IMPORTANT:** At the time of writing, the specification is being enhanced due to security concerns and there are no available libraries implementing these improvements. For this reason, the phpwebsocket library we are proposing to use now only works on Chrome and probably will be out of date when you read these lines. We recommend you check our website for links or search the web for new WS servers available.

Because the selection and configuration of a WS server depends on the configuration of your server, we are going to test our examples using XAMPP and a PHP script. XAMPP is an easy-to-install Apache server that includes all the applications you need to run PHP scripts in your own computer. To download and install XAMPP, go to:
www.apachefriends.org/en/xampp.html

Once you have XAMPP installed, you need to get the PHP script to run the WS server. There are several versions, but for the purposes of our test, we are going to use phpwebsocket available at http://code.google.com/p/phpwebsocket/.

> **Do It Yourself:** Go to www.apachefriends.org/en/xampp.html in order to download and install the version of the software for your operating system. You will also need the **server.php** file available at http://code.google.com/p/phpwebsocket/. Copy the file in the **htdocs** directory generated by XAMPP (This directory will be your localhost and allocate all the files you need to run.). We are not going to modify this file to simplify our codes, but you can always try to adapt it to your purposes or even avoid this procedure and use the API to access your own WS server.

WebSocket uses a persistent connection, so the script for the WS server has to be running all the time, capturing requests and sending updates to users. To run the PHP file to start the WS server, you have to open the XAMPP control panel and run the Shell application (There is usually a "Shell" button at the top.). In the opened console, you have to find the **htdocs** directory where you saved the **server.php** file and run this command: **php -q server.php** (In Windows, the console is operated by DOS commands: to select a directory, use the command **CD**, and to list the content, use **DIR**.).

The WS server is now running and ready. Because this is running in your computer, you have to access the files through the localhost. To run our examples, you will have to copy every file into the **htdocs** directory and open the HTML templates in your browser using the host http://localhost/ (for example, http://localhost/example.html).

Constructor

Before programming our code to interact with the WS server, let see what the API provides for this purpose. The specification declares only one interface with a few methods, properties and events, plus a constructor to set the connection:

> **WebSocket(url)**—This constructor starts a connection between the application and the WS server targeted by the **url** attribute. It returns a WebSocket object referencing this connection. A second attribute may be specified to provide an array with communication sub-protocols.

Methods

The connection is initiated by the constructor, so there are only two methods to work with it:

send(data)—This is the method necessary to send a message to the WS server. The `data` attribute represents a string with the information to be transmitted.

close()—This is the method to close the connection.

Properties

A few properties let us know about the connection's configuration and status:

url—It shows the URL to which the application is connected.

protocol—This returns the sub-protocol used, if any.

readyState—This returns a number representing the state of the connection: 0 meaning that the connection has not been established yet, 1 meaning the connection is opened, 2 meaning the connection is being closed and 3 meaning the connection was closed.

bufferedAmount—This is a very useful property that allows us to know the data requested but not yet sent to the server. The value returned helps us regulate the amount of data and frequency of the requests in order not to saturate the server.

Events

To know the status of the connection and listen to messages sent by the server, we have to use events. The API provides the following:

open—This event is fired when the connection is opened.

message—This event is fired when there is a message from the server available.

error—This event is fired when an error occurs.

close—This event is fired when the connection is closed.

Template

The `server.php` file offered on Google Codes has a `process()` function that processes a small list of predefined commands and sends back the proper answer. For testing purposes, we are going to use a form to insert and send these commands to the server:

```
<!DOCTYPE html>
<html lang="en">
<head>
  <title>WebSocket</title>
  <link rel="stylesheet" href="websocket.css">
  <script src="websocket.js"></script>
</head>
```

```
<body>
  <section id="formbox">
    <form name="form">
      <p>Command:<br><input type="text" name="command"
id="command"></p>
      <p><input type="button" name="button" id="button"
value="Send"></p>
    </form>
  </section>
  <section id="databox"></section>
</body>
</html>
```

Listing 13-20: *inserting commands*

We will also create a CSS file with the following styles and the name
websocket.css:

```
#formbox{
  float: left;
  padding: 20px;
  border: 1px solid #999999;
}
#databox{
  float: left;
  width: 500px;
  height: 350px;
  overflow: auto;
  margin-left: 20px;
  padding: 20px;
  border: 1px solid #999999;
}
```

Listing 13-21: *the usual styles for the boxes*

Start Communication

As always, the Javascript code is responsible for the entire process. Let's create our first
communication application to check how the API works:

```
function initiate(){
  databox=document.getElementById('databox');
  var button=document.getElementById('button');
  button.addEventListener('click', send, false);

  socket=new WebSocket("ws://localhost:12345/server.php");
  socket.addEventListener('message', received, false);
}
```

```
function received(e){
  var list=databox.innerHTML;
  databox.innerHTML='Received: '+e.data+'<br>'+list;
}
function send(){
  var command=document.getElementById('command').value;
  socket.send(command);
}
window.addEventListener('load', initiate, false);
```

Listing 13-22: sending messages to the server

In the **intiate()** function, the WebSocket object is constructed and saved in the **socket** variable. The **url** attribute points to the location of the **server.php** file in our localhost. Also, the port of connection is declared in this URL. Usually the host is specified with the IP number of the server, and the value of the port is 8000 or 8080, but that depends or your needs, the configuration of your server, the ports available, the location of the file in your server, etc. The use of the IP instead of a domain is intended to avoid DNS translation (You should always use this technique to access your application to avoid the time spend by the network translating the domain into the correspondent IP address.).

After we get the WebSocket object, a listener for the **message** event is added to this object. The **message** event will be fired every time the WS server sends a message to the browser and the **received()** function will be called to handle the event. As in other Communication APIs, this event includes the **data** property that holds the content of the message. In the **received()** function, we use it to show the message on the screen.

To send messages to the server, we included the **send()** function. The value of the <input> element named **command** is taken by this function and sent to the WS server using the **send()** method.

> **IMPORTANT:** The **server.php** file has the **process()** function to process every call and send back an answer. You can change this function to satisfy your needs, but for our examples we kept it as it's offered at Google Codes. The function is checking the message received and compares its value with a list of predefined commands. The commands available in the version we used to test these examples are **hello**, **hi**, **name**, **age**, **date**, **time**, **thanks**, and **bye**. For instance, if you send the message "hello", the server will send back the message "hello human".

Full Application

In our first example, you can easily see how the communication process works for this API. The connection is started by the WebSocket constructor, the **send()** method sends every message we want to be processed by the server and the **message** event will inform the application of the arrival of new messages from this server. However, we didn't close the connection, check for errors or even detect when the connection was ready to work. Let's now see an example that takes advantage of all the events provided by this API to inform about the status of the connection at every step of the process.

```
function initiate(){
    databox=document.getElementById('databox');
    var button=document.getElementById('button');
    button.addEventListener('click', send, false);

    socket=new WebSocket("ws://localhost:12345/server.php");
    socket.addEventListener('open', opened, false);
    socket.addEventListener('message', received, false);
    socket.addEventListener('close', closed, false);
    socket.addEventListener('error', error, false);
}
function opened(){
    databox.innerHTML='CONNECTION OPENED<br>';
    databox.innerHTML+='Status: '+socket.readyState;
}
function received(e){
    var list=databox.innerHTML;
    databox.innerHTML='Received: '+e.data+'<br>'+list;
}
function closed(){
    var list=databox.innerHTML;
    databox.innerHTML='CONNECTION CLOSED<br>'+list;

    var button=document.getElementById('button');
    button.disabled=true;
}
function error(){
    var list=databox.innerHTML;
    databox.innerHTML='ERROR<br>'+list;
}
function send(){
    var command=document.getElementById('command').value;
    if(command=='close'){
        socket.close();
    }else{
        socket.send(command);
    }
}
window.addEventListener('load', initiate, false);
```

Listing 13-23: *informing state of the connection*

There are a few improvements in the code in Listing 13-23 from the previous example. Listeners for all the events available in the WebSocket object were added and the proper functions to handle the events were created. We also show the status when the connection is opened using the value of the **readyState** property, close the connection using the `close()` method when the "close" command is sent from the form and disable the "Send" button when the connection is closed (`button.disabled=true`).

> **Do It Yourself:** This last example requires the HTML document and CSS styles in Listings 13-20 and 13-21. Copy all these files to the `htdocs` directory created by the XAMPP application and start the Shell console clicking on the "Shell" button at the XAMPP control panel. In the console, you have to find the `htdocs` directory and run the PHP server with the command: `php -q server.php`. Open your browser and go to http://localhost/client.html (where client.html is the name of your HTML file with the document of Listing 13-20). Insert commands in the form and press the "Send" button. You should get answers from the server according to the command inserted (`hello`, `hi`, `name`, `age`, `date`, `time`, `thanks`, and `bye`). Send the command "close" to close the connection.

> **IMPORTANT:** At this moment, the `server.php` file from Google Codes is not working properly. It doesn't implement the new security measures and probably you will have to refresh your HTML page several times in order to get the message "Connection Opened" and be able to start sending messages. To find new WS servers available, go to our website and check the links for this chapter or search the web.

Quick Reference
Communication API

HTML5 includes three different APIs for communication purposes. The XMLHttpRequest Level 2 is an improvement on the old XMLHttpRequest for Ajax applications. The Web Messaging API offers communication between windows, tabs, frames and even other APIs. And the WebSocket API provides new alternatives to establish a fast and effective client/server connection.

XMLHttpRequest Level 2

This API has a constructor for XMLHttpRequest objects and a few methods, properties and events to process the connection.

XMLHttpRequest()—This constructor returns the XMLHttpRequest object we need to start and process a connection with the server.

open(method, url, async)—This method opens the connection between the application and the server. The **method** attribute determines which HTTP method will be used to send the information (e.g., **GET**, **POST**). The **url** attribute declares the path for the script that will receive the information. And the **async** attribute is a boolean value to establish a synchronous or asynchronous connection (**true** for asynchronous).

send(data)—This method sends the value of the **data** attribute to the server. The **data** attribute may be an ArrayBuffer, a blob, a document, a string or a FormData.

abort()—This method cancels the request.

timeout—This property sets the time in milliseconds the request can take to be processed.

readyState—This property returns a value representing the status of the connection: 0 meaning the object has been constructed, 1 meaning the connection has been opened, 2 meaning the header of the response has been received, 3 meaning the response is being received, 4 meaning the data transfer has been completed.

responseType—This property returns the type of the response. It can be set to change the response type. Possible values are **arraybuffer**, **blob**, **document**, and **text**.

response—This property returns the response to the request in a format declared by the **responseType** property.

responseText—This property returns the response to the request as text.

responseXML—This property returns the response to the request as if it were an XML document.

loadstart—This event is fired when the request starts.
progress—This event is fired periodically while a request is processing.
abort—This event is fired when the request is aborted.
error—This event is fired when an error occurs.
load—This event is fired when the request has been successfully completed.
timeout—This event is fired when the request takes more time to be processed than that specified by the `timeout` property.
loadend—This event is fired when the request has been completed (either in success or failure).

A special attribute was included to get an XMLHttpRequestUpload object instead of a regular XMLHttpRequest object with the purpose of uploading data.

upload—This attribute returns an XMLHttpRequestUpload object. This object uses the same methods, properties and events of the XMLHttpRequest object but for uploading processes.

The API also includes an interface for creating FormData objects representing HTML forms.

FormData()—This constructor returns a FormData object to represent an HTML form.

append(name, value)—This method adds data to the FormData object. Every data appended to the object represents a form field with its name and value declared in the attributes. A string or a blob may be provided for the `value` attribute.

This API uses a common ProgressEvent interface (also used by other APIs to control the progress of an operation) that includes the following properties:

lengthComputable—This property returns a boolean value to determine if the values of the rest of the properties are valid.
loaded—This property returns the total amount of bytes already downloaded or uploaded.
total—This property returns the total size in bytes of the data to be downloaded or uploaded.

Web Messaging API

This API consists of only one interface, which provides a few methods, properties and events to communicate applications allocated in different windows, tabs, frames or even other APIs.

postMessage(message, target)—This method sends a message to a specific `contentWindow` and the document declared as target by the `target` attribute. The `message` attribute is the message to be transmitted.

message—This event is fired when a message is received.

data—This property of the `message` event returns the content of the message received.

origin—This property of the `message` event returns the origin of the document that sent the message.

source—This property of the `message` event returns a reference to the `contentWindow` from which the message was sent.

WebSocket API

This API includes a constructor that returns a WebSocket object and starts the connection. As well, it provides a few methods, properties and events to control the communication between client and server.

WebSocket(url)—This constructor returns a WebSocket object and starts the connection with the server. The `url` attribute declares the path to the script that is running the WS server and the port of communication. An array with sub-protocols may be specified as a second attribute.

send(data)—This method sends a message to the WS server. The `data` attribute must be a string with the information to be transmitted.

close()—This method closes the connection with the WS server.

url—This property shows the URL the application is using to connect to the server.

protocol—This property returns the sub-protocol used for the connection, if any.

readyState—This property returns a value representing the state of the connection. 0 means the connection has not yet been established, 1 means the connection is opened, 2 means the connection is being closed and 3 means the connection was closed.

bufferedAmount—This property returns the total amount of data waiting to be sent to the server.

open—This event is fired when the connection is opened.
message—This event is fired when the server sends a message to the application.
error—This event is fired when an error occurs.
close—This event is fired when the connection is closed.

Chapter 14
Web Workers API

Doing the Hard Work

Javascript has turned into the primary tool for building successful applications on the web. As we explained in Chapter 4, it is no longer just an alternative for creating nice (or sometimes annoying) tricks for web pages. The language has become an essential part of the web and a technology everybody has to understand and implement.

Javascript has already reached the status of general-purpose language—a condition in which it's forced to provide elemental features that by nature it doesn't have. This language was conceived of as a script language, intended to be processed one code at a time. The absence of multithreading in Javascript (processing of multiple codes at the same time) reduces efficiency, limits its scope and makes some desktop applications impossible to emulate on the web.

Web Workers is an API designed with the specific purpose of turning Javascript into a multithreading language and solving this problem. Now, thanks to HTML5, we are able to execute time-consuming codes in the background while the main script continues running on the web page, receiving the user's input and keeping the document responsive.

Creating a Worker

The way Web Workers works is simple: the worker is built in a separate Javascript file and the codes communicate with each other through messages. Usually, the message sent to the worker from the main code is the information we want to be processed, and the messages sent back by the worker represents the result of this processing. To send and receive these messages, the API takes advantage of techniques implemented in other APIs studied before. Events and methods that you already know about are used to send and receive messages from one code to another:

> **Worker(scriptURL)**—Before communicating with the worker, we have to get an object pointing to the file in which the code of the worker is located. This method returns a Worker object. The `scriptURL` attribute is the URL of the file with the code (worker) that will be processed in the background.

postMessage(message)—This method is the same studied before in Chapter 13 for the Web Messaging API, but now implemented over the Worker object. It sends a message toward or from the worker code. The `message` attribute is a string or a JSON object representing the message to be transmitted.

message—This is an event already studied that listens for messages sent to the code. As with the `postMessage()` method, it can be applied in the worker or the main code. It uses the `data` property to retrieve the message sent.

Sending and Receiving Messages

To learn how workers and the main code communicate with each other, we are going to use a simple template to send our name as a message to the worker and print its answer.

Even a basic example of Web Workers requires at least three files: the main document, the main Javascript code and the file with the code for the worker. Here is our HTML document:

```
<!DOCTYPE html>
<html lang="en">
<head>
  <title>WebWorkers</title>
  <link rel="stylesheet" href="webworkers.css">
  <script src="webworkers.js"></script>
</head>
<body>
  <section id="formbox">
    <form name="form">
      <p>Name:<br><input type="text" name="name" id="name"></p>
      <p><input type="button" name="button" id="button"
value="Send"></p>
    </form>
  </section>
  <section id="databox"></section>
</body>
</html>
```

Listing 14-1: template to test Web Workers

In the template, we included a CSS file called **webworkers.css** with the following rules:

```
#formbox{
  float: left;
  padding: 20px;
  border: 1px solid #999999;
}
```

```
#databox{
   float: left;
   width: 500px;
   margin-left: 20px;
   padding: 20px;
   border: 1px solid #999999;
}
```

Listing 14-2: styling the boxes

The Javascript for the main document has to be able to send the information we want processed by the worker. This code also has to be able to listen for the answer.

```
function initiate(){
   databox=document.getElementById('databox');
   var button=document.getElementById('button');
   button.addEventListener('click', send, false);

   worker=new Worker('worker.js');
   worker.addEventListener('message', received, false);
}
function send(){
   var name=document.getElementById('name').value;
   worker.postMessage(name);
}
function received(e){
   databox.innerHTML=e.data;
}
window.addEventListener('load', initiate, false);
```

Listing 14-3: a simple use of the API

Listing 14-3 presents the code for our document (the one that goes inside the **webworkers.js** file). After the creation of the necessary references for the **databox** and the button in the **initiate()** function, the Worker object was constructed. The **Worker()** constructor takes the **worker.js** file as the file with the code for the worker and returns a Worker object with this reference. Every interaction with the object will be, actually, an interaction with the code in this particular file.

Once we get the proper object, a listener for the **message** event has to be added to listen for messages coming from the worker. When a message is received, the **received()** function is called and the value of the **data** property (the message) is shown on the screen.

The other part of the communication is done by the **send()** function. When the user clicks the "Send" button, the value of the **name** input is taken and sent as a message for the worker using **postMessage()**.

With the **received()** and **send()** functions in charge of communications, we are ready to send messages to the worker and process its answers. Now it's time to prepare the worker:

```
addEventListener('message', received, false);

function received(e){
   var answer='Your name is '+e.data;
   postMessage(answer);
}
```

Listing 14-4: *code for the worker (*`worker.js`*)*

As well as the code in Listing 14-3, the code for the worker has to listen constantly for messages coming from the main code using the **message** event. The first line of the code in Listing 14-4 is adding a listener for this event to the worker. This listener will execute the **received()** function every time the event is fired (a message is received). In this function, the value of the **data** property is added to a predefined string and sent back to the main code using again the **postMessage()** method.

> **Do It Yourself:** Compare the codes in Listings 14-3 and 14-4 (the main code and the worker). Notice how the communication procedure works and how the same method and event are applied for this purpose in both codes. Create the files using Listings 14-1, 14-2, 14-3 and 14-4, upload them to your server and open the HTML document in your browser.

> **IMPORTANT:** You can use **self** or **this** to reference the worker (e.g., **self.postMessage()**), or just declare the methods as we did in Listing 14-4.

This worker is, of course, extremely elementary. Nothing is really processed; the only processing performed is the construction of a string from the message received that is immediately sent back as the answer. However, this example is useful for understanding how the codes communicate with each other and how to take advantage of this API.

Despite their simplicity, there are a few important things you have to consider before to create your workers. Messages are the only possible way to communicate directly with workers. Messages have to be created using strings or JSON objects, because workers are not allowed to receive other types of data. Also, they can't access the document or even manipulate any HTML element, and Javascript functions and variables from the main code are not accessible to workers. Workers are like canned codes that can only process information received through messages and send back the result using the same mechanism.

Detecting Errors

Despite all the limitations mentioned before, workers are still flexible and powerful. We can use functions, predefined methods and entire APIs from inside a worker. Considering how complex a worker may become, the Web Workers API incorporates a specific event to check for errors and return as much information as possible about the situation.

> **error**—This event is fired by the Worker object in the main code every time an error occurs in the worker. It uses three properties to provide information: **message**, **filename** and `lineno`. The **message** property represents the error message. It's a string that lets us know what went wrong. The `filename` property shows the name of the file with the code that causes the error. This is useful when external files are loaded from the worker, as we will see later. Finally, the `lineno` property returns the line number in which the error occurred.

Let's create a code to show errors returned by a worker:

```
function initiate(){
  databox=document.getElementById('databox');
  var button=document.getElementById('button');
  button.addEventListener('click', send, false);

  worker=new Worker('worker.js');
  worker.addEventListener('error', error, false);
}
function send(){
  var name=document.getElementById('name').value;
  worker.postMessage(name);
}
function error(e){
  databox.innerHTML='ERROR: '+e.message+'<br>';
  databox.innerHTML+='Filename: '+e.filename+'<br>';
  databox.innerHTML+='Line Number: '+e.lineno;
}
window.addEventListener('load', initiate, false);
```

Listing 14-5: *using the* `error` *event*

The last code is similar to the main code in Listing 14-3. It constructs a worker but it only uses the **error** event because we don't want to listen for answers from the worker this time, but rather only check for errors. It's useless, of course, but it will show you how the errors are returned and what kind of information is provided in these situations.

To deliberately generate an error, we call a non-existent function within the worker:

```
addEventListener('message', received, false);

function received(e){
  test();
}
```

Listing 14-6: a worker that doesn't work

In the worker, we have to use the **message** event to listen for messages coming from the main code because it's what makes the process begin. When a message is received, the **received()** function is executed and the non-existent **test()** function is called, thus generating an error.

As soon as the error occurs, the **error** event is fired in the main code and the **error()** function is called, showing on the screen the values of the three properties provided by the event. Check the code in Listing 14-5 to see how the function takes and processes this information.

> **Do It Yourself:** For this example, we are using the HTML document and CSS rules in Listings 14-1 and 14-2. Copy the code in Listing 14-5 in the **webworkers.js** file and the code in Listing 14-6 in the **worker.js** file. Open the template of Listing 14-1 in your browser and send any random string to the worker using the form. The error returned by the worker will be shown on the screen.

Terminating Workers

Workers are special units of codes that are always running in the background, waiting for information to be processed. Workers will be, most of the time, required in specific circumstances and for special purposes. Usually their services won't be necessary or required all the time, and it is a good practice to stop or terminate their processing if we don't need them anymore.

For this purpose the API provides two different methods:

> **terminate()**—This method terminates the worker from the main code.
> **close()**—This method terminates the worker from inside the worker.

When a worker is terminated, any process running is aborted and any task in the event loop is discarded. To test both methods, we are going to create a small application that works exactly as our first example, but it also responds to two specific commands: "close1" and "close2". If the strings "close1" or "close2" are sent from the form, the worker will be terminated by the main code or the code of the worker using **terminate()** or **close()** respectively.

```
function initiate(){
  databox=document.getElementById('databox');
  var button=document.getElementById('button');
  button.addEventListener('click', send, false);

  worker=new Worker('worker.js');
  worker.addEventListener('message', received, false);
}
function send(){
  var name=document.getElementById('name').value;
  if(name=='close1'){
    worker.terminate();
    databox.innerHTML='Worker Terminated';
  }else{
    worker.postMessage(name);
  }
}
function received(e){
  databox.innerHTML=e.data;
}
window.addEventListener('load', initiate, false);
```

Listing 14-7: terminating the worker from the main code

The only difference between the code in Listing 14-7 and the code in Listing 14-3 is the addition of the conditional **if** to check for the insertion of the "close1" command. If this command is inserted in the form instead of a name, the **terminate()** method is executed and a message is shown on the screen indicating the termination of the worker. On the other hand, if the string is different from the command expected, it is sent as a message to the worker.

The code for the worker will perform a similar task. If the message received contains the string "close2", the worker will terminate itself using the **close()** method or send a message back otherwise:

```
addEventListener('message', received, false);

function received(e){
  if(e.data=='close2'){
    postMessage('Worker Terminated');
    close();
  }else{
    var answer='Your name is '+e.data;
    postMessage(answer);
  }
}
```

Listing 14-8: worker terminating itself

Do It Yourself: Use the same HTML document and CSS rules in Listings 14-1 and 14-2. Copy the code from Listing 14-7 into the `webworkers.js` file and the code from Listing 14-8 into the `worker.js` file. Open the template in your browser, and using the form, send the commands "close1" or "close2". After this, the worker won't respond anymore.

Synchronous APIs

Workers may have limitations in working with the main document and accessing its elements, but when it comes to processing and functionality, as we said before, things get better. For instance, we can use regular methods such as `setTimeout()` or `setInterval()`, load additional information from servers using `XMLHttpRequest` and use some APIs to create powerful codes. The last possibility is the most promising of all, but it has a catch: we will have to learn a different implementation of the APIs available for workers.

When we studied some APIs before, the implementation presented in those chapters was the one called asynchronous. Most APIs have an asynchronous and synchronous version available. These different versions of the same API perform the same tasks but using specific methods according to the way they are processed. Asynchronous APIs are useful when the operations performed are time–consuming and require resources the main document can't provide. The asynchronous operations are performed in the background while the main code continues processing without interruption. Because workers are new threads running at the same time as the main code, they are already asynchronous, and these types of operations are not necessary anymore.

> **IMPORTANT:** Several APIs have synchronous versions, such as File API and IndexedDB API, but most of them are under development or unstable at this moment. Check the links in our website for more information and examples.

Importing Scripts

Something that is worth mentioning is the possibility of loading external Javascript files from a worker. A worker can hold all the code necessary to perform any task we need, but because several workers may be created for a single document, there is the chance that some parts of this code will become redundant. We can select these parts, put them into one single file and load that file from every worker with a the new `importScripts()` method:

> **importScripts(file)**—This method loads an external Javascript file to incorporate new code into a worker. The `file` attribute indicates the path to the file to be included.

If you ever used methods from other languages, you will notice the similarities between `importScripts()` and functions such as `include()` from PHP, for example. The code in the file is incorporated into the worker as if it were part of the worker's file.

To use the new `importScripts()` method, you just need to declare it at the beginning of the worker. The code for the worker won't be ready until these files are completely loaded.

```
importScripts('morecodes.js');

addEventListener('message', received, false);

function received(e){
  test();
}
```

Listing 14-9: loading external Javascript codes for the worker

The code in Listing 14-9 is non-functional, but just an example of how to use the `importScripts()` method. In this hypothetical situation, the file `morecodes.js` containing the function `test()` is loaded as soon as the worker's file is loaded. After this process, the `test()` function (and any other function inside the `morecodes.js` file) becomes available for the rest of the worker's code.

Shared Worker

What we have seen so far is called a Dedicated Worker. This type of worker only responds to the main code from which it is created. There is another type of worker called a Shared Worker, which responds to multiple documents from the same origin. Working with multiple connections means that we can share the same worker from different windows, tabs or frames, and we can keep everyone updated and synchronized for the construction of complex applications.

The connections are made through ports and these ports can be saved inside the worker for future reference. To work with Shared Workers and ports, this part of the API incorporates new properties, events and methods:

SharedWorker(scriptURL)—This constructor replaces the previous `Worker()` constructor used for Dedicated Workers. As always, the `scriptURL` attribute declares the path for the Javascript file with the code for the worker. An optional second attribute could be added to specify a `name` for the worker.

port—When the SharedWorker object is constructed, a new port is created for this document and assigned to the `port` property. This property will be used later to reference the port and communicate with the worker.

connect—This is a specific event to check for new connections from inside the worker. The event will be fired every time a document starts a connection with the worker. It is useful to keep track of all the connections available for the worker (to reference all the documents that are using this worker).

start()—This method is available for MessagePort objects (one of the objects returned in the construction of a shared worker) and its function is to begin dispatching messages received on a port. After the construction of the SharedWorker object, this method must be called to start the connection.

The `SharedWorker()` constructor returns a SharedWorker object and a MessagePort object with the value of the port through which the connection to the worker will be made. The communication with the shared worker must be done through the port referenced by the value of the **port** property.

To test Shared Workers, we will have to use at least two different documents from the same origin, two Javascript codes for each document and one file for the worker.

The HTML document for our example includes an iframe to load a second document in the same window. Both the main document and the document within the iframe will share the worker.

```
<!DOCTYPE html>
<html lang="en">
<head>
  <title>WebWorkers</title>
  <link rel="stylesheet" href="webworkers.css">
  <script src="webworkers.js"></script>
</head>
<body>
  <section id="formbox">
    <form name="form">
      <p>Name:<br><input type="text" name="name" id="name"></p>
      <p><input type="button" name="button" id="button"
value="Send"></p>
    </form>
  </section>
  <section id="databox">
    <iframe id="iframe" src="iframe.html" width="500"
height="350"></iframe>
  </section>
</body>
</html>
```

Listing 14-10: template to test Shared Workers

The document for the iframe will be a simple HTML document with a `<section>` for our familiar **databox** and the **iframe.js** file with the code to connect with the worker:

```
<!DOCTYPE html>
<html lang="en">
<head>
  <title>iframe window</title>
  <script src="iframe.js"></script>
</head>
<body>
  <section id="databox"></section>
</body>
</html>
```

Listing 14-11: template for the iframe (iframe.html)

Each HTML document has its own Javascript code to start the connection with the worker and process its answers. These codes have to construct the SharedWorker object and use the port referenced by the value of the **port** property to send and receive messages. First, let's see the code for the main document:

```
function initiate(){
  var button=document.getElementById('button');
  button.addEventListener('click', send, false);

  worker=new SharedWorker('worker.js');
  worker.port.addEventListener('message', received, false);
  worker.port.start();
}
function received(e){
  alert(e.data);
}
function send(){
  var name=document.getElementById('name').value;
  worker.port.postMessage(name);
}
window.addEventListener('load', initiate, false);
```

Listing 14-12: connecting from the main document (webworkers.js)

Every document wanting to work with a shared worker has to create the SharedWorker object and set a connection with the worker. In the code in Listing 14-12, the object is constructed using the **worker.js** file as the file for the worker, and then the communication operations are done through the corresponding port using the **port** property.

After a listener for the **message** event is added to listen for answers from the worker, the **start()** method is called to begin dispatching messages. The connection to a shared worker is not established until this method is executed (unless we use event handlers, such as **onmessage**, instead of the **addEventListener()** method).

Notice that the **send()** function is similar to previous examples, except this time the communication is made through the value of the **port** property.

For the iframe, the code doesn't change too much:

```
function initiate(){
   worker=new SharedWorker('worker.js');
   worker.port.addEventListener('message', received, false);
   worker.port.start();
}
function received(e){
   var databox=document.getElementById('databox');
   databox.innerHTML=e.data;
}
window.addEventListener('load', initiate, false);
```

Listing 14-13: connecting from the iframe (`iframe.js`)

In both codes, the SharedWorker object is constructed referencing the same file (**worker.js**), and the connection has to be established using the **port** property (albeit through different ports). The only noticeable difference between the code for the main document and the code for the iframe is how the response from the worker is processed. In the main document, the **received()** function pops up an alert message (see Listing 14-12), while within the iframe, the answer is printed as a simple text inside the **databox** (see Listing 14-13).

Now it is time to see how the shared worker takes care of every connection and sends messages back to the proper document. Remember that there is only one worker for both documents, hence it is a shared worker. Therefore every request for connection to the worker has to be differentiated and saved for future reference. We are going to save the references to the ports for each document in an array called **myports**:

```
myports=new Array();

addEventListener('connect', connect, false);

function connect(e){
   myports.push(e.ports[0]);
   e.ports[0].onmessage=send;
}
function send(e){
   for(f=0; f < myports.length; f++){
      myports[f].postMessage('Your Name is '+e.data);
   }
}
```

Listing 14-14: the code for the shared worker (`worker.js`)

The procedure is similar to the one for Dedicated Workers. We just have to consider this time which document we are going to answer to, because several may be connected to the worker at the same time. To do this, the **connect** event provides the **ports** array with the value of the newly created port (The array contains only this value located at index 0.).

Every time a code requests a connection to the worker, the **connect** event is fired. In the code in Listing 14-14, this event calls the **connect()** function. In this function, we performed two operations: first, the value of the port is taken from the **ports** property (index 0) and saved in the **myports** array (initialized at the beginning of the worker). Second, the **onmessage** event handler is registered for this particular port and the **send()** function is set as the one to be called when a message is received.

As a result, every time a message is sent to the worker from the main code, no matter from which document, the **send()** function in the worker is executed. In this function, we use a **for** loop to retrieve from the **myports** array all the ports opened for this worker and send a message to each document connected. The process is exactly as in Dedicated Workers, but this time several documents are answered instead of just one.

> **Do It Yourself:** To test this example, you have to create several files and upload them to your server. Create an HTML file with the template in Listing 14-10 and the name you like. This template will load the same **webworkers.css** file used throughout this chapter, the **webworkers.js** file with the code in Listing 14-12, and the **iframe.html** file as the source of the iframe with the code in Listing 14-11. You also have to create a file called **worker.js** for the worker with the code in Listing 14-14. Once all these files are saved and uploaded to the server, open the first file in your browser. Use the form to send a message to the worker and see how both documents (the main document and the document in the iframe) process the answer.

> **IMPORTANT:** At the moment of this writing, Shared Workers were only implemented by browsers based on the WebKit engine, such as Google Chrome and Safari.

The Web Workers API brings multithreading to Javascript. It's the API that lets us process codes in the background without interrupting the normal operation of the code in the main document.

Workers

There are two different types of workers: Dedicated Workers and Shared Workers. Both share the following methods and events:

postMessage(message)—This method sends a message to the worker, the main code or the corresponding port. The **message** attribute is the string or the JSON object to be sent.

terminate()—This method terminates the worker from the main code.

close()—This method terminates the worker from inside the worker.

importScripts(file)—This method loads an external Javascript file to incorporate new code to a worker. The **file** attribute indicates the path for the file to be included.

message—This event is fired when a message is sent to the code. It can be used in the worker to listen for messages from the main code or the other way around.

error—This event is fired when an error occurs in the worker. It's used in the main code to watch for worker's errors. It returns information using three properties: **message**, **filename** and **lineno**. The **message** property represents the error message, the **filename** property shows the name of the file with the code that causes the error and the **lineno** property returns the line number in which the error occurred.

Dedicated Workers

Dedicated Workers have their own constructor:

Worker(scriptURL)—This constructor returns a Worker object. The **scriptURL** attribute is the path of the file containing the worker.

Shared Workers

Due to the Shared Workers' nature, the API has to provide a few methods, events and properties specific for this type of workers:

> **SharedWorker(scriptURL)**—This constructor returns a SharedWorker object. The `scriptURL` attribute is the path of the file containing the shared worker. An optional second attribute could be added to specify a **name** for the worker.
>
> **port**—This property returns the value of the port for the connection to the shared worker.
>
> **connect**—This event is fired in the shared worker when a new connection is requested from a document.
>
> **start()**—This method begins dispatching messages. It's used to start the connection with the shared worker.

Chapter 15
History API

History Interface

What in HTML5 we usually call History API is in fact just an improvement on an old API that never had an official implementation but was supported by browsers for years. This old API was in fact a little group of methods and properties, part of which was the History object. The new History API is an improvement on this object and was included in the official HTML5 specification as the History interface. This interface combines all the old methods and properties plus a few new ones to work and modify browser history according to our needs.

Navigating the Web

A browser history is a list of all the web pages (URLs) visited by the user in one single session. It's what makes the navigation possible. Using the navigation buttons at the left of the navigation bar in every browser we can go back and forward in this list and see previous documents. This list is built with real URLs generated by websites and included in every hyperlink inside their documents. With browser arrows, we can load the web page we visited before or come back to the last one.

Despite the practicality of browser buttons, sometimes is useful to be able to navigate through the history list from inside the document. To emulate browser navigation arrows from Javascript, we always had the following methods and properties available:

> **back()**—This method takes the browser one step back in the session history (emulating the left arrow).
>
> **forward()**—This method takes the browser one step forward in the session history (emulating the right arrow).
>
> **go(steps)**—This method takes the browser back or forward the specified steps in the session history. The **steps** attribute may be a negative or positive value according to the direction we choose to go.
>
> **length**—This property returns the number of entries in the session history (the total of URLs on the list).

These methods and properties have to be declared as part of the History object, with an expression such as `history.back()`. We can also use the Window object to refer to the window, but this is not necessary. For example, if we want to go back to the previous web page, we can use the code `window.history.back()` or `window.history.go(-1)`.

> **IMPORTANT:** This part of the API is already known and used by most of web designers and programmers nowadays. We are not going to see any sample code of these methods, but you can always go to our website and check the links for this chapter to find more information about it.

New Methods

By the time using the XMLHttpRequest object became standard and Ajax applications became an extraordinary success for the web, the way people navigated and accessed documents had changed forever. Now it is common practice to program small scripts to retrieve information from servers and show the information within the current document without refreshing the page or loading a new one. Users interact with modern websites and applications from the same URL, receiving information, entering data and getting processing results always from the same page. The web has begun to emulate desktop applications.

However, the way browsers keep track of the user's activity is through URLs. URLs are, in fact, the data inside the navigation list, the addresses that indicate where the user is currently located. Because new web applications avoided the use of URLs to point to the user's location on the web, it soon became evident that important steps were lost in the process. Users could update data on a web page dozens of times and yet no trace was left in the History list to indicate the steps followed.

New methods and properties were incorporated to the existing history API with the intention of manually modifying the URL in the Location bar as well as the history list using Javascript code. From now on, we have the possibility of adding fake URLs to the history list and keeping an eye on the user's activity.

> **pushState(state, title, url)**—This method creates a new entry in the session history. The `state` attribute declares a value for the state of the entry. It is useful to identify the entry later and it may be specified as a string or a JSON object. The `title` attribute is the title of the entry, and the `url` attribute is the URL for the entry we are generating (This value will replace the current URL in the Location bar.).
> **replaceState(state, title, url)**—This method works exactly like `pushState()`, but it doesn't generate a new entry. Instead, it replaces the information for the current one.

state—This property returns the value of the state for the current entry. This value will be **null** unless it was declared by one of the previous methods through the **state** attribute.

Fake URLs

The URLs generated using methods such as **pushState()** are like fake URLs in the sense that browsers never check for the validity of these addresses and the existence of the document that they are pointing at. It depends on us to make sure that these fake URLs are in fact valid and useful.

To create a new entry in the browser history and change the URL inside the Location bar, we have to use the **pushState()** method. Let's see an example of how it works:

```
<!DOCTYPE html>
<html lang="en">
<head>
  <title>History API</title>
  <link rel="stylesheet" href="history.css">
  <script src="history.js"></script>
</head>
<body>
  <section id="maincontent">
    This content is never refreshed<br>
    <span id="url">page 2</span>
  </section>
  <aside id="databox"></aside>
</body>
</html>
```

Listing 15-1: basic template to test the History API

In Listing 15-1, we have the HTML code with the basic elements necessary to test the History API. There is permanent content inside a **<section>** element identified as **maincontent**, a text that we will turn into a link to generate the virtual second page of the website and the usual **databox** for the alternative content.

Let's include the styles for the document:

```
#maincontent{
  float: left;
  padding: 20px;
  border: 1px solid #999999;
}
```

```
#databox{
   float: left;
   width: 500px;
   margin-left: 20px;
   padding: 20px;
   border: 1px solid #999999;
}
#maincontent span{
   color: #0000FF;
   cursor: pointer;
}
```

Listing 15-2: styles for the boxes and the `<span>` *elements (*`history.css`*)*

What we are going to do in this example is add a new entry with the **pushState()** method and update content without refreshing the page or loading another document.

```
function initiate(){
   databox=document.getElementById('databox');
   url=document.getElementById('url');
   url.addEventListener('click', changepage, false);
}
function changepage(){
   databox.innerHTML='the url is page2';
   window.history.pushState(null, null, 'page2.html');
}
window.addEventListener('load', initiate, false);
```

Listing 15-3: generating a new URL and content (`history.js`*)*

In the **initiate()** function in Listing 15-3, we created the proper reference to the **databox** and added a listener for the **click** event to the **<span>** element. Every time the user clicks on the text inside **<span>**, the **changepage()** function is called.

The **changepage()** function performs two tasks: it updates the content of the page with new information and it inserts a new URL in the history list. After the function is executed, the **databox** shows the text "the url is page2" and the URL of the main document is replaced in the Location bar by the fake URL "page2.html".

The **state** and **title** attributes for the **pushState()** method were declared as **null** this time. The **title** attribute is not used at this moment by any browser and will always be declared as **null**, but we will apply and use the **state** attribute in the following examples.

> **Do It Yourself:** Copy the template in Listing 15-1 into an HTML file. Create a CSS file called **history.css** with the styles in Listing 15-2 and a Javascript file called **history.js** with the codes in Listing 15-3. Upload them to your server and open the HTML file in your browser. Click on the text "page 2" and check how the URL in the Location bar changes to the one generated by the code.

Keeping Track

What we have done so far is just a manipulation of the session history. We made the browser believe that the user visited a URL that, at this point, doesn't even exist. After you clicked on the "page 2" link, the fake URL "page2.html" was shown on the Location bar and new content inserted in the **databox**, everything without refreshing or loading another page. It's a nice trick but not complete. The browser doesn't consider the new URL a real document yet. If you go back and forward in the session history using the navigation buttons, the URL changes from the new one to the one of the main document, but the content of the document doesn't change at all. We need to detect when the fake URLs are revisited and perform the right modifications in the document to show the corresponding state.

We mentioned before the existence of the **state** property. The value of this property may be set during the generation of a new URL, and this is the way we can identify later what is the current web address. To work with this property, the API provides a new event:

> **popstate**—This event is fired in certain circumstances when a URL is revisited or the document is loaded. It provides the **state** property with the value of the state declared when the URL was generated with the **pushState()** or **replaceState()** methods. This value is **null** when the URL is real unless we changed it before using **replaceState()**, as we will see next.

In the following code, we will improve the previous example by implementing the **popstate** event and the **replaceState()** method to detect which URL the user is requesting at the moment.

```
function initiate(){
  databox=document.getElementById('databox');
  url=document.getElementById('url');
  url.addEventListener('click', changepage, false);
  window.addEventListener('popstate', newurl ,false);
  window.history.replaceState(1, null);
}
function changepage(){
  showpage(2);
  window.history.pushState(2, null, 'page2.html');
}
function newurl(e){
  showpage(e.state);
}
function showpage(current){
  databox.innerHTML='the url is page '+current;
}
window.addEventListener('load', initiate, false);
```

Listing 15-4: keeping track of the user's position (`history.js`)

There are two things we have to do in our application to have full control over the situation. First, we must declare a state value for every URL we are going to use, the fake and the real ones. And second, we must update the content of the document according to the current URL.

In the `initiate()` function in Listing 15-4, a listener was added for the `popstate` event. This listener will call the `newurl()` function every time a URL is revisited. The function will simply update the content of the `databox` indicating the current page. It takes the value of the `state` property and sends it to the `showpage()` function to be shown on the screen.

This will work for every fake URL, but as we said before, the real URLs don't have a state value by default. By using the `replaceState()` method at the end of the `initiate()` function, we change the information of the current entry (the real URL for the main document) and declare the value 1 for its state. Now, every time the user revisits the main document, we will be able to detect it checking this value.

The `changepage()` function is the same, except this time it uses the `showpage()` function to update the document's content and declare the value 2 for the state of the fake URL.

The application works as follows: when the user clicks on the "page 2" link, the message "the url is page 2" is shown on the screen and the URL in the Location bar is changed to "page2.html" (including the full path, of course). This is what we had done so far, but here is where things get interesting. If the user hits the left arrow in the browser navigation bar, the URL in the Location bar will change to the previous in the history list (that is the real URL of our document) and the `popstate` event will be fired. This event calls the `newurl()` function that reads the value of the `state` property and sends it to the `showpage()` function. Now the state's value is 1 (the value we declared for this URL using the `replaceState()` method) and the message shown on the screen will be "the url is page 1". If the user goes back to the fake URL using the right arrow in the navigation bar, the state's value will be 2 and the message shown on the screen will be again "the url is page 2".

As you can see, the value of the `state` property is any value you want to control which URL is the current one and to adapt the document's content to this situation.

> **Do It Yourself:** Use the files with the codes from Listings 15-1 and 15-2 for the HTML document and CSS styles. Copy the code of Listing 15-4 into the `history.js` file and upload the files to your server. Open the HTML template in your browser and click on the "page 2" text. The URL and the content of the `databox` will change according to the corresponding URL. Push the back and forward buttons on the navigation bar several times to see the URL changing and the content associated with that URL updated on the screen (The document's content is shown according to the current state.).

> **IMPORTANT:** The URL "page2.html" generated with the `pushState()` method in previous examples is considered fake, but it should be real. The purpose of this API is not to create fake URLs but to provide the alternative for programmers of preserving the user's activity in the browser history to be able

to go back to a previous state anytime that is required (even after the browser was closed). You will have to be sure that the code in your server is returning this state and providing the proper content for every URL requested (the real and the fake ones).

Real Example

The following is a more practical application. We are going to use the History API and all the methods studied before to load a set of four images from the same document. Each image is associated with a fake URL that can be used to return a specific image from the server later.

The main document is loaded with an image by default. This image will be associated with the first of four links that are part of the permanent content. All these links will be pointing to fake URLs referencing a state, not a real document, including the link for the main document that will be changed to "page1.html". This will make sense soon.

```
<!DOCTYPE html>
<html lang="en">
<head>
  <title>History API</title>
  <link rel="stylesheet" href="history.css">
  <script src="history.js"></script>
</head>
<body>
  <section id="maincontent">
    This content is never refreshed<br>
    <span id="url1">image 1</span> -
    <span id="url2">image 2</span> -
    <span id="url3">image 3</span> -
    <span id="url4">image 4</span> -
  </section>
  <aside id="databox">
    <img id="image"
src="http://www.minkbooks.com/content/monster1.gif">
  </aside>
</body>
</html>
```

Listing 15-5: template for a "real" application

The only difference between this new application and the previous one is the number of links and new URLs we are generating. In the code in Listing 15-4, there were two states, the state 1 corresponding to the main document and the state 2 for the fake URL "page2.html" generated by the **pushState()** method. In this case, we have to automate the process and generate a total of four fake URLs corresponding to each image available.

```
function initiate(){
   for(var f=1;f<5;f++){
     url=document.getElementById('url'+f);
     url.addEventListener('click', function(x){
         return function(){ changepage(x);}
       }(f), false);
   }

   window.addEventListener('popstate', newurl ,false);

   window.history.replaceState(1, null, 'page1.html');
}
function changepage(page){
   showpage(page);
   window.history.pushState(page, null, 'page'+page+'.html');
}
function newurl(e){
   showpage(e.state);
}
function showpage(current){
   if(current!=null){
     image=document.getElementById('image');
     image.src='http://www.minkbooks.com/content/monster' +
current + '.gif';
   }
}
window.addEventListener('load', initiate, false);
```

Listing 15-6: *manipulating history (*`history.js`*)*

As you can see, we are using the same functions, but with a few visible changes. First, the **replaceState()** method in the **initiate()** function has the **url** attribute set to "page1.html". We decided to program our application this way, declaring the state of the main document as 1 and the URL as "page1.html" (independently of the real URL of the document). This way makes it simple to jump from one URL to another, always using the same format and the values of the **state** property to build each URL. You can see this in practice by looking at the **changepage()** function. Every time the user clicks on one of the links in the template, this function is executed and the fake URL is constructed with the value of the **page** variable and added to the history list. The value received by the function was previously set in the **for** loop at the beginning of the **initiate()** function. This value is set to 1 for the "page 1" link, 2 for the "page 2" link, and so on.

Every time a URL is visited, the **showpage()** function is executed to update the content (image) according to that URL. Because the **popstate** event sometimes is fired in circumstances when the **state** property is **null** (such as after the main document is loaded for the first time), we checked the value received by the **showpage()** function before doing anything else. If the value is different from **null**, it means the **state** property was defined for that URL and the image corresponding to that state is shown on the screen.

The images used for this example are named monster1.gif, monster2.gif, monster3.gif and monster4.gif, following the same order as the values of the state property. Thus, by using this value, we can select the image to be shown. However, always remember that the value may be anyone you want, and the process to create the fake URLs and content associated with them will have to be set according to the needs of your application.

Also remember that users should be able to return to any of the URLs generated by the application and see the proper content on the screen anytime they want. You must prepare your server to process these URLs in order to make any state always available and accessible. For example, if a user opens a new window and types the URL "page2.html", the server should return the main document with the image "monster2.gif", and not just the template in Listing 15-5. The main idea behind this API is to provide the alternative for users to come back to any previous state any time they want, and we can only achieve that by turning the fake URLs into valid ones.

> **IMPORTANT:** The `for` loop we used in the code in Listing 15-6 to add a listener for the `click` event to every `<span>` element in the document takes advantage of a Javascript technique available to send real values to a function. To send a value to a callback function in an `addEventListener()` method, we have to specify the real value. If we send a variable instead, what is really sent is not the value of the variable but its reference. So, in this case, to send the current value of the `f` variable of the `for` loop, we have to use two anonymous functions. The first function is executed in the moment the `addEventListener()` method is called. It receives the current value of the `f` variable (check the parentheses at the end) and puts that value in the `x` variable. Then, the function returns a second anonymous function with the value of the variable `x`. This second function is what will be executed with the right value when the event is fired. For more information about this subject, visit our website and check the links for this chapter.

> **Do It Yourself:** To try the last example, use the HTML document in Listing 15-5 with the CSS file in Listing 15-2. Copy the code in Listing 15-6 in the `history.js` file and upload the files to your server. Open the template in your browser and click on the links. Navigate through the URLs you selected using the navigation buttons. The images on the screen should change according to the URL in the Location bar.

Quick Reference
History API

The History API lets us manipulate session history in the browser to keep track of the user's activity. This API is included in the official specification as the History interface. This interface combines new and old methods and properties.

length—This property returns the total number of entries in the history list.

state—This property returns the state for the current URL.

go(step)—This method takes the browser back or forward in the history list according to the value of the **step** attribute. This value may be negative or positive depending on the direction of the navigation.

back()—This method loads the previous URL in the history list.

forward()—This method loads the next URL in the history list.

pushState(state, title, url)—This method inserts new data into the history list. The **state** attribute is the value of the state we want to give to this new entry. The **title** attribute is the title for the entry. And the **url** attribute is the new URL we want to generate in the history list.

replaceState(state, title, url)—This method modifies the current entry. The **state** attribute is the value of the state we want to give to the current entry. The **title** attribute is the title for the entry. And the **url** attribute is the new URL we want to give to the current entry.

popstate—This event is fired in certain circumstances to inform the current state.

Chapter 16
Offline API

Cache Manifest

The offline working days are over. Because this chapter is about the Offline API, that statement might sound contradictory, but just think about it. You have been working offline almost all of your life. Desktop applications were your primary production tools. And now, suddenly, the web has emerged as the new working platform. Online applications are getting more and more complex, and HTML5 is making things harder in the offline versus online battle. Databases, files access and storage, graphic tools, image and video editing, and multiprocessing are, among others, a set of essential features now available for the web. Our daily activity is turning toward the web and our production environment is becoming online. The offline days are over.

However, as the transition continues, web applications become more sophisticated, requiring bigger files and more time for downloading. By the time applications on the web replace desktop applications, working online will be impossible. Users won't be able to download several megabytes of files every time they need to use each application and won't be able to count on having Internet access available 100% of the time. Offline applications will soon disappear, but under the current conditions online applications are destined to fail.

The Offline API came to save the day. Basically, this API provides the alternative to saving applications and web files in the user's computer for future use. One access is enough to download all the files required to run the application and use it with or without being connected to the network. Once the files are downloaded, the application runs in the browser but using these files, like a desktop application would do, independently of what happens with the server or the connection.

The Manifest File

A web application or a sophisticated website will consist of several files, but not all of them are necessary to run the application and not all of them need to be stored in the user's computer. The API assigns a specific file to declare the list of files that are needed to work offline. This is just a text file called a "manifest", with a list of URLs pointing to the location of the requested files. The "manifest" may be created with any text editor.

It has to be saved with the `.manifest` extension and start with the line **CACHE MANIFEST** as in the following example:

```
CACHE MANIFEST
cache.html
cache.css
cache.js
```

Listing 16-1: cache manifest file

The files listed under **CACHE MANIFEST** are all the files the application needs to run from the user's computer without requesting any external resources. In our example, we have the `cache.html` file as the main document for the application, the `cache.css` file with CSS styles and the `cache.js` file for the Javascript codes.

Categories

In the same way that we need to specify the files required for the application to run offline, we could also need to declare specific files only available online. This could be the case for part of the application only useful when connected—for example, a chat room.

To identify the type of files listed in the manifest file, the API introduces three categories:

CACHE—This is the category by default. All the files under this category will be saved in the user's computer for future use.

NETWORK—This category is considered a whitelist; all the files under it are only available online.

FALLBACK—This category is for files that might be useful to get from the server while online, but they may be replaced by an offline version. If the browser detects a connection, it will try to use the original file. Otherwise, the replacement will be loaded from the user's computer.

Using categories, our manifest file could be something like this:

```
CACHE MANIFEST

CACHE:
cache.html
cache.css
cache.js

NETWORK:
chat.html
```

```
FALLBACK:
newslist.html nonews.html
```

Listing 16-2: declaring files by category

In the new manifest file in Listing 16-2, files are listed under the corresponding categories. The three files in the **CACHE** category will be downloaded, saved in the user's computer and used for this application from now on (unless we specify something different later). The `chat.html` file specified in the **NETWORK** category will be only available when the browser is online. And the `newslist.html` file under the **FALLBACK** category will be used online; however, if it cannot be accessed, it will be replaced by the `nonews.html` file. As well as the files under the **CACHE** category, the `nonews.html` file is cached and saved in user's computer to be available when it's required.

The **FALLBACK** category is useful not only to replace individual files, but also to indicate full directories. For example, the line `/ noconnection.html` will replace any file not available in the cache by the file `noconnection.html`. This is a nice way to diverts users to a document that recommends them go online when they try to access the part of the application that is not available for offline use.

Comments

Comments may be added in a manifest file using the # symbol (one per line). Because files are ordered by category, comments might look useless but are important for updates. The manifest file not only declares which files must be cached, but when. Every time the application files are updated, there is no way for the browser to know this except through the manifest file. If the updated files are the same and no new ones were added to the list, the manifest file will look the same and the browser won't be able to recognize the difference and will continue using the old files already cached. However, to force the browser to download the application files again, we can indicate the update using comments. Usually one comment with the date of the last update will be enough, as shown in the following example:

```
CACHE MANIFEST

CACHE:
cache.html
cache.css
cache.js

NETWORK:
chat.html

FALLBACK:
newslist.html nonews.html
```

Listing 16-3: comment to inform about updates

Let's suppose you add more code to the current functions of the `cache.js` file. Users will have the file already cached in their computers and browsers will use this old version instead of the new one. Changing the date at the end of the manifest file or adding new comments will inform browsers about the update and all the files will be downloaded again, including the improved version of the `cache.js` file. After the cache is updated, the new copies of the files will be used by the browser to run the application.

Using the Manifest File

After selecting all the files necessary to run the application offline and preparing the full list of URLs pointing to those files, we have to include the manifest file in our documents. The API provides a new attribute for the `<html>` element to indicate the location of this file:

```
<!DOCTYPE html>
<html lang="en" manifest="mycache.manifest">
<head>
  <title>Offline API</title>
  <link rel="stylesheet" href="cache.css">
  <script src="cache.js"></script>
</head>
<body>
  <section id="databox">
    Offline Application
  </section>
</body>
</html>
```

Listing 16-4: loading the manifest file

Listing 16-4 shows a small HTML document including the `manifest` attribute for the `<html>` element. The `manifest` attribute is indicating the location of the manifest file necessary to generate the cache for the application. As you can see, nothing changes for the rest of the document: the files for CSS styles and Javascript codes are included as usual, independently of the content of the manifest file.

The manifest file has to be saved with the `.manifest` extension and the name you want (in our example, `mycache`). Every time the browser finds the `manifest` attribute in a document, it will try to download the manifest file first and then all the resources listed inside. The `manifest` attribute must be included in every HTML document that has to be part of the cache for the application. The process is transparent for users and may be controlled through programming using the API, as we will see soon.

As well as the extension and the internal structure of the manifest file, there is another important requisite to consider. The manifest file must be served by servers with the proper MIME type. Every file has a MIME type associated to indicate the format of its content. For instance, the MIME type for an HTML file is `text/html`. A manifest file must be served using the `text/cache-manifest` MIME type or the browser will return an error.

> **IMPORTANT:** The `text/cache-manifest` MIME type is not part of the configuration by default of any server at this moment. You must add it to your server manually. How to include this new file type depends on which kind of server you have. For some versions of Apache, for example, the addition of the following line in the `httpd.conf` file is enough to start serving these files with the proper type: `AddType text/cache-manifest .manifest`.

Offline API

The manifest file by itself should be enough to generate a cache for small websites or simple codes, but complex applications demands more control. The manifest file declares the files necessary to be cached, but it can't inform how many of those files were already downloaded, the errors found in the process or when an update is ready to be used, among other critical situations. Considering these possible scenarios, the API provides the new ApplicationCache object with methods, properties and events to manage the whole process.

Errors

Probably the most important event of the ApplicationCache object is **error**. If an error occurs during the process of reading files on the server, the application won't be cached or the cache won't be updated. It's extremely important to be aware of these situations and act according to the circumstances.

Using the HTML document presented in Listing 16-4, we are going to build a small application to see how the **error** event works.

```
function initiate(){
  var cache=window.applicationCache;
  cache.addEventListener('error', showerror, false);
}
function showerror(){
  alert('error');
}
window.addEventListener('load', initiate, false);
```

Listing 16-5: checking for errors

The **applicationCache** attribute for the window used in the code in Listing 16-5 returns the ApplicationCache object for this document. After saving a reference to the object in the **cache** variable, a listener for the **error** event is added to the object. The listener will call the **showerror()** function when the event is fired and this function will pop up an alert informing us of the error.

> **Do It Yourself:** Create an HTML file with the code in Listing 16-4, a Javascript file called **cache.js** with the code from Listing 16-5, and a manifest file called **mycache.manifest**. As we studied before, you have to include in the manifest file the list of the files to be cached under the **CACHE** category. For our example,

these files are the HTML file, the `cache.js` file, and the `cache.css` file with the styles for the document. Upload the files to your server and open the HTML file in your browser. If you erase the manifest file or forgot to add the correspondent MIME type for this file on the server, the `error` event will be fired. You can also interrupt Internet access or use the Work Offline option of Firefox to see the application running offline from the new cache.

IMPORTANT: The implementation of the Offline API is at the experimental stage in most browsers at this point. We recommend you test the examples of this chapter in Firefox and Google Chrome. Firefox provides the option to deactivate the connection and work offline (Click the Work Offline option in the Developer Menu.). As well, Firefox is the only browser that will let you erase the cache to facilitate its study (Go to Options / Advanced / Network, and select the cache to erase.). On the other hand, Google Chrome has implemented almost every event available and will let you experiment with all the possibilities.

The CSS file has to include styles for the `<section>` element of our document. You can create your own styles or use the following:

```
#databox{
  width: 500px;
  height: 300px;
  margin: 10px;
  padding: 10px;
  border: 1px solid #999999;
}
```

Listing 16-6: *CSS rule for the* `databox`

Online and Offline

There is a new property for the Navigator object called `onLine` that indicates the current status of the connection. This property has two events associated that will be fired when its value changes. The property and the events are not part of the ApplicationCache object, but are useful for this API.

> **online**—This event is fired when the value of the `onLine` property changes to `true`.
> **offline**—This event is fired when the value of the `onLine` property changes to `false`.

Here is an example of how to use them:

```
function initiate(){
  databox=document.getElementById('databox');

  window.addEventListener('online', function(){ state(1); },
false);
  window.addEventListener('offline', function(){ state(2); },
false);
}
function state(value){
  switch(value){
    case 1:
      databox.innerHTML+='<br>We are ONline';
      break;
    case 2:
      databox.innerHTML+='<br>We are OFFline';
      break;
  }
}
window.addEventListener('load', initiate, false);
```

Listing 16-7: checking the connection status

In the code in Listing 16-7, we used anonymous functions to handle the events and send a value to the **state()** function to show the correspondent message in the **databox**. The events will be fired every time the value of the **onLine** property changes.

> **IMPORTANT:** There is no guarantee that the property will have the proper value all the time. Listening for these events on a desktop computer probably will produce no effect, even when the computer is completely disconnected from the Internet. To test this example on a PC, we recommend you use the Work Offline option provided by Firefox.

> **Do It Yourself:** Use the same HTML and CSS files from the previous example. Copy the code from Listing 16-7 in the **cache.js** file. Using Firefox, erase the cache for your website and load this application. To test the events, you can use the Work Offline option on the Firefox menu. Every time you click this option, the condition changes and a new message is appended to the **databox**.

Cache Process

To create or update a cache could take from a few seconds to several minutes, depending on the size of the files that must to be downloaded. The entire process goes through different stages according to what the browser is able to do at each moment. In a regular update, for example, browsers will try to read the manifest file first to check for possible updates, download all the files listed in the manifest if an update exists and inform when the process is finished. To inform the current step in the process, the API offers the **status** property. This property may take the following values:

> **UNCACHED (value 0)**—This value indicates that no cache was created yet for this application.
> **IDLE (value 1)**—This value indicates the cache for the application is the newest and is not obsolete.
> **CHECKING (value 2)**—This value indicates the browser is checking for new updates.
> **DOWNLOADING (value 3)**—This value indicates the files for the cache are being downloaded.
> **UPDATEREADY (value 4)**—This value indicates the cache for the application is available and not obsolete, but it is not the newest; an update is ready to replace it.
> **OBSOLETE (value 5)**—This value indicates the current cache is obsolete.

You can check the value of the **status** property any time you want, but it's better to use the events provided by the ApplicationCache object to check for the state of the process and the cache. The following events are usually fired in sequence and some of them are associated with a specific application cache status:

> **checking**—This event is fired when the browser is checking for updates.
> **noupdate**—This event is fired when no changes were found in the manifest file.
> **downloading**—This event is fired when the browser finds a new update and starts downloading the files.
> **cached**—This event is fired when the cache is ready.
> **updateready**—This event is fired when the downloading process for an update is complete.
> **obsolete**—This event is fired when the manifest file is not available anymore and the cache is being deleted.

The following example will help you to understand the process. In this code, every time an event is fired, a message is added to the **databox** with the value of the event and the **status** property:

```
function initiate(){
  databox=document.getElementById('databox');

  cache=window.applicationCache;
  cache.addEventListener('checking', function(){ show(1); },
false);
  cache.addEventListener('downloading', function(){ show(2); },
false);
```

```
  cache.addEventListener('cached', function(){ show(3); },
false);
  cache.addEventListener('updateready', function(){ show(4); },
false);
  cache.addEventListener('obsolete', function(){ show(5); },
false);
}
function show(value){
  databox.innerHTML+='<br>Status: '+cache.status;
  databox.innerHTML+=' | Event: '+value;
}
window.addEventListener('load', initiate, false);
```

Listing 16-8: checking the connection

We used anonymous functions for every event to send a different value to identify each event in the **show()** function. This value and the value of the **status** property are shown on the screen every time the browser reaches a new step in generating the cache.

> **Do It Yourself:** Use the HTML and CSS files from previous examples. Copy the code in Listing 16-8 into the **cache.js** file. Upload the application to your server and see how different steps of the process are shown on the screen according to the status of the cache every time the document is loaded.

> **IMPORTANT:** If the cache was already created, it is important to follow different steps to clear the cache and load a new version. Modifying the manifest file is one step, but is not the only one. Browsers keep a copy of the files for a few hours before even consider checking again for updates, so no matter how many new comments or files were added to the manifest file, the browser will run the old cache version for a while. To test each example, we recommend you change the names of every file. For instance, adding a number at the end of the name (such as **cache2.js**) will make the browser consider this a new application and create a new cache. This is only good for testing purposes, of course.

Progress

Applications that include images, several code files, information for databases, videos or any other big file may take a long time to download. To follow this process, the API provides the already known **progress** event. This event is the same we have used previously in other APIs.

The **progress** event is only fired while the files are being downloaded. In the following example, we are going to use **noupdate** along with the **cached** and **updateready** events seen before to inform when the process is over.

```
function initiate(){
   databox=document.getElementById('databox');
   databox.innerHTML='<progress value="0"
max="100">0%</progress>';

   cache=window.applicationCache;
   cache.addEventListener('progress', progress, false);
   cache.addEventListener('cached', show, false);
   cache.addEventListener('updateready', show, false);
   cache.addEventListener('noupdate', show, false);
}
function progress(e){
   if(e.lengthComputable){
      var per=parseInt(e.loaded/e.total*100);
      var progressbar=databox.querySelector("progress");
      progressbar.value=per;
      progressbar.innerHTML=per+'%';
   }
}
function show(){
   databox.innerHTML='Done';
}
window.addEventListener('load', initiate, false);
```

Listing 16-9: download progress

As always, the **progress** event is fired periodically to inform about the state of the process. In the code in Listing 16-9, every time **progress** is fired, the **progress()** function is called and the information on the screen is updated using a **<progress>** element.

There are different possible situations at the end of the process. The application could have been cached for the first time, so the **cached** event is fired. It could be that the cache already existed and an update was available, so when the files are finally downloaded the **updateready** event is fired instead. And a third possibility is that a cache was already in use and no update was available, so the **noupdate** event will be fired. We listen to events for every one of these situations and called the **show()** function in each case to print the message "Done" on the screen, thus indicating the process is over.

You can find an explanation for the **progress()** function in Chapter 13.

> **Do It Yourself:** Use the HTML and CSS files from previous examples. Copy the code in Listing 16-8 into the **cache.js** file. Upload the application to your server and load the main document. You have to include a big file in the manifest file to be able to see the progress bar working (Browsers have limitations at this moment over the size of the cache. We recommend you to try with files of a few megabytes, no more than five). For example, using the

`trailer.ogg` video introduced in Chapter 5, the manifest file should look like this:

```
CACHE MANIFEST
cache.html
cache.css
cache.js
trailer.ogg
# date 2011/06/27
```

IMPORTANT: We used `innerHTML` to add a new `<progress>` element to the document. This is not the recommended practice but it's useful and convenient for our example. Usually elements are added to the DOM using the Javascript method `createElement()` along with `appendChild()`.

Updating the Cache

So far we have seen how to create a cache for our application, how to inform the browser when an update is available and how to control the process every time a user accesses the application. This is useful but not completely transparent for users. The cache and its updates are loaded as soon as the user runs the application, which could produce delays and annoying behavior. The API solves this problem by providing new methods to update the cache while the application is already running:

> **update()**—This method initiates an update of the cache. It indicates to the browser to download the manifest file first and then continue with the rest of the files if a change in the manifest is detected (the files for the cache were modified).
>
> **swapCache()**—This method switches to the most recent cache after an update. It doesn't run new scripts or replace resources, but rather indicates to the browser that a new cache is available for future readings.

To update the cache, we just have to call the **update()** method. The **updateready** and **noupdate** events are useful to know the result of the process. For the next example, we are going to use a new HTML document with two buttons to request the update and test the current code in the cache.

```html
<!DOCTYPE html>
<html lang="en" manifest="mycache.manifest">
<head>
  <title>Offline API</title>
  <link rel="stylesheet" href="cache.css">
  <script src="cache.js"></script>
</head>
```

```
<body>
  <section id="databox">
    Offline Application
  </section>
  <button id="update">Update Cache</button>
  <button id="test">Test</button>
</body>
</html>
```

Listing 16-10: HTML document to test the update () *method*

The Javascript code implements techniques already studied; we have just included two new functions for the buttons:

```
function initiate(){
  databox=document.getElementById('databox');
  var update=document.getElementById('update');
  update.addEventListener('click', updatecache, false);
  var test=document.getElementById('test');
  test.addEventListener('click', testcache, false);

  cache=window.applicationCache;
  cache.addEventListener('updateready', function(){ show(1); },
false);
  cache.addEventListener('noupdate', function(){ show(2); },
false);
}
function updatecache(){
  cache.update();
}
function testcache(){
  databox.innerHTML+='<br>change this message';
}
function show(value){
  switch(value){
    case 1:
      databox.innerHTML+='<br>Update Ready';
      break;
    case 2:
      databox.innerHTML+='<br>No Update Available';
      break;
  }
}
window.addEventListener('load', initiate, false);
```

Listing 16-11: updating the cache and checking the current version

In the **initiate()** function, a listener for the **click** event was added to both buttons. A click on the **update** button will call the **updatecache()** function and execute the **update()** method. And a click on the **test** button will call the `testcache()` function and append a text to the **databox**. This is a text you can change later to create a new version of the code and check whether it was updated or not.

> **Do It Yourself:** Create a new HTML document with the code in Listing 16-10. The manifest and the CSS files are the same from previous examples (unless you changed some file names, in which case you will have to update the file's list in the manifest file). Copy the code in Listing 16-11 into a file called **cache.js**, and upload all these files to your server. Open the main document in your browser and test the application.

Once the HTML document is loaded, the window shows our typical **databox** and two buttons under it. As we explained before, the "Update Cache" button has the `click` event associated with the **updatecache()** function. If the button is clicked, the **update()** method is executed inside this function and the updating process starts. The browser downloads the manifest file and compares it with the same file already in the cache. If this file was modified, all the files listed inside are downloaded again. When the process is over, the **updateready** event is fired. This event calls the **show()** function with the value 1, corresponding to the message "Update Ready". On the other hand, if the manifest file didn't change, no update is detected and the **noupdate** event is fired. This event calls the **show()** function with the value 2. In this case, the message "No Update Available" is shown in the **databox**.

You can check how the code works by modifying or adding comments in the manifest file. Every time you hit the button to update the cache after any modification, the message "Update Ready" will appear in the **databox**. You can also play with the text in the **testcache()** function to detect when an update is already running.

> **IMPORTANT:** This time there is no need to erase the cache from your browser to download a new version. The **update()** method forces the browser to download the manifest file and the rest of the files if an update is detected. However, the new cache is still not available until the user refreshes the page.

The Offline API is a set of techniques that involves a special file called "manifest" and several methods, events and properties to create a cache for running applications in the user's computer. The API was meant mainly to provide permanent access to applications and the possibility of working while disconnected from the Internet.

Manifest File

The manifest file is a text file with the `.manifest` extension and a list of the files necessary for the cache. It has to start with the line `CACHE MANIFEST` and its content may be organized into the following categories:

> **CACHE**—This category includes the files to be cached.
> **NETWORK**—This category includes the file that can only be accessed while online.
> **FALLBACK**—This category provides an offline alternative for online files that are not accessible at the moment.

Properties

The Navigator object provides a new property to check for the status of the connection:

> **onLine**—This property returns a boolean value to indicate the connection's condition. It's `false` if the browser is offline and `true` otherwise.

The API provides the `status` property to check for the status of the application cache. This property is part of the ApplicationCache object and may take the following values:

> **UNCACHED (value 0)**—This value indicates no cache was created yet for this application.
> **IDLE (value 1)**—This value indicates the cache for the application is the newest and is not obsolete.
> **CHECKING (value 2)** —This value indicates the browser is checking for new updates.
> **DOWNLOADING (value 3)**—This value indicates the files for the cache are being downloaded.

UPDATEREADY (value 4)—This value indicates the cache for the application is available and not obsolete, but it is not the newest; an update is ready to replace it.

OBSOLETE (value 5) —This value indicates the current cache is obsolete.

Events

There are two window events to check for the status of the connection:

online—This event is fired when the value of the `onLine` property changes to `true`.

offline—This event is fired when the value of the `onLine` property changes to `false`.

The API provides several events, as part of the ApplicationCache object, to inform about the condition of the cache:

checking—This event is fired when the browser is checking for updates.

noupdate—This event is fired when no update is found.

downloading—This event is fired when the browser has found a new update and starts downloading the files.

cached—This event is fired when the cache is ready.

updateready—This event is fired when the downloading process for an update is complete.

obsolete—This event is fired when the manifest file is not available anymore and the cache is being deleted.

progress—This event is fired during the process of downloading the files for the cache.

error—This event is fired if an error occurs during the creation or update of the cache.

Methods

Two methods are provided by the API to request an update of the cache:

update()—This method initiates an update of the cache. It indicates to the browser that has to download the manifest file and the rest of the files if an update is detected.

swapCache()—This method switches to the most recent cache after an update. It doesn't run new scripts or replace resources, but rather indicates to the browser that a new cache is available for future readings.

Conclusion

Working for the World

This is a book about HTML5. It was meant to be a guide for developers, designers and programmers who want to build revolutionary websites and applications. It was meant to be for the genius everybody has inside. For Masterminds. But we are in a transition process, a moment in time in which old technologies are merged with new ones, and markets are getting behind. At the same moment that millions and millions of copies of new browsers are downloaded from the web, millions and millions of people are not even aware of their existence. The market is still full of old computers running Windows 98 and Internet Explorer 6, or even worse.

Creating for the web has always been a challenge, and it's not getting any easier. Despite the long, hard efforts to build and implement standards for the web, not even the new browsers consistently support them. And old browsers with no standards at all are still there, running, all around the world, making our lives impossible.

So it's time to see what we can do to bring HTML5 to the people, to innovate and create, to be Masterminds in a world that seems indifferent. It's time to see how can we work with the new technologies and make them available for everyone.

The Alternatives

When it comes to alternatives, we have to decide which position to take. We can be rude, polite, smart or hard workers. A rude developer would say: "Hey, this was programmed to work in new browsers. New browsers are free, don't be lazy; just download a copy." The polite developer would say: "This was developed taking advantage of new technologies; if you want to enjoy my work to its full potential, upgrade your browser. In the meantime, here is an old version you can use." The smart developer would say: "We make cutting-edge technology available for everyone. You don't need to do anything; we did it for you." And finally, a hard-working developer would say: "This is a version of our website adapted to your browser, here is another version with more features special for new browsers, and here is the experimental version of our super-evolved application."

For the most useful and practical approach, here are the options available when the user's browser is not ready for HTML5:

Inform—Ask the user to upgrade the browser if some features your application needs are not available.

Adapt—Select different styles and codes for the document according to the features available in the user's browser.

Redirect—Redirect users to an entirely new document designed especially for old browsers.

Emulate—Use libraries to make HTML5 features available in old browsers.

Modernizr

Regardless of what option you choose, the first thing you have to do is detect whether the HTML5 features your application needs are available in the user's browser or not. The features are independent and easy to identify, but the techniques required to detect them are as diverse as the features themselves. Developers must consider different browsers and versions and depend on codes that are often unreliable.

A small library called Modernizr was developed to solve this problem. This library creates an object called Modernizr that offers properties for every HTML5 feature. These properties return a boolean value that will be `true` or `false` depending on whether the features are available or not.

The library is open-source, made in Javascript and available for free at www.modernizr.com. You just have to download the Javascript file and include it in the head of your document, as in the following example:

```
<!DOCTYPE html>
<html lang="en">
<head>
  <title>Modernizr</title>
  <script src="modernizr.min.js"></script>
  <script src="modernizr.js"></script>
</head>
<body>
  <section id="databox">
    content
  </section>
</body>
</html>
```

Listing C-1: including Modernizr in our documents

The file called **modernizr.min.js** is a copy of the file for the Modernizr library downloaded from the Modernizr website. The second file included in the HTML document in Listing C-1 is our own Javascript code to check the values of the properties provided by the library:

```
function initiate(){
  var databox=document.getElementById('databox');
  if(Modernizr.boxshadow){
    databox.innerHTML='Box Shadow is available';
  }else{
    databox.innerHTML='Box Shadow is NOT available';
  }
}
window.addEventListener('load', initiate, false);
```

Listing C-2: detecting the availability of CSS styles for box shadows

As you can see in the code in Listing C-2, we can detect any HTML5 feature using just a conditional **if** and the corresponding property of the Modernizr object. Every feature has its own property available.

> **IMPORTANT:** This is just a small introduction to this useful library. By using Modernizr, for example, you can also select a set of CSS styles from CSS files without using Javascript. Modernizr provides special classes to implement in our style sheets to select the proper CSS properties according to the features available. To learn more, visit www.modernizr.com.

Libraries

Once the features available are detected, you have the option of using only what has been detected to work in the user's browser or recommending the user upgrade his or her software. However, imagine you are a stubborn developer or a mad programmer who (along with your users and clients) doesn't care about the browser's vendors or browser's version or beta versions or unimplemented features or anything else; you just want to run the latest technology available, no matter what!

Well, this is where independent libraries can help. Dozens of programmers in the world are probably more stubborn than you and your clients, and they are developing and improving libraries to emulate HTML5 features in old browsers, especially Javascript APIs. Thanks to this effort, we already have available new HTML elements, CSS3 selectors and styles and even complex APIs such as Canvas or Web Storage in every browser in the market.

There is an up-to-date list of libraries available at:

www.github.com/Modernizr/Modernizr/wiki/HTML5-Cross-browser-Polyfills

> **IMPORTANT:** Visit our website and follow the links for this chapter for more information about this topic.

Google Chrome Frame

Google Chrome Frame is probably a last resort. Personally, I think it was a good idea at the beginning, but now it is just better to recommend users upgrade their browsers rather than make them download a plugin such as Google Chrome Frame.

Google Chrome Frame was specifically developed for old versions of Internet Explorer. It was designed to bring all the power and possibilities of Google Chrome into browsers that are not prepared for these technologies but are still running in users' computers and are part of the market.

As I said it was a good idea. Inserting just a simple HTML tag in your documents, a message was shown to your users to recommend them to install the Google Chrome Frame before running your website or application. After this simple step, all the features supported by Google Chrome were automatically available. However, users had to download software from the web anyway. I can't see any difference between this and downloading a new browser version, especially now that Internet Explorer has its own HTML5 compatible edition available for free. These days, with so many browsers HTML5-ready, it is better to guide users to this new software than to send them to obscure and confusing plugins.

To know more about Google Chrome Frame and how to use it go to:
code.google.com/chrome/chromeframe/

Working for the Cloud

In this new world of mobile devices and cloud computing, no matter how current the browser, we will always have something else to worry about. Probably the iPhone was the innovation that started it all. Since its appearance, several things changed for the web. The iPad followed the iPhone, and all kind of imitations emerged later to fulfill this new market. Thanks to this radical change in the electronic world, mobile access turned into a common practice. Suddenly these new devices became an important target for websites and web applications, and the diversity of platforms, screens and interfaces forced developers to adapt their products to every specific case.

These days, independent of what kind of technology we use, our websites and applications must still be adapted to every possible platform to preserve consistency and make our work available for everyone. Fortunately, HTML always considered these situations and provided the **media** attribute in the **<link>** element to select external resources according to predetermined parameters:

```
<!DOCTYPE html>
<html lang="en">
<head>
  <title>Main Document</title>
  <link rel="stylesheet" href="webstyles.css" media="all and
(min-width: 769px)">
  <link rel="stylesheet" href="tablet.css" media="all and (min-
width: 321px) and (max-width: 768px)">
  <link rel="stylesheet" href="phone.css" media="all and (min-
width: 0px) and (max-width: 320px)">
</head>
<body>
  ...
</body>
</html>
```

Listing C-3: *different CSS files for different devices*

Selecting CSS styles is an easy way to get our job done. According to the device or the size of the screen, the CSS files are loaded and the proper styles applied. HTML elements can be resized and entire documents adapted and rendered into a specific space and circumstances.

In Listing C-3, three different CSS files are incorporated for three different situations. The situations are detected by the values of the attribute **media** in every **<link>** tag. By using the properties **min-width** and **max-width**, we are able to determine the CSS file that will be applied to this document according to the resolution of the screen in which the document is being displayed. If the horizontal size of the screen is between 0 and 320 pixels, the **phone.css** file is loaded. For a resolution between 321 and 768 pixels, the **tablet.css** file is the one included. And finally, for a resolution bigger than 768 pixels, the **webstyles.css** file is used to render the document.

In this example, we contemplated three possible scenarios: the document is displayed in a small smartphone, a tablet PC and a full-scale computer. The values used are usually found in these devices.

Of course, the adaptation process does not involve only CSS styles. The interfaces provided by these devices are slightly different from a desktop computer due to the elimination of physical parts, such as the keyword and mouse. Regular events such as **click** or **mouseover** have been modified or in some cases replaced by touch events. And there is another important feature usually present in mobile devices that allows the user to change the orientation of the screen and therefore the space available for the document. All these changes from the old computer interface make it almost impossible to get a good adaptation of the design and operability just by adding or modifying some CSS rules. Javascript has to be used to adapt codes or even detect the situation and redirect users to a version of the website specific for the device that is accessing the application.

> **IMPORTANT:** This topic is beyond the purpose of this book. For more information, please visit our website.

Final Recommendations

There will be always developers who will say to you: "If you use technologies that are not available for 5% of the browsers in the market, you are going to lose 5% of customers." My answer is: "If you have clients to satisfy, then adapt, redirect, or emulate, but if you work for yourself, inform."

You always have to find the way to succeed. If you work for others, in order to succeed you have to provide a full working solution, a product that the clients of your clients are able to access, no matter what choices they make about computers, browsers or systems. But if you work for yourself, in order to succeed, you have to create the best of the best, you have to innovate, be ahead of everyone, independent of what the 5% of the users have installed in their computers. You have to work for the 20% that already downloaded the last version of Firefox, the 15% that already have Google Chrome running in their PCs, the 10% that have Safari in their mobile devices. You have millions of users ready to become your customers. While the developer asked you why you would lose the 5% of the market, I ask why you would lose the chance to succeed.

You will never conquer 100% of the market, and that's a fact. You are not developing your websites in Chinese or Portuguese. You are not working for 100% of the market; you are already working for a small part of it. Why continue limiting yourself? Develop for the market that allows you to succeed. Develop for that portion of the market that is continuously growing and will let you free the genius inside you. In the same way that you don't worry about markets that speak other languages, don't worry about the part of the market that is still using old technologies. Inform them. Let them know what they are missing. Take advantage of the latest technologies available and be a Mastermind. Develop for the future and you will succeed.

13207179R00239

Made in the USA
Lexington, KY
19 January 2012